THE CONNOISSEUR

THE CONNOISSEUR

A Cultural History

PETER BURKE

REAKTION BOOKS

For Maria Lúcia

Published by
REAKTION BOOKS LTD
2–4 Sebastian Street
London EC1V 0HE, UK
www.reaktionbooks.co.uk

First published 2026

EU GPSR Authorised Representative
Logos Europe, 9 rue Nicolas Poussin, 17000, La Rochelle, France
email: contact@logoseurope.eu

Printed and bound in Great Britain by Bell & Bain, Glasgow

A catalogue record for this book is available from the British Library

ISBN 978 1 83639 195 1

CONTENTS

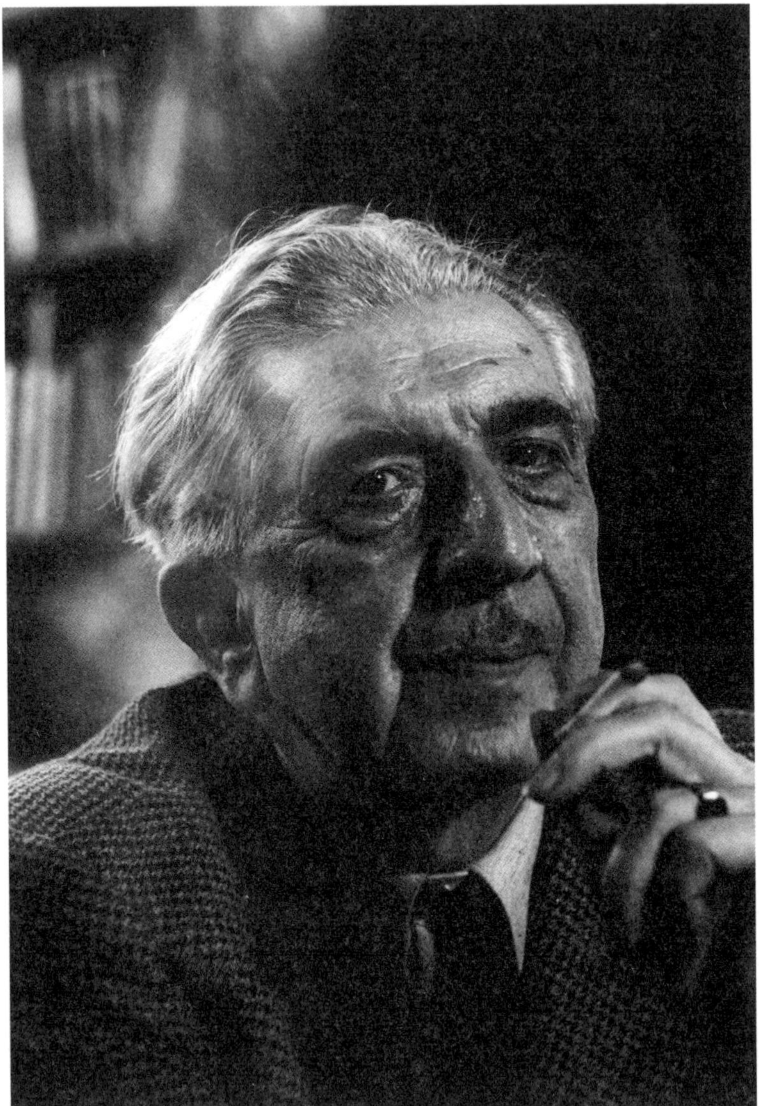

1 Roberto Longhi, 1962.

Preface

> There is a sort of contentment in knowing that a given work is from a given time and by a given hand.
>
> PIERRE-JEAN MARIETTE

This book presents a history of connoisseurship – in other words, the collective practice of judging works of art – in the West over the last four or five centuries, focusing, like so many of the connoisseurs themselves, on paintings and drawings by the Old Masters.

The need for such a history has long been felt. It was noted by Roberto Longhi (illus. 1), himself a distinguished connoisseur, in 1954. Four decades later, the art historian Enrico Castelnuovo, speaking at a conference in honour of another distinguished example of the species, Giovanni Morelli (see illus. 4), specified the need for a social history of connoisseurs.[1] Nevertheless, despite many excellent monographs and some collections of essays on aspects of this substantial topic, no one, so far as I know, has yet responded to these pleas for a general history, a big picture, a bird's eye view.

In what follows the bird will descend from time to time to complement the distant eye with some close-ups, including a number of case studies of the practice of individuals such as Morelli and Longhi. Like the artists they studied, these connoisseurs had their distinctive styles. Some of them focused on works produced by a particular artist or in a particular period, while others ranged widely. Some made extensive use of documents, photographs and scientific evidence, others did not. The case studies will focus on their methods, their strengths and weaknesses and the experiences that drew or drove them to engage in this career.

I should explain right at the start where I am speaking from. I am not an art historian and cannot claim to be a connoisseur. I am a 'plain' or general historian who loves art, tried his best to draw and paint when he was a teenager and still enjoys the game of guessing who painted the works on display at the National Gallery and elsewhere (although, unlike a true connoisseur, I usually trust the information on the labels). Plain historians have so far shown little interest in this field of enquiry (with a few exceptions such as Carlo Ginzburg, J. H. Plumb, John Brewer, Brian Cowan and Carol Helstosky). Nevertheless, I believe that our profession does have something to contribute to this domain, notably a sense of the various contexts in which the 'culture of connoisseurship' (as it is now known) developed, together with a sense of the changes in that culture over the long term, in step with changes in the world of art and its institutions, which range from workshops, academies and auction rooms to museums and universities. From outside, this world seems glamorous. From inside, it appears to be an arena for cutthroat competition in which both fortunes and reputations can be won or lost.

The main purpose of this study is to historicize the connoisseurial eye, in other words to show that it is neither an ahistorical constant nor a sudden invention, but rather the patient accumulation of a variety of skills over the long term, especially from their codification in the seventeenth century through the rise of the amateur in the eighteenth and the professional in the nineteenth century to a later age of crisis. The book is also intended as a contribution to the growing field of the history of practices, which has become a major form of cultural history in the wake of the theories of the French sociologist Pierre Bourdieu.[2]

My particular approach comes from the history of knowledge, a topic on which I have already published several books. In this case, I am especially concerned with the different forms of knowledge (or better, knowledges) that are involved in the practice of connoisseurship. These knowledges were and still are based on varieties of experience – those of artists, dealers, collectors, restorers, forgers and art historians. One might say that each of these groups has its own way of looking at pictures, its own 'occupational eye' or gaze.[3] However, the groups overlap and cannot help interacting or even colliding. Their 'mindful eyes' resemble the 'mindful hands' of the artists whose works they study.[4]

This family of knowledges may be located in a much wider group of practical knowledges that depend on judgements by the eye. These forms of what is known as 'expert intuition' include medical diagnoses and the *coup d'oeil* that the military theorist Carl von Clausewitz attributed to Napoleon and defined as the 'rapid discovery' of something that remains invisible to other people. Widening out still further, we might include the bundle of skills that make a good chess player, a good footballer or a good judge of wine. These very different skills all exemplify what Bourdieu called 'knowing through the body' (*la connaissance par corps*), in these cases knowing the next move in chess or recognizing a wine 'without thinking', or, more exactly, without conscious thought.[5] They may also be described as examples of decision-making in conditions of uncertainty, of a kind that is familiar in the domains of business and politics.

Comparing these skills helps to demystify the traditional idea of intuition as a special gift granted to a few outstanding individuals whom I shall call the 'stars'. These arts of judgement are all based on past experiences that facilitate pattern recognition in a particular domain. The knowledge on which judgements are based is what the philosopher Michael Polanyi called 'personal' or 'tacit' knowledge, underlying performances 'achieved by the observance of a set of rules which are not known as such to the person following them'.[6]

In similar fashion to Polanyi, the economist-psychologist Daniel Kahneman contrasted a form of thinking, rapid and unconscious, which he called 'System One', with 'System Two', a mode of conscious thought that moves more slowly to its conclusions.[7] One might say that connoisseurs have usually begun with System

One but justified or modified their rapid judgements with System Two, combining the slow and careful examination of works of art with other forms of evidence that range from X-rays of a given painting to documents such as contracts, letters and inventories. As Max Friedländer, a famous early twentieth-century connoisseur, famously remarked, 'One should retain, and steel, one's courage of subjective opinion, but one should also sceptically and coolly put this opinion to the test.'[8]

The reliability of the methods of connoisseurship, which have been elaborated over the centuries, cannot be taken for granted. Indeed, the problem of reliability will resurface on many occasions in the course of the book and especially in its conclusion. The methods themselves will be described in more detail in the first chapter.

1

What Is Connoisseurship?

The abstract noun 'connoisseurship' is an eighteenth-century term, recorded in English a little later than the word 'connoisseur'. Although it is somewhat ungainly (more so than its German equivalent, *Kennerschaft*) the English word has been adopted by French and Italian scholars. It refers to a practice, or more exactly a bundle or even a system of practices, that have traditionally included three in particular. The first is judging the quality of a work of art. In the second place comes dating and placing the work and attributing it to a particular artist, 'baptizing' it, as the nineteenth-century connoisseurs Otto Mündler and Giovanni Morelli used to say.[1] The third involves distinguishing original works from copies and forgeries.[2]

As in the case of war, politics and business, the attribution of works of art is a form of decision-making in conditions of uncertainty. There is a tendency to ascribe works in a particular style to famous artists, a special case (often driven by pride or greed) of a general trend that the sociologist Robert Merton called the 'Matthew Effect', attributing discoveries by others to the most celebrated scientists, illustrating the axiom in the Gospel of St Matthew that 'To him who hath shall be given.'[3]

Attribution includes its opposite, *dis*attribution or *de*-attribution (emphasizing its negative side) or *re*-attribution, which sounds more positive. This process sometimes involves breaking the news to collectors that their prized Raphael or Rembrandt was actually painted by a less important artist. Understandably enough, they have not always taken this news well. The collector Hans-Heinrich Thyssen told Ivan Gaskell, whose catalogue had disattributed a Rembrandt self-portrait in his collection, 'You have cost me a great deal of money!' Less politely, the famous American connoisseur Bernard Berenson (see illus. 6) was once shown the door by a British collector, Lord Wemyss, immediately after disattributing his Leonardo.[4]

Today, in an age of increasing specialization, the scope of the term 'connoisseurship' is often restricted to the art of attribution, leaving quality to be assessed by professional art critics. Such a restriction would have shocked leading connoisseurs such as Longhi or Berenson, both of whom were passionately concerned with quality.

To call the whole package of skills 'connoisseurship' emphasizes what the French call *connaissance*, in other words knowledge derived from experience, especially the experience of a few individuals with hypersensitivity to works of art. This 'hands-on', or more exactly 'eyes-on', knowledge may be contrasted with *savoir*, knowledge derived from research or scientific testing. For connoisseurs, everything begins with personal encounters with objects, what a British expert on manuscripts, Christopher de Hamel, calls 'meetings' or even 'interviews'.[5] However, this book will suggest that as the methods of connoisseurs have been refined over the centuries (in this case more than five centuries, from the year 1500 or thereabouts to the present), *connaissance* has come to include an ever-increasing dose of *savoir*.

There are five obvious questions to ask at this point. What were the objects of connoisseurship? By whom has connoisseurship been practised? How are connoisseurial judgements formed? Where and when can this system of practices be found?

What?

The objects of connoisseurship have been many and various. In China, for instance, favourite collectibles included calligraphy, ancient bronze vessels, jade and porcelain, while treatises on connoisseurship also discussed the quality of different kinds of incense and tea.[6] In eleventh-century Japan, members of the elite engaged in competitions to guess the ingredients of different perfumes, a practice described in the classic *The Tale of Genji*. Calligraphy was also favoured but the distinctive feature of Japanese connoisseurship was the interest in swords, linked to the culture of the samurai. The situation in Japan changed in the eighteenth century, which was the age of amateurs, as it was in Europe. Groups met in order to produce and also to discuss paintings and calligraphy, a form of sociability that could also be found, as we shall see in Chapter Three, in early modern Italy, France and Spain. However, the 'salon culture' of Japan was more open to ordinary townspeople, including women, than its European equivalent.[7]

In Europe, painting has been central to connoisseurship, though individuals have also been concerned with drawings and prints (woodcuts, engravings, etchings and so on) and with sculpture (including coins, medals and cameos). Other collectibles such as furniture, ceramics, textiles and book-bindings will be omitted from this study, like the oriental rugs studied by the famous German connoisseur Wilhelm Bode (see illus. 24).[8] So will flowers (especially tulips), wine and tea, although they all had, or still have, their connoisseurs.[9]

A relatively short study of some five hundred years of connoisseurship needs a focus. In this case, the spotlight will fall on paintings, especially those by European Old Masters, leaving other forms of art in the penumbra.

Who?

To become a successful connoisseur of art, it is necessary to possess a number of qualities, above all what is known as 'the eye', in other words a sharp eye that notices details and is able to discriminate between objects that look almost the same. To this eye we should add a love of art that allows total immersion in a given painting, and an unusually powerful visual memory that makes it possible to compare different works, some of them seen as long as several years earlier.

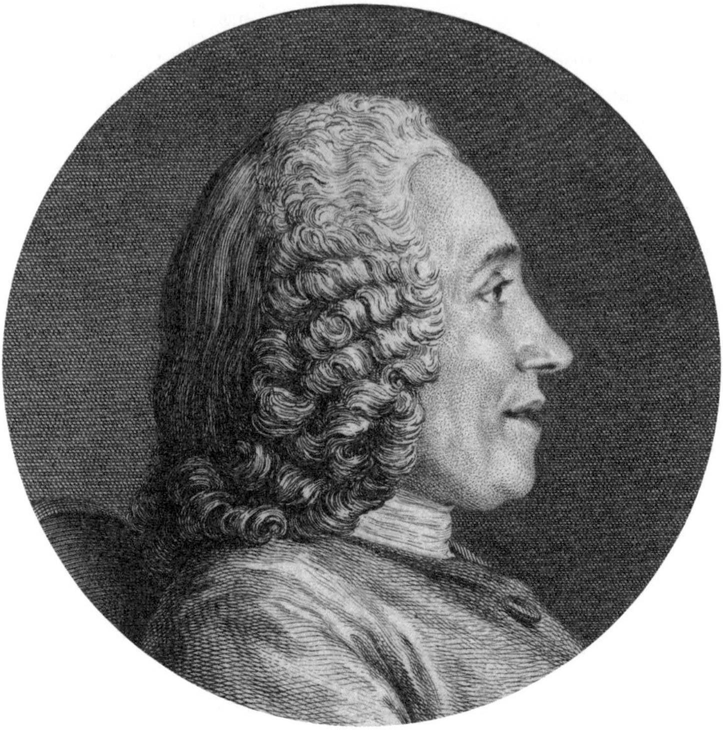

2 Augustin de Saint-Aubin, *Pierre-Jean Mariette*, 1765, etching and engraving.

A social historian of connoisseurs needs to ask, like the French sociologist Bernard Lahire, who has the eye?[10] A number of groups – artists, dealers, collectors, restorers, forgers, art historians and curators – have a special interest in one or more connoisseurial skills. Artists study the styles of both their idols and rivals. They have often been asked to appraise paintings or to advise a patron on whether a work commissioned from a particular artist was painted by that artist or by members of his workshop. Indeed, for most of the period with which this book is concerned, some artists argued that they were the only people fit to judge works of art, dismissing connoisseurs as people who 'have never held a brush'.[11] Forgers look closely at the works of the artists they wish to counterfeit; dealers need to know what will sell. A few of the latter stand out for the quality of their eye, among them Pierre-Jean Mariette (illus. 2), who sold prints in eighteenth-century Paris before he retired in order to have more time to spend on his passion, his own collection. Restorers have opportunities for even closer looking than other experts. Art historians make use of documents to help with attribution, but some of them also rely on their eye. So do some collectors. Denis Mahon, for example, an Englishman who has been described as 'the incarnation of the eye', had private means that enabled him to devote his life to connoisseurship and form his own collection of Old Masters.[12]

The large group of 'semi-connoisseurs' – as one might call the majority of collectors and other regular visitors to art galleries – offers a reminder that connoisseurship, like other skills, comes in different degrees. This study will have most to say about the stars, the small number of people who have become famous for their eye. These 'eyes', as they are sometimes known, include a number of colourful individuals, among them three Italians, two Americans and an Englishman, all of whom will figure in later chapters.

The career as a connoisseur of Italian Giovanni Battista Cavalcaselle (illus. 3) nearly ended before it began. As a young man in 1848, he joined the rising against Austrian rule in northern Italy.

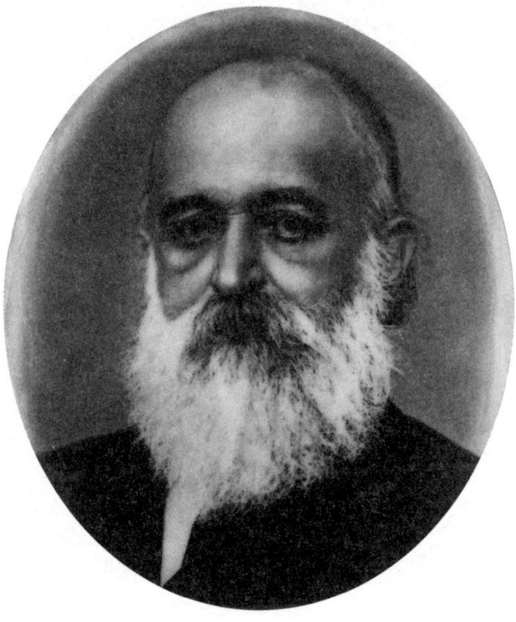

3 Giovanni Battista Cavalcaselle, 19th century.

He was captured and condemned to be shot, only to be saved at the last moment when the firing squad was suddenly ordered to retreat. A second stroke of luck for Cavalcaselle was meeting the English journalist and connoisseur Joseph Crowe on a coach in Berlin, a meeting that led to their fruitful collaboration on histories of Italian art that became standard works on the subject.[13]

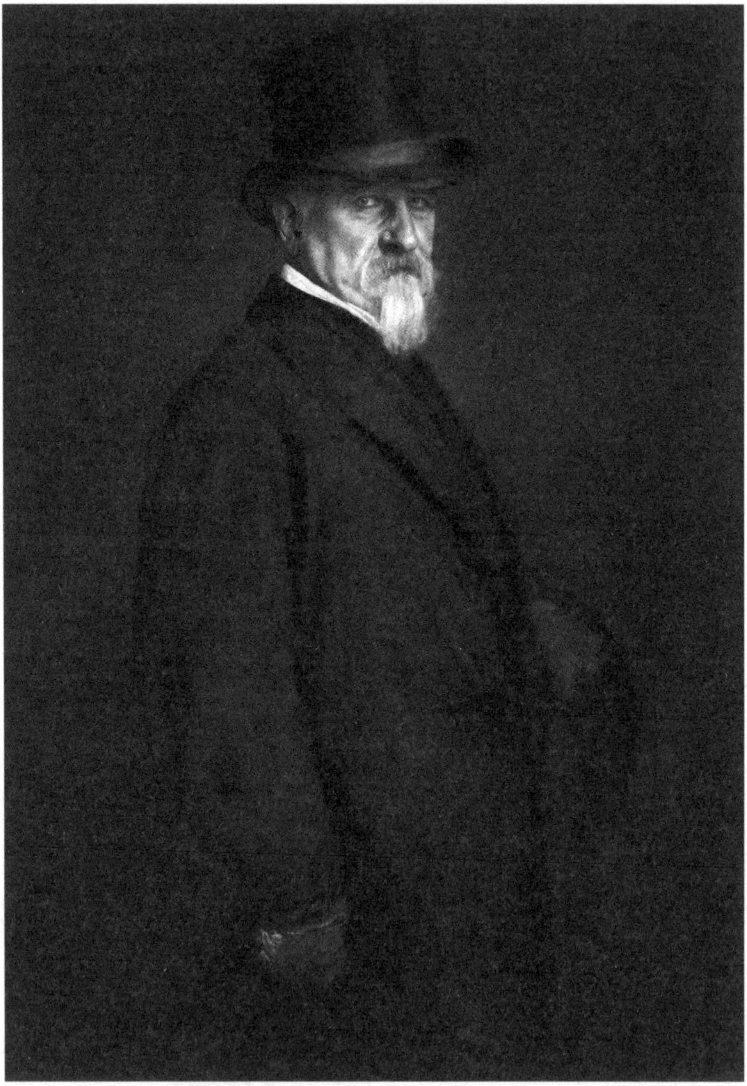

4 After Franz von Lenbach, *Giovanni Morelli*, 1886, photogravure.

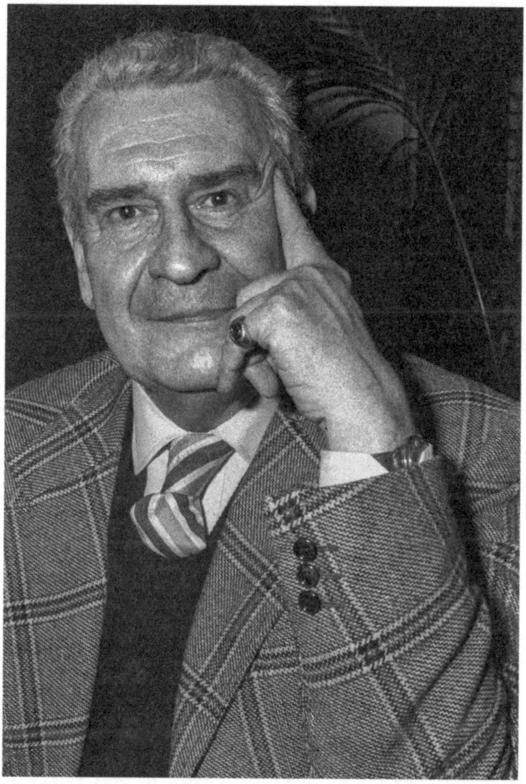

5 Federico Zeri, 1981.

Cavalcaselle's rival Giovanni Morelli (illus. 4) was a many-sided man who was trained as an anatomist and active as a soldier, a politician and a playwright as well as a connoisseur. A lover of irony and satire, Morelli liked to try on different identities and present himself in various disguises writing his best-known works in the name of an imaginary Russian, Ivan Lermolieff.[14]

The third Italian, Federico Zeri (illus. 5), who published a book on *Eccentrici fiorentini* (1962), was something of an eccentric himself, described by a fellow connoisseur as 'a complete madman' (*un pazzo completo*).[15] Like Morelli, he enjoyed creating alternative identities, sometimes making telephone calls in the name of an imaginary female journalist called Wanda.[16] He also enjoyed playing the role of an *enfant terrible*, both on television and in private life. It was characteristic of Zeri that when he was first shown the so-called 'Getty Kouros', a statue of a young man in the

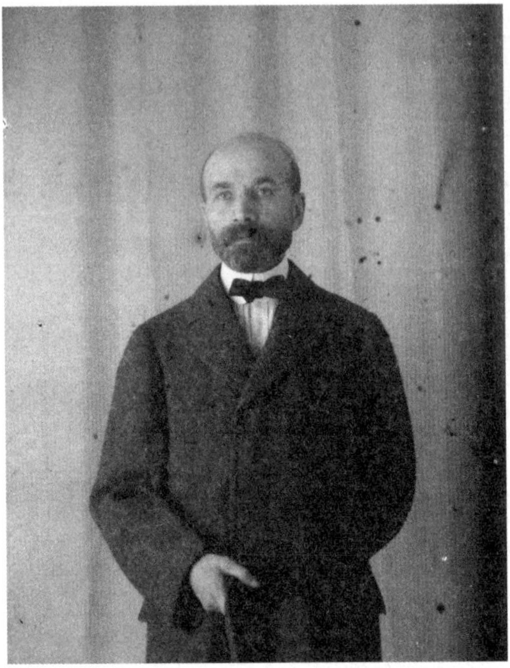

6 Bernard Berenson, 1917.

archaic Greek style bought by the J. Paul Getty Museum in 1985, his immediate reaction was to say, 'I hope that you haven't paid for it yet!' (They had, $10 million). Today, Zeri's doubts about the statue's authenticity are shared by many specialists on ancient art.

The life of Bernard Berenson (illus. 6), who remains the best known of connoisseurs, can be described as one of rags to riches. He was born into a poor Jewish family in a village in what is now Lithuania, grew up in Boston in the United States, studied at Harvard and ended his long career as the wealthy owner of a villa in Tuscany, a place of pilgrimage for a number of young people who later became well-known connoisseurs in their own right. He became famous for his lists of attributions, especially of painters of the Italian Renaissance, although he would have preferred to be known as a philosopher of art.

The second American was the curator Thomas Hoving (illus. 7), a flamboyant, ebullient individual who specialized in medieval sculpture but expressed an infectious enthusiasm for a variety of works of art. Following a stint as head of New York Parks, he became director of the Metropolitan Museum of Art at the age of 36, expanding both the building and the collections and organizing spectacular, popular and sometimes controversial exhibitions. After leaving the Met, Hoving set up a consulting firm for museums and became the editor of *Connoisseur* magazine, alongside writing on art forgeries, about which he had learned much from Frank X. Kelly, a restorer who doubled as a forger of works by Monet. As a connoisseur, Hoving's greatest achievement was the discovery and recognition of the Bury St Edmunds Cross. He bought the cross from a dealer (who kept it in the vault of a Swiss bank), dated it to the late twelfth century and discovered its original location in the medieval abbey in Bury in Suffolk.

The youngest of this group was the Englishman Eric Hebborn, an artist and restorer who is best known for his drawings in the style of famous masters, which he sold as originals, sometimes deceiving leading connoisseurs. Hebborn boasted that his code was 'Never sell to a person who was not a recognized expert, or acting on expert advice.' He viewed forgery as a game in which the point was to outwit the experts as well as to make money. As he wrote,

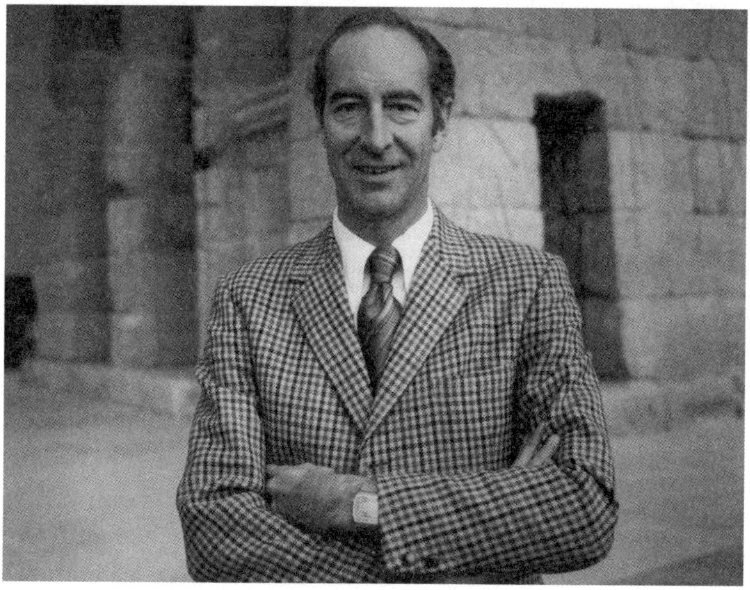

7 Thomas Hoving, 1978.

'there is no satisfaction in deceiving the neophyte.'[17] One night in Rome, Hebborn was murdered as he walked home. The assassin remains unknown, like the motive – perhaps a former client who discovered that he had been deceived, or a colleague who resented the revelation of trade secrets in Hebborn's *Art Forger's Handbook*, published only a few weeks prior to his death.[18]

Some individual connoisseurs will be discussed at greater length in the chapters that follow, as case studies that reveal the varieties of connoisseurship and the elaboration of its techniques over the centuries.

How?

The distinctive method of connoisseurs is the analysis of style for the purpose of attribution. It is often explained as a kind of intuition that a few people possess while the rest do not. The seventeenth-century Florentine connoisseur Filippo Baldinucci (see illus. 15) referred to the 'learned eye' (*occhio erudito*). Morelli called this gift the 'practised eye' (*oeil exercé*). The German art historian Wilhelm Vöge preferred to speak of the 'sensitive eye' (*empfindsame Auge*). This expert eye is exercised at two moments, one brief and the other lengthy.

Individuals with a practised eye, especially the stars, are often able to recognize the work of a particular artist in a flash, a kind of epiphany, eureka moment or *coup d'oeil*. The French connoisseur Roger de Piles emphasized what he called 'the first glance' (*le premier coup d'oeil*), from 'a reasonable distance', though he noted that this glance should be followed by viewing the work more carefully from close up.[19] The English connoisseur Jonathan Richardson (illus. 8) also recommended beginning by looking at a picture from a distance in order to get an impression of the whole, the 'Tout-Ensemble'. The German connoisseur Max Friedländer stressed the importance of the 'first impression' because 'The receptiveness of the eye is heightened by what is new, strange, unexpected, different.'[20]

An immediate sense of something 'off' often leads to the judgement that a certain work is a fake, as it did when Zeri first

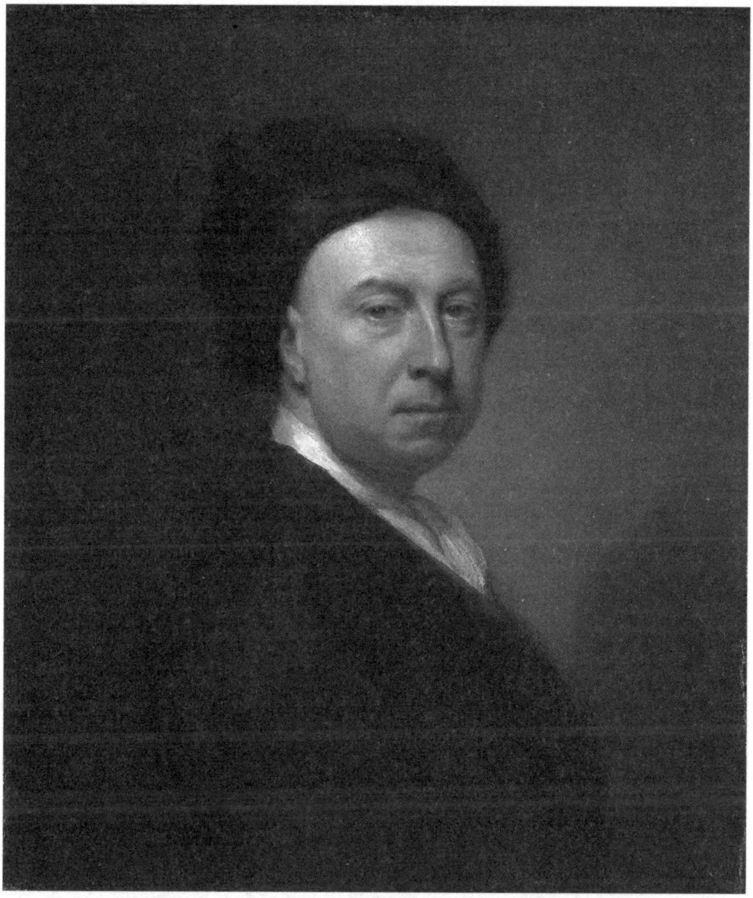

8 Jonathan Richardson, *Self-Portrait*, 1733, oil on canvas.

saw the Getty Kouros.[21] On other occasions, what flashes into the mind of the connoisseur is the name of an artist.

The Dutch connoisseur Abraham Bredius (illus. 9) recorded his discovery of the *Polish Rider*, which he claimed was 'one of Rembrandt's greatest masterpieces', in Poland in 1897. 'One look at the whole and a few seconds' study of the technique were enough to convince me instantly.'[22] Berenson described his recognition of a work by the Renaissance painter Antonello da Messina: 'The instant I looked at the fresco with a seeing eye, I mean with all faculties cooperating, I felt that it must be by Antonello.'[23] When the Japanese connoisseur Yukio Yashiro (see illus. 28) visited the

Fitzwilliam Museum in Cambridge in 1923, he was shown a painting of the *Annunciation* and 'instantly recognized that it was by Domenico Veneziano'. Other experts confirmed this judgement.[24] When Mina Gregori (illus. 10), an Italian expert on Caravaggio, saw a painting of *Mary Magdalen in Ecstasy*, she 'had an immediate, instinctive reaction. They laid it down on the floor, I got down on my knees, and when I saw her hands, I said, "yes, that's it."'[25]

Other senses might also be involved in judging works of art. In the case of sculpture, touch, sometimes described as 'tactile apprehension', is obviously crucial.[26] The eighteenth-century connoisseur Cardinal Alessandro Albani, whose sight was weak, is said to have 'acquired a remarkable capacity for judging antiques by touch'. The British connoisseur John Pope-Hennessy emphasized the importance of the hands-on approach in the literal sense of that term. 'One learns about bronzes only by handling them,' he wrote: 'Sculptures . . . convey a message to the eye, but it is a message that must be confirmed by touch.' Edmund de Waal, a connoisseur who is also a potter, has written about objects that 'invited touch with

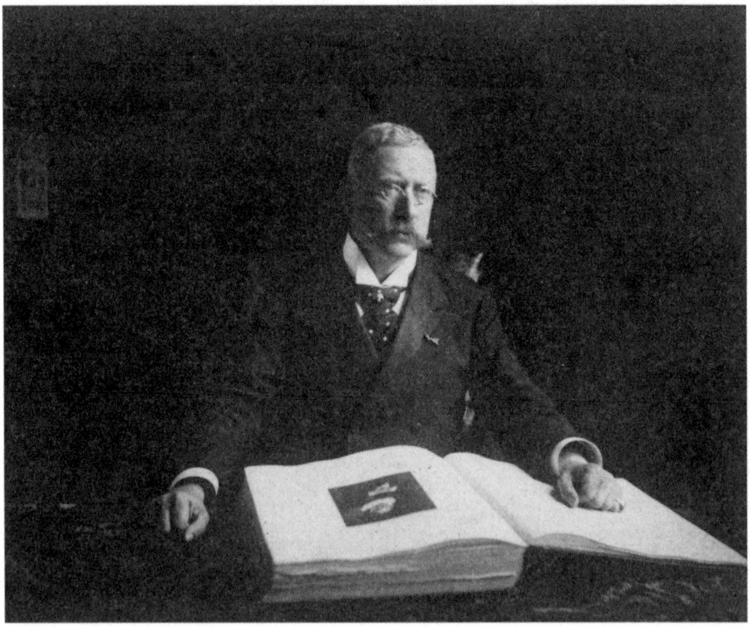

9 Abraham Bredius, 1905.

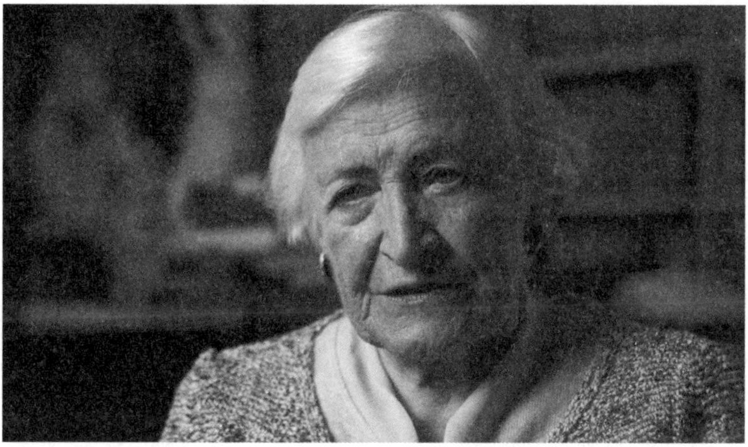

10 Mina Gregori in the documentary *Caravaggio: The Soul and the Blood* (2018, dir. Jesus Garcès Lambert).

the whole hand or just the fingers', or, on the contrary, 'asked you to stay away'.[27]

In a dialogue on medals and coins, the eighteenth-century English writer Joseph Addison noted that in order to date these objects, some antiquaries would listen to the ring of the metal, smell the coin and even lick it 'to distinguish the age of it by its taste'.[28] It was said of Berenson that in the presence of a fake, 'his stomach felt wrong' and 'He had a curious ringing in his ears,' a remarkable example of knowing through the body. In similar fashion, it was said of Hanns Swarzenski, a specialist on medieval sculpture, that he 'experiences objects with all his senses, not with his eyes alone. He does not know a work of art until he has touched it, caressed it, weighed it in his hands, smelled it, and yes, even listened to it.'[29] The common metaphor of artistic 'taste' was taken literally by the seventeenth-century artist and critic Marco Boschini, who compared paintings to spices, marzipan and pasta.[30]

We should not forget smell, both literal and metaphorical. In ancient Rome, the poet Martial referred to connoisseurs who literally smelled bronze statues to discover whether or not they were Greek (*Epigrammata*, Book IX, 59). King Charles I was described by a papal diplomat as having 'a good nose' (*buon naso*) for paintings.[31] In similar fashion, a nineteenth-century French artist and collector asked his readers, 'Do you have the nose of a hunting dog to catch a masterpiece as the dog catches a partridge?'[32]

Rapidity of judgement is not of course confined to art. The best doctors, for example, are able to offer rapid diagnoses, recognizing the symptoms of an illness without being aware that they have done so. Carlo Ginzburg has described the 'fusion of the clinician's and connoisseur's eye' in Morelli, who had a medical training before turning to paintings. He also compared Morelli to Freud and to the fictional detective Sherlock Holmes, since all three made use of small details as clues to interpretation.[33] Psychologists describe rapidity of judgement as a form of 'thin slicing', in other words 'the ability of our unconscious to find patterns ... based on very narrow slices of experience'.[34]

In a second moment, after the flash of recognition, connoisseurs engage in slow looking in order to confirm or reject their original hypothesis. As Richardson put it, after the first impression, 'let the Composition be Examin'd Near', allowing the observer to notice significant details that support the attribution of a work of art to a particular artist.[35] Hence connoisseurship also requires training in what may be called 'close looking', a term coined on the analogy of 'close reading' in literary studies. Examining a work from different angles and in different lights cannot be done in a hurry.

This point has been made again and again by the connoisseurs themselves. Pierre-Jean Mariette, one of the stars in eighteenth-century France, told beginners that before judging works, 'it is necessary to have examined them for a long time.'[36] Mary Berenson called her husband Bernard 'a *slow* looker, willing to give a picture time to make its full impression', while Berenson himself declared that 'We must look and look and look till we live the painting and for a fleeting moment become identified with it.'[37] A French colleague was surprised to see the British art historian Paul Joannides spending hours observing a single drawing by Michelangelo. 'When I expressed my surprise about the time he took', she remembers, Joannides replied that 'One never finishes looking at a drawing.'[38]

This second practice might be described as feeling a painting all over with one's eyes. Virginia Woolf vividly described her friend

Roger Fry looking at paintings, 'plunging his eyes into them as if he were a humming-bird hawkmoth hanging over a flower, quivering yet still'.[39] As a German art historian, Adolph Goldschmidt, used to say to his students, 'imagine that you are a fly.'[40] No wonder then that connoisseurs have so often been represented with a magnifying glass in their hand, examining the brushwork of a painting in the hope of recognizing the distinctive hand of the artist. Like the hermeneutic circle, close and distant looking reinforce each other in a process of moving backwards and forwards so as not to miss anything important. As Max Friedländer warned his readers, 'the eye tires if it stays too long in the same place,' so that it is best 'to look at a picture periodically for six seconds rather than once for a whole minute'.[41]

Experience is crucial in acquiring a good eye. Indeed, connoisseurship requires constant practising. Berenson once explained that 'I must keep myself in constant training by contact with works of art' and that 'If I stop my researches I shall lose my eye.'[42] Zeri agreed that 'It is necessary to practise looking every day.'[43] Philip Pouncey, a specialist on Italian drawings, 'felt again and again how his own hypersensitivity to distinct styles of drawing might be blunted by an interruption of even one or two weeks' vacation'.[44] In similar fashion, as the celebrated violinist Jascha Heifetz once confessed, 'If I don't practise one day, I know it; two days, the critics know it; three days, the public knows it.'

Another means for connoisseurs to acquire a good eye is by learning to draw and paint themselves. According to one eighteenth-century artist and biographer of artists, to become an 'expert connoisseur' (*esperto conoscitore*), what was needed was 'continual practice in drawing'.[45]

Attribution depends on comparison between the style of a given work and that of possible candidates for its maker. The stars usually have extraordinary visual memories, archives in their mind that allow them to make comparisons at great speed without being aware that they have done so. The rapid judgements are based on decades of close looking together with a sensitivity to small differences in style between masters and their followers. Pope-Hennessy singled out two of his colleagues for these qualities: Roberto Longhi, he wrote, had 'an eye of great speed and often of great accuracy', while the Austrian-American Richard Offner's eye 'was the most rapid I have ever known'.[46] Thanks to his remarkable eye and his no less remarkable memory, Longhi, for instance, was able to show that some paintings by Giotto that had come to rest in different parts of the world over the years were actually parts of the same altarpiece. Longhi was able to reassemble them in his imagination as if they were pieces of a jigsaw puzzle.

Having made their judgement, connoisseurs need to communicate it, to put it into words, describing what they have seen, however doubtful they may be about the possibility of translating the visual into the verbal. Longhi was the master of this kind of description, practised from ancient Greece onwards and known by the Greek term *ekphrasis*.[47]

Needless to say, the reliability of the eye has often been challenged. The French critic Jean-Baptiste Dubos, for instance, described attribution as guesswork and connoisseurship as 'the least reliable of the arts after medicine'. In similar fashion another eighteenth-century critic, Marc-Antoine Laugier, described attribution as conjectural and uncertain.[48] Many connoisseurs agree that attributions based on the eye need to be supplemented by other forms of evidence wherever this is possible. As Berenson admitted in the case of his attribution of a fresco to Antonello da Messina, 'Such a spontaneous recognition is not yet knowledge. It must first withstand every challenge. Has it got the mood, the music, the *tempo* of the Master? Does it resemble him in essential details?'[49]

To answer questions such as these, connoisseurs have often turned to the deliberate comparison of the work in question with known works by the same artist. This method was facilitated by the rise of prints reproducing paintings and later by the rise of photographs. Most connoisseurs also look for documentary evidence. It is particularly important to establish what is now known as a work's 'provenance', in other words its pedigree, the chain of owners from the time that the work was first painted until the present.[50] In this way, as we shall see in detail later, a practice that began as more or less pure *connaissance* has become a mixture of *connaissance* with *savoir*.

When and Where? Rome and China

Discriminating collectors of art can be found in ancient Greece, Rome and China. In ancient Rome, an art market already existed and collecting Greek statues, or Roman copies (generally free copies), became a fashion.[51] Some copies were sold as originals, encouraging the art of discriminating between the two. Cicero, for example, was a connoisseur of Greek sculpture who was aware of unreliable attributions, remarking on one occasion that 'they say it is by Polykleitos' (*Polyclitum esse dicebant*).[52] An epigram by the poet Martial makes fun of a man who pretended to be a connoisseur and 'took counsel of his nose whether the bronzes smelt of Corinth and condemned even your statues, Polykleitos' (*Epigrammata*, Book IX, 59). The fashion for collecting also encouraged *ekphrasis*, a modern name for a literary genre describing works of art, in the tradition of Homer's famous description of the shield of Achilles in the *Iliad*. Examples of the genre include texts by the polymath Pliny the Elder in the first century after Christ, the satirist Lucian of Samosata in the second century and the rhetorician Callistratus in the third. Pliny described works of art in the biographies of artists in books 34–6 of his *Natural History*, inspiring biographies by Giorgio Vasari in the Renaissance.[53]

As for painting, an aristocrat named Vindex was supposed to have been particularly skilled at attributions.[54] In the third century, the Greek philosopher Philostratus of Lemnos wrote a dialogue, *Eikones* (Images), in which a teacher instructs a student in the interpretation of 64 paintings (real or imaginary) displayed in a house in the Greek city of Neapolis (now Naples). This dialogue (or better, monologue, since the ten-year-old student is silent) was continued by the philosopher's grandson, Philostratus the Younger. Both writers concentrate on describing the subjects of the paintings, making only occasional reference to their style or quality in brief phrases that drew attention to 'the dewy look of the roses' or the 'high degree of skill' in representing shadows.[55] The *Eikones* inspired a number of early modern dialogues on art.

In East Asia, there is a long tradition of connoisseurship, especially in China and Japan. In the so-called Edō period (when the capital of Japan was moved from Kyōto to Edō, the modern Tokyo) from the early seventeenth to the mid-nineteenth century, families of connoisseurs emerged who specialized in the knowledge of particular styles of both Chinese and Japanese ink paintings and signed or sealed certificates of attribution. The expert was known as *tsu*. A history of painting was published in 1678 discussing the styles of more than four hundred artists. The vocabulary to describe these styles in Japanese included *wabi* (austere beauty) and *sabi* (a simple rustic style).

Let us look at the Chinese case in a little more detail. The dominant elite of gentlemen scholars, whether or not employed in the civil service, practised both calligraphy and painting as well as collecting examples of both, thus training their eyes to discriminate between the works of different artists. By Chinese standards, the European connoisseurs described in this book arrived rather late at the feast. Discussions of fakes go back at least as far as the fifth century, when Yu He informed the emperor of the many forged examples of calligraphy in the imperial collection and described how forgers 'used drippings from thatched roofs to change the colour of the paper' and so make an example of modern calligraphy 'look like an old piece of writing'.[56]

In response, from the Tang dynasty (618–907 CE) onwards, seals and comments written on the work itself were used to authenticate paintings. In the sixth century, Xie He wrote a guide to what collectors should look for and in it he formulated six 'laws' or 'principles' of painting, including ways of using the brush; in the late Tang, Zhang Yangyuan wrote biographies of painters, like Giorgio Vasari much later.

As in Europe, Chinese collectors respected the 'masters': in this case the 'Four Masters of the Yuan Dynasty' (1271–1368), the 'Four Masters of the Ming Dynasty' (1368–1644), and the 'Four Wangs' of the seventeenth century. Around the year 1300, the scholar Tang

Hou wrote an 'Examination of Painting', in which he declared that while the power of money makes a collector, 'the power of a good eye makes a connoisseur' (someone with discrimination, or *muli* (power of the eye)).[57]

Discussions of *shangjian* (from *shang*, judging quality, and *jian*, judging authenticity) go back at least as far as the Song dynasty (960–1279 CE), when the painter, calligrapher and collector Mi Fu made attributions of works in the imperial collection and boasted of the number of fakes that he had recognized. His attitude to fakes has been described as 'sportsmanlike' rather than judgmental.[58]

Authentication by experts included the study of the material of the work (such as paper or silk), the inscriptions on it and also the personal seals of earlier collectors, an important aid to the study of provenance. In one case, that of a work by the monk Huaisu, the chain of collectors who owned it stretches – with occasional gaps – from the tenth century to the present.[59] Catalogues of collections were produced during the Song dynasty, including one of the collection of Emperor Huizong. The eleventh-century scholar Guo Xi enriched the language available for the criticism of paintings, a vocabulary that had become 'extensive' by the fourteenth century.[60]

There is even more evidence for connoisseurship in the late Ming period in the sixteenth and early seventeenth centuries. For example, an official described in his diary a visit he made to a collector where he was shown a copy of a famous tenth-century painting and a work by a twelfth-century master. 'Both were pieces I had been hoping to appreciate all my life,' so this was 'a rare experience in connoisseurship'. It was at this time that the collector Wen Zhenheng wrote his *Treatise on Superfluous Things*, in which he discussed calligraphy and painting, including the manner in which they should be displayed.[61] And the care and display of paintings and calligraphy were discussed by the artist Dong Qichang: 'In displaying calligraphy or paintings, there are five don'ts: don't show it under a light, on a rainy day, after drinking, in the presence of a vulgar person, or in the presence of a woman.' Dong also recommended that the scrolls should be regularly exposed to the air, to avoid mould.[62] Visual evidence supports the impression left by these texts that viewing paintings in the right way, at leisure and in company, was considered to be a pastime for gentlemen.[63]

Fakes appear to have proliferated in the late Ming period, as the art market expanded along with increasing demand. When he was in Nanjing, the sixteenth-century Jesuit missionary Matteo Ricci noted that the Chinese were 'greatly given to forging antique things, with great artifice and ingenuity'.[64] A poem describing the art market in Suzhou suggests that forgeries continued to proliferate during the seventeenth century:

> Buffalo and horses are invariably signed Dai Song and
> Han Gan
> Landscapes are always called the Elder and Younger Li . . .
> People in high places are so proud of their connoisseurship
> They will keep buying with all the money they have.
> How many authentic antiques can there be?[65]

The methodical detection of forgeries also went back a long way and included not only attention to style but the study of the material, the inscription, the provenance (via the seals of earlier collectors) and other documents.[66]

When and Where? The West

Turning now to Europe, we find connoisseurship gradually emerging between the sixteenth and the nineteenth centuries, first in Italy and then in France, Spain, the Netherlands, Germany and Britain. From the late nineteenth century onwards, it spread more widely, to the United States, Latin America and – in its new form – back to China and Japan, as well as coming to include modern and, more recently, contemporary art.

It is important not to assume that the system of practices described above has remained the same everywhere over the centuries, despite many instances of continuity. There have been many innovations as well as more subtle changes in meaning when traditional terms are employed, among them the phrase 'by his hand', which may sometimes refer to a product of an artist's workshop.[67] In the course of time, concepts that are often taken for granted (including, as we shall see, the ideas of 'original', 'copy', 'restoration' and 'fake') have changed their meaning, a point that underlines the need to historicize the practice of connoisseurship. For example, the term 'originality' itself originated as late as the eighteenth century.[68]

Any attempt to decide when the practice that we know as connoisseurship emerged in modern Europe faces obvious problems. The great French historian Marc Bloch was surely wise to warn his colleagues against what he called 'the idol of origins', which often leads scholars to ignore or at least to underestimate later changes in ideas, practices and institutions.[69] As in the case of other practices, the moment when they were first recorded, the moment of 'textualization', is likely to be much later than the practice itself. The importance of textualization – apart from leaving sources for scholars to study – is that it assists the transition from tacit knowledge to a conscious knowledge that can be criticized and verified.

At what moment connoisseurship in the sense of a system of practices emerged in Europe is a matter of controversy, even if the question is limited to the knowledge of paintings and drawings by the Old Masters, the main topic in what follows. Although a concern with both attribution and copies can be found among collectors of ceramics and furniture, for instance, it was in painting that connoisseurship developed and that most of the stars were active. Here too historicization is needed. Today the term 'Old Masters' (*Altmeister, maîtres d'autrefois*) refers to major artists working between 1400 and 1800, including Jan van Eyck, Raphael, Dürer, Titian, Rembrandt, Rubens, Velázquez, Watteau and Tiepolo. They are followed by 'Modern Masters' such as Delacroix, Turner, the Impressionists and the Post-Impressionists.

Which painters count as 'old' is of course a relative matter. When Peter Paul Rubens died in 1640, for instance, the inventory of his collection of paintings was divided into 'les Pieces des vieux Maistres' and the 'Maistres modernes' of his own time. This is one of the first uses of the phrase in any language, followed in English by the art lover John Evelyn in 1684.[70] By the 1790s, at least in Britain, the phrase 'Old Masters' had become 'widely accepted' to refer to works that had been made before 1789, allowing Antoine Watteau and Giovanni Battista Tiepolo – not to mention Rubens himself – to enter the club.[71] It is on these masters, at work between the fifteenth and the eighteenth century, that the stars have concentrated their attention, as this study will do, though the final chapter addresses the question of the challenges to traditional connoisseurship posed by the rise of modernism and still more by contemporary art.

It is likely that the first connoisseurs were artists, followed by dealers, then amateurs and finally by professionals such as curators or art historians. Artists have long been aware of the styles of their colleagues and rivals, their strengths and especially their weaknesses, and since the fifteenth century, if not before, they have been asked to appraise the work of other artists. In 1457, for instance, the painter Pietro da Milano was asked by the patron who had commissioned the frescos painted in the Ovetari Chapel in Padua to distinguish the hand of Mantegna in those works from that of another artist, Nicolò Pizzolo. Pietro certified that the paintings of the Assumption and of St James were Mantegna's work, 'not that the witness saw him painting them but out of long experience', since 'among painters, it is always known by whose hand any painting is, especially when it is by the hand of any established master.'[72]

For these reasons, it is odd that the rise of connoisseurship (rather than the rise of professional connoisseurs) is sometimes dated to the early nineteenth century, the age of Karl Friedrich von Rumohr, Johann David Passavant and Gustav Waagen – or even later in the century, to the age of Giovanni Battista Cavalcaselle and Giovanni Morelli.[73] This dating is much too late. A case has also been made for the eighteenth century, thanks to the Mariettes, father and son, in Paris, and the Richardsons (once again, father and son) in London, but even this date is surely too late.[74] The three essential parts of connoisseurship – judging quality, attributing works and distinguishing between originals and copies or forgeries – were already discussed in treatises on art in the seventeenth century as well as practised by connoisseurs such as Filippo Baldinucci in Florence, Sebastiano Resta in Rome and Everard Jabach and Roger de Piles in Paris. Their methods were refined later, but the essentials were already present at this time.

At this point, readers may well be asking themselves, as I did at the beginning of my research, were there no connoisseurs during the Renaissance? To answer this question is the purpose of the next chapter.

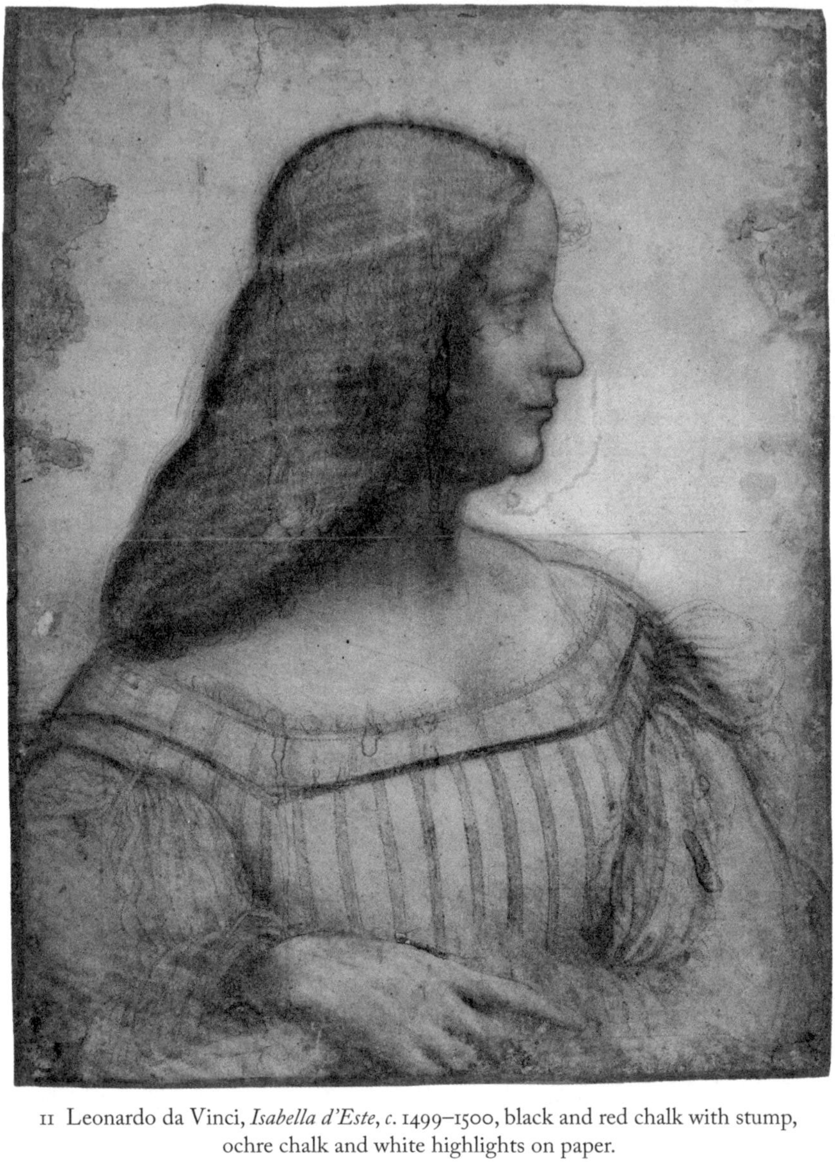

11 Leonardo da Vinci, *Isabella d'Este*, *c.* 1499–1500, black and red chalk with stump, ochre chalk and white highlights on paper.

2

The Birth of the Connoisseur

Looking back, the first connoisseurs about whose activities we are reasonably well informed lived in the period that we know as the Renaissance. This was a great age of art patronage, especially in Italy around the year 1500. Among the most famous patrons of the time were Pope Julius II, the patron of Michelangelo; Pope Leo X, the patron of Raphael; and Isabella d'Este, the Marchioness of Mantua, who collected works by the most famous painters of her time.

Whether this period can also be described as an age of connoisseurship in a strict sense of the term is a more difficult question. To answer it, we should distinguish between an interest in collecting classical antiquities and an interest in commissioning contemporary paintings, as well as consider the three domains of connoisseurship identified in the previous chapter: the sense of quality, the concern with attribution and the discrimination between original works and copies or forgeries.

Collecting Antiquities

The demand for antiquities – especially marble statues, ancient Roman coins and antique cameos and gems – was high at this time, especially in Rome, Venice and Florence.

One major collector was Pietro Barbo (Pope Paul II), who owned about 3,300 objects, including '47 antique bronzes and 227 cameos'. A contemporary described him as having 'an immense knowledge of ancient coins', while an inscription on the frame of a Byzantine sculpture in ivory (now known as the 'Quirin Diptych') refers to his love for these 'works of great skill (*ingenium*)'.[1] A second major collector was Isabella d'Este (illus. 11), who admitted to her 'insatiable desire' for ancient objects (*lo insaciabile desiderio nostro de cose antique*). Isabella (who was advised by her goldsmith, Gian Cristoforo Romano, and by fra Sabba da Castiglione, author of the *Ricordi*, an early guide to collecting) owned more than 1,500 such objects (not counting coins) at her death in 1539, including what an inventory described as 'A cupid who sleeps on a lion's skin, made by Praxiteles'.[2] A third famous collector was Lorenzo de' Medici, whose interest is well documented in his letters. Lorenzo owned at least 43 classical sculptures as well as coins, cameos, gems and vases, some of them made of alabaster or jasper.[3]

Although Paul II and Lorenzo de' Medici are known to have recognized the quality of the pieces they collected, references to the beauty of coins and statues or the skill that went into their making were relatively rare at this time. Antiquities were mainly viewed as relics of a much-admired past and so treated with the respect that was formerly reserved for the relics of the saints. Surviving fragments were a stimulus to reconstruction, supporting the dream of making antiquity whole again.

As for attribution, the fifteenth-century humanist Poggio Bracciolini, an enthusiastic collector on the small scale that his pocket allowed, was sceptical about attributions to the famous artists of the ancient world, whose names were known thanks to the descriptions of their works by the ancient Roman writer Pliny the Elder. Poggio tried to buy marble heads of Juno, Minerva and Bacchus that some Greek dealers attributed to the ancient Greek sculptors Praxiteles and Polykleitos, but he believed that the dealers had simply 'made up the names in order to sell the heads more dearly'.[4] Less critical was the fifteenth-century collector Niccolò Niccoli (or his biographer). Niccoli is praised for his judgement 'in painting and in sculpture' but described as buying a gem 'engraved by the hand of Polykleitos'. Equally uncritical was the anonymous individual who made the inventory of Isabella's possessions, including the Cupid 'made by Praxiteles'.[5]

It took centuries for scholars to realize that what had been thought (sometimes by their original purchasers) to be 'Greek' statues, and even works by certain masters, were usually ancient Roman copies.[6] For a plausible positive attribution of an ancient work, it is necessary to wait until the year 1506, when Michelangelo and his colleague the Florentine sculptor Giuliano da Sangallo identified the newly discovered statue of Laocoön (acquired by Pope Julius II and displayed in his sculpture garden in the Vatican) as the work of three Greek sculptors mentioned by Pliny, though some scholars now suspect that this famous statue is actually an early work by Michelangelo, in other words a successful fake.[7]

Forgery was also discussed at this time. Two contemporary biographies of Michelangelo (one by the patrician Ascanio Condivi and the other by the artist Giorgio Vasari) tell the story of the young artist making a statue of a sleeping Cupid (as Praxiteles had done) and selling it as an antique to a collector, Cardinal Riario. The artist then revealed his forgery, but the client was not convinced. Indeed, Riario ordered Michelangelo to make another fake in order to prove that the Cupid was his own work (a twist in the tale that recurs in biographies of later forgers, as we shall see).[8] It is worth noting that in his biography of Michelangelo, Vasari tells this story not to condemn deception but to illustrate the skill of the artist. Like the Chinese connoisseur Mi Fu, discussed in Chapter One, Vasari's attitude to fakes seems to have been 'sportsmanlike', at least in this case.

Ancient coins were easier to fake than statues. A treatise on ancient coins and medals published in 1555 by the Italian engraver Enea Vico, which was doubtless written with collectors in mind, explains how the forgeries were artificially aged by soaking them in urine and burying them in the earth for a few months.[9]

This brief survey suggests that although there were many collectors of antiquities active at this time, there were few connoisseurs in this field. One was Ambrogio Traversari, the head of the Camaldolese order of monks, who appreciated the quality of ancient coins and was able to date the objects he collected.[10] A second, as we have seen, was Pope Paul II. A third was Lorenzo de' Medici. He too cared for quality and was apparently able to date pieces and to recognize fakes.[11]

Collecting Paintings

Were patrons concerned with quality in painting? They had various reasons for commissioning works of art. One purpose was to display their 'magnificence', a central value for rulers and aristocrats at this time. Another was interior decoration: Isabella d'Este once asked Giovanni Bellini for a picture 'to decorate a study of ours' (*per ornamento d'uno nostro studio*). A third motive was devotion. What most patrons wanted was a painting of a particular religious subject, such as an Annunciation or a Crucifixion. It was only around the year 1500 that a few of them became interested in acquiring works by particular painters, as Isabella's correspondence shows.[12] A few patrons took an interest in the styles of different artists. For example, a report addressed to Ludovico Sforza, Duke of Milan, by one of his agents offered him the choice between the 'virile air' of Botticelli, the 'sweeter air' of Filippino Lippi, the 'angelic air' of Perugino or the 'good air' of Ghirlandaio.[13] It is likely that the agent was paraphrasing the views of some Florentines, who were already vigorous critics of art.[14]

In Venice, the collector Marcantonio Michiel noted what he called the 'graceful air' (*gratia dell'aeri*) in a Madonna by Bellini. However, the term 'air' (*aria*) would soon be replaced by the word 'style' (*maniera*).[15] Michiel himself noted *la maniera del maestro* when describing a portrait by Gentile da Fabriano.[16] In the preface to his famous biographies of artists, Giorgio Vasari (illus. 12) noted the need to discriminate between the styles of different painters (*discernere tra maniera e maniera*). For example, he described the style of the master he most admired, Michelangelo, as the 'grand manner' (*maniera grande*). Again, he noted the 'softness' (*morbidezza*) in works by Giorgione, while condemning other Venetian painters for styles that he describes as 'dry', 'crude' and 'stunted' (*maniera secca, cruda, stentata*).

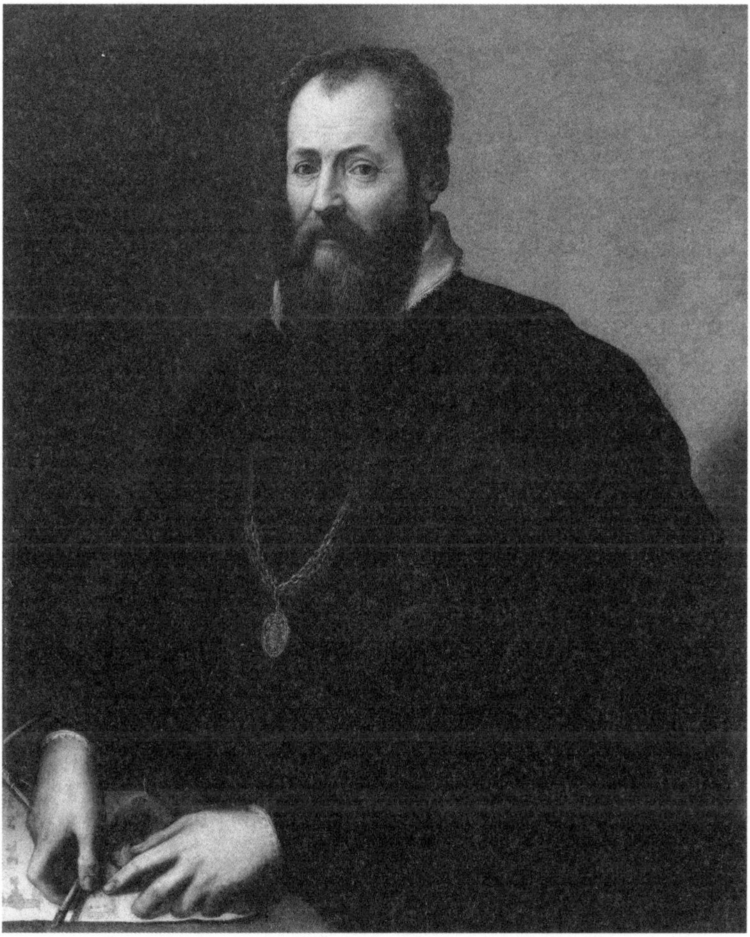

12 Stradanus (attrib.), *Giorgio Vasari*, *c.* 1571, oil on panel.

The interest in attribution on the basis of style is an essential part of connoisseurship. Indeed, some would say that it is *the* essential part. Hence it is worth noting that Vasari used the term *maniera* over 1,300 times in his *Lives*, sometimes to refer to collective styles (the 'Greek' or 'German' manner, for instance) and more often to describe the style of individual artists, rebuking Jacopo da Pontormo, for instance, for changing his style under the influence of Dürer.[17] Another keyword of the time was 'grace' (*grazia*). It was of course a central term in the nobleman Baldassare Castiglione's famous conduct book in the form of a dialogue, *The Courtier* (1528). Since the author was a friend of Raphael, who painted his portrait, it remains unclear whether the language of art was indebted to the language of behaviour in this case or the other way round. The debate on language in this dialogue makes a brief reference to the differences in the style of five famous painters (Leonardo, Mantegna, Raphael, Michelangelo and Giorgione), concluding that 'each was perfect in his style' (*ciascun nel suo stil essere perfettissimo*).[18]

This interest in individual styles, like the rise in this period in the number of paintings signed by the artists, is surely part of the 'development of the individual' emphasized by Jacob Burckhardt in his famous study of the Italian Renaissance.[19] The writing and publishing of biographies, which was becoming increasingly common, or even fashionable, in the sixteenth century, was another consequence of this trend. Vasari was encouraged to write his famous collection of the lives of artists by another biographer, Paolo Giovio, and like him practised what is now called 'oral history', interviewing older people and noting down their memories of the time when they were young.[20] An increasing interest in individuals is also revealed by the rise in the attributions of unsigned paintings to particular artists. The fifteenth-century sculptor Lorenzo Ghiberti made a list of works by earlier Tuscan artists such as Giotto, Taddeo Gaddi, Andrea Orcagna and Ambrogio Lorenzetti (there was little practical need for attributions of contemporary works at this time, since patrons were well aware whom they had commissioned).[21]

Should we speak of connoisseurs of painting at this time? Let us take the case of Vasari. Scholars have noted his collection and attribution of drawings and engravings as well as his remark that the work of individual artists 'is recognized by their style' (*che si conoscono all suo già detto segno*).[22] Vasari also offered many attributions in the course of his famous *Lives*, though he does not seem to have felt any need to justify them.[23] When he revised his book for a second edition, Vasari emphasized his travels to view paintings and 'judge them with my own eyes'.[24] In some cases, though, the attributions must have been made by other people, since it is clear that Vasari had not seen all the works that he mentioned. For this reason, I hesitate to describe him as a connoisseur in the strict sense of the term.

If anyone in this period may safely be described in this way, it is surely the Venetian patrician Marcantonio Michiel. His interest in style has already been mentioned, while he was praised by the writer Pietro Aretino for his judgement of architecture, painting and sculpture.[25] Michiel loved to find out who made the works that he saw, either in public spaces (Donatello's statue of Gattamelata in Padua, for instance) or in private houses, adding notes such as 'was painted by' (*fu dipinto da*) or 'by the hand of' (*di mano di*). Visiting the house of Andrea Odoni, for instance, he noted that the portrait of the owner (a painting that is now in the National Gallery, London) was 'by the hand of Lorenzo Lotto'.[26] Michiel also mentioned pictures on which two artists collaborated, as in the case of Giorgione's *Three Philosophers*, which according to him was 'completed by Sebastiano Venetiano'. He sometimes expressed doubts. In the case of a painting of St Jerome, 'some people believe that it is by Antonello da Messina, but others attribute it [*l'attrbuiscono*, an early use of this term in the context of art] to Hans Memling.' So did Michiel himself, because the work 'reveals the artist's style' (*mostra quella maniera*).

Originals, Copies and Fakes

There is also evidence of discrimination between originals and copies at this time, including copies that were sometimes made, or at least employed, to deceive. Andrea del Sarto, for example, was commissioned to copy Raphael's famous portrait of Pope Leo x. When his patron, Ottaviano de' Medici, was requested to send the original to the Duke of Mantua, Ottaviano sent the copy instead. According to Vasari, no one noticed. Still more remarkable, Giulio Romano, who had assisted Raphael in painting the original portrait, believed that he recognized his own brushstrokes in this copy, although they were actually the work of Andrea. As in the case of Michelangelo's *Cupid*, it was the skill, not the deceit, that interested Vasari.[27] As for Michiel, he once remarked on a painting by Giorgione that a fellow collector, Giovanni Ram, 'possesses a copy of it, which he believes to be the original' (*egli creda che sii el proprio*).[28] Unfortunately, Michiel did not explain how he knew that the Ram version was a copy.

There is curiously little to say about forged paintings at this time, perhaps because collectors still concentrated their attention on contemporary art. An exception to the rule was noted by a sixteenth-century Spanish writer, Felipe de Guevara, who referred to a number of fakes of the work of Hieronymus Bosch and may have been the first writer on art to mock the ignorance of collectors. King Philip of Spain was known to be an enthusiast for Bosch, which may explain why that artist's work appealed to forgers.[29]

It is difficult to deny the title of 'connoisseur' to Michiel or indeed to Vasari, thanks in particular to his interest in drawings and engravings, despite the fact that Vasari refused to believe that some woodcuts attributed to Dürer were works by the master, calling them 'inferior designs' (today, they are accepted as works by Dürer).[30] How many people shared their interests in their day is not easy to say. When Dürer was in Venice, he was delighted to meet a number of people who, in his words, were 'knowledgeable in painting'. He does not name them, but we are surely entitled to suspect that he met Michiel and other members of his circle, including the patricians Taddeo Contarini and Gabriele Vendramin, the owner of Giorgione's famous *Tempest*.[31] Other knowledgeable individuals to be found in Florence and Rome include Paolo Giovio, a professional physician who became a bishop and was described by Vasari as having 'great knowledge and judgement in matters of our arts'.

The examples given in this chapter suggest that the different elements in what is now known as 'connoisseurship' – the eye for quality, an interest in dating and attribution, and the ability to identify copies or fakes – already existed separately in Italy in the fifteenth and sixteenth centuries in the case of antiquities, and were coming to do so in that of painting. Indeed, it might be argued that the growing knowledge of painting on the part of patrons and collectors was a displacement of the skills developed in the course of studying classical antiquities.

Given this separation, we may conclude that as late as the sixteenth century, if there were connoisseurs, there was still no connoisseurship. The different elements would only be combined into a system in the seventeenth century, when a number of treatises testify to the crystallization or codification of older practices. Antiquities would still be collected for centuries, but the focus of interest moved to paintings. A kind of hybridization took place, involving on one side more attention to the aesthetic side of antiquities, and on the other a more scholarly approach to pictures, as we shall see in the following chapter.

3

Codifying Connoisseurship

As we saw in Chapter One, scholars differ about the date for the emergence of connoisseurship, whether as early as the Renaissance or as late as the nineteenth century. The central argument of this chapter is that it was in the seventeenth century that connoisseurship developed into a system of practices and that there was increasing awareness of its methods. A phrase such as the 'codification of connoisseurship' seems appropriate to describe this process.[1]

New words are often indicators of other changes. At this time, the term *conoscitore* came into use in Italy and *connoisseur* in France (where both André Félibien and Roger de Piles used the word in their treatises on art). In the Netherlands the equivalent was *const-verstandigen*, a term employed by the Dutch artist and writer Karel van Mander in 1604 and derived from the Italian *intendente*, someone who understands painting or antiquities.[2] The spread of these words suggests that amateur collectors as well as artists and dealers were now assessing and attributing works of art.[3] Antiquities were still collected with enthusiasm, often by the same individuals who bought pictures, among them Lord Arundel, whose collection will be described below, and Peter Paul Rubens, whose correspondence with another collector (the British diplomat Sir Dudley Carleton) reveals his interest in offering some of his own paintings in return for some 'marbles'.[4]

It was for the guidance of this growing group of collectors that so many treatises on the art of judging paintings appeared at this time, together with biographies of artists and general reflections on art and its history. They form part of a larger movement for textualization, in other words setting down in writing, for a wider public, forms of practical knowledge that had previously been transmitted to apprentices by word of mouth or by example. Such 'how to do it' books can be found in Europe from around the year 1400 onwards, an early example being the *Craftsman's Handbook* (*Libro dell'arte*) by the Florentine painter Cennino Cennini.[5] The trend was amplified by the invention of printing. Famous texts of this kind range from Castiglione's *Cortegiano* (1528) on the perfect courtier to Vannoccio Biringuccio's *Pirotechnia* (1540), a handbook of metalworking, and from Bernard Palissy's *Recepte véritable* (1563), a 'true recipe' for making pottery, to Samuel Quiccheberg's *Inscriptiones* (1565), a guide for would-be collectors of paintings and other objects that includes instructions for displaying them. Paradoxically some of these books claimed that the knowledge they described was secret, while making it widely available, and put into words what (so the authors asserted) could only be communicated by observation.[6] An early example, written in 1586, explains that the text has been written for collectors in order to make explicit the implicit knowledge of artists, in whose memories are lodged 'many fine secrets and suggestions' (*molti bei secreti e avvertimenti*).[7]

In the seventeenth century, we find a whole series of texts on judging paintings, testifying to a growing demand from collectors. These collectors were known either in Italian as *virtuosi* or in French as *curieux*, emphasizing their wide interests, or more specifically as 'art lovers': *amateurs* in French, *liefhebbers* in Dutch or *dilettanti* (those who delight in something) in Italian. At this time, *dilettante* did not yet have the pejorative meaning that it would acquire in the age of professionalization.

Texts on Painting

1604	Karel van Mander, *Het Schilderboek*
c. 1612–17	Giulio Mancini, *Considerazioni sulla pittura* (written)
c. 1615	Giambatista Agucchi, *Trattato della pittura* (written)
1626	Juan de Butron, *Ingenuidad de la Pintura*
1632	Antoon van Dyck, *Icones*
1633	Vicente Carducho, *Diálogos de la pintura*
1637	Franciscus Junius, *De pictura veterum*
1642	Philips Angel, *Lof der Schilderkunst*
1642	Giovanni Baglioni, *Vite de'Pittori*
1642	Carlo Ridolfi, *Vita di Jacopo Robusti*
1648	Carlo Ridolfi, *Maraviglie dell'arte*
1649	Abraham Bosse, *Sentiments sur la distinction des diverses manières de peinture*
1649	Francisco Pacheco, *Arte de Pintura*
1658	Alexander van Fornenbergh, *Den Antwerpschen Protheus* [Quentin Matsys]
1660	Marco Boschini, *Carta del navegar pittoresco*
1662	Cornelis de Bie, *Het Gulden Cabinet*
1666	André Félibien, *Entretiens*
1667	Carlo Roberto Dati, *Vite de'pittori antichi*
1672	Giovanni Pietro Bellori, *Vite de'Pittori*
c. 1673	Giovanni Battista Passeri, *Vite de'Pittori* (written)
1674	Marco Boschini, *Breve Instruzione per intender le maniere*
1674	Raffaele Soprani, *Vite de'Pittori*
1675–80	Joachim von Sandrart, *Teutsche Academie*
1677	Roger de Piles, *Conversation sur la connoissance de la peinture*
1678	Carlo Cesare Malvasia, *Felsina Pittrice*
1678	Samuel van Hoogstraten, *Inleyding tot de hooge schoole der schilderkonst*

c. 1679	Giovanni Battista Passeri, *Vite de'Pittori* (completed)
1681	R. de Piles, *Vie de Rubens*
1681	Filippo Baldinucci, *Vocabolario toscano dell'arte di disegno*
1682	Baldinucci, *Vita de Bernini*
1685	William Aglionby, *Painting Illustrated in Three Dialogues*
1695	Giovanni Pietro Bellori, *Descrizione delle immagini dipinte da Raffaele*
1699	R. de Piles, *Idée du peintre parfait*

These authors wrote in seven languages: Italian, Spanish, Dutch, German, French, English and Latin. Besides celebrating the lives of individual artists and their regions of origin, some of them discussed the skills that were mentioned earlier: the sense of quality, attributions to particular artists and the way to distinguish originals from copies. It appears that the seventeenth century was the time when close looking at paintings was first recommended to art lovers, to observe and appreciate details (including the brushwork) in addition to viewing the painting as a whole.[8]

The number of treatises in the form of a dialogue between teacher and student is worth noting: Carducho, Boschini, Félibien, Piles and Aglionby. They are genuine dialogues in the sense of including questions from the student. In other words, they are closer to the model of Plato than to that of the ancient writer Philostratus, mentioned in Chapter One. Dialogue offered a bridge between oral and written culture, making it appropriate for a topic that drew on the practical knowledge of artists as well as on the historical and theoretical knowledge of scholars. Like Philostratus, the authors of these treatises have much to say about the iconography of paintings, which are sometimes described in detail in a revival of the classical tradition of *ekphrasis*. This interest in description is particularly clear in *La galeria*, a collection of poems by the fashionable baroque writer Giambattista Marino, who praised works by Raphael, Correggio and Titian as well as by masters of his own time such as Guido Reni.

These paintings were supposed to be displayed in a house in Naples (as in the text by Philostratus, whose *Images* Marino was trying to imitate and surpass).[9]

Why the years around 1600 should have been a turning point in the history of connoisseurship is an intriguing question with various possible answers. One of these is that the treatises were a response to demand on the part of the increasing number of amateur collectors of art. Another answer is to point to the rise of academies of art in this period, in Milan, Rome, Paris (where Abraham Bosse and Roger de Piles were members), Nuremberg, Berlin, Antwerp and London. In these academies, students not only practised drawing but attended lectures on art and they may also have read books on the subject.[10] A third possible reason for the timing of this turning point is that the rise of the art market encouraged judgements on paintings by making comparisons easier than before, since many works would be displayed together in the shops of dealers or in the annual exhibition shown in Rome in the Pantheon. In the growing city of Amsterdam, the art market was also expanding rapidly at this time. It also expanded in Venice, where leading dealers in art included two Netherlanders, Daniel Nijs and Jan Reynst.[11]

Yet another explanation for the turning point is to note that the interest in old paintings was a new one. Thanks to the achievement of artists of the Renaissance, especially Raphael, Dürer and Titian, old paintings now competed with new ones for the attention of collectors. They became 'Old Masters', a term that first appears in the seventeenth century. In contrast, an interest in what was originally known as 'ancient music' only developed in the eighteenth century, in England, before spreading elsewhere and becoming known as 'classical'.[12]

The Discovery of Old Paintings

Connoisseurship of these 'Old Masters' – who were still relatively new masters – became necessary once collectors of pictures began to take an interest in works that had been painted before their own time. A few examples can be found before the year 1600. On one occasion, Isabella d'Este revealed an interest in a work by a master who had lived in the preceding century: Jan van Eyck's lost painting of the drowning of Pharaoh's army in the Red Sea.[13] Marcantonio Michiel recorded viewing a painting by Hans Memling 'made in 1450', and a portrait by 'Roger of Brussels' (Roger van der Weyden), 'the celebrated ancient painter' (*pittor antico celebre*).[14] Other early examples come from the Habsburg family. Margaret of Austria, regent of the Netherlands and herself an amateur artist, owned the famous Arnolfini portrait by Jan van Eyck, who died four decades before she was born. Her niece Mary of Hungary, who inherited her collection, also loved fifteenth-century Flemish art. A third Habsburg, Philip II of Spain, collected works by Hieronymus Bosch, as was noted earlier, as well as owning a *Crucifixion* by Roger van der Weyden.[15]

Yet another member of the Habsburg family, the emperor Rudolf II, owned a number of paintings by Dürer, including the *Adoration of the Magi* and the *Rosenkranzfest* (obtained in 1606, a century after it was painted). He also owned works by Titian, Correggio and Parmigianino, and tried, unsuccessfully, to acquire paintings by Matthias Grünewald, Hans Holbein and Lucas van Leyden. His rival in this respect was Maximilian of Bavaria, who acquired Dürer's *Lamentation of Christ* and the so-called 'Heller Altarpiece' (a painting, now lost, of the assumption and coronation of the Virgin Mary).[16] Copies were commissioned by these collectors to replace the originals in the churches from which they had been taken. What for pious viewers were primarily holy images, representations of sacred events, were now viewed by collectors as examples of the skill of their makers. It was for this reason that the German scholar Hans Belting argued that the history of art only begins at the end of the Middle Ages.[17]

The growing art market responded to this new demand for old art. By the end of the sixteenth century, dealers specializing in old paintings begin to appear in Italian cities such as Rome, where a certain Costantino Spata described himself in this way (as *regattiero de quadri vecchi*) in 1597.[18] Demand encouraged supply and supply in its turn encouraged demand by the display of these old paintings.

Some artists now produced works in the manner of famous predecessors as a means of showing off their skill. The Dutch engraver Hendrick Goltzius, for instance, made prints that were inspired by the work of Dürer.[19] To describe works such as these, which are sometimes treated as fakes, connoisseurs such as Filippo Baldinucci and Roger de Piles employed a new term, 'pastiche' (in Italian, *pasticcio*, originally a pie or pastry with a mixed filling).[20] However, some art dealers sold copies of paintings as if they were originals, as the Dutch artist and dealer Gerrit van Uylenburgh was accused of doing in 1675.[21] No wonder then that the treatises on art discussed how to discriminate between originals and copies, though some authors dismissed copies as inferior while others valued them.[22]

Two leading Venetian painters of this period, Pietro della Vecchia and Luca Giordano, became famous for their pastiches of Renaissance masters, whose work they imitated but also tried to surpass. Vecchia was known as 'the ape of Giorgione', but also as his 'twin' (*gemello*), while his work was sometimes mistaken for that of the master.[23] The market also included fakes, in the sense of imitations intended to deceive the customer, whether the intention was that of the artist or a dealer. Fake paintings by the masters were mentioned rarely in the sixteenth century but frequently in the seventeenth, notably fake Dürers, Giorgiones, Ruisdaels and Claudes. Indeed, forgeries of landscapes by Claude Lorrain were so common that they provoked the artist to produce a catalogue of his genuine paintings, entitled the *Liber veritatis*.[24]

The Growing Interest in Attribution

The seventeenth-century evidence for interest in attribution is rich and various. As the list above suggests, published biographies of artists on the model of Vasari's *Lives* became increasingly common in the seventeenth century, especially in Italy, where regional responses to Vasari's notorious privileging of Tuscany include

Giovanni Baglione on Rome, Carlo Ridolfi on Venice, Raffaele Soprani on Genoa and Carlo Malvasia on Bologna. As in the case of Vasari, these biographies included many attributions of works of art, whether these were documented or depended on the eye. The growing interest in attributions is surely linked to a similar interest in the biographies of writers and in the attribution of anonymous writings at this time. For example, a biography of Montaigne was prefixed to the 1608 edition of his *Essays*, while the German scholar Vincent Placcius published a list identifying the authors of a number of anonymous and pseudonymous works.[25]

In the case of paintings, evidence of interest in attribution comes from inventories of the goods of the upper class. In seventeenth-century Venice, for instance, we find cautious phrases such as the following: 'An old portrait, a copy of Raphael'; 'An old painting in the style of Giorgione'; 'An old painting on wood, believed to be by Giovanni Bellini'.[26]

In Spain, too, inventories of collections offered attributions. The inventory of the collection of the Duke of Medina, for instance, made in 1647, refers to paintings 'by the hand' of Correggio, Dürer and Raphael, but describes another work as 'not by the hand of Titian but a copy', and yet another as 'school of Titian'.[27] An inventory of the famous collection of Gaspar de Haro, Marquis of Carpio, emphasizes authenticity with the phrases 'original by Leonardo', 'original by Titian', 'original by Tintoretto' and so on.[28] One appraisal of the value of a collection, carried out by an artist, has been described as 'an exercise in connoisseurship', while a case has been noted where the appraiser 'seems to have been forced to use attributions provided by the collector himself', but used his valuations to criticize some of them.[29]

In the Dutch Republic, inventories made following the death of collectors also offered attributions, especially after the middle of the seventeenth century, though 'only in the more valuable estates' such as that of Herman Becker, who owned a work by Dürer, several Rembrandts and what was originally described as 'A wedding by Bruegel'. In this case 'by' was crossed out and replaced with 'in the style of', testifying to an argument about attribution.[30]

In Flanders at this time, inventories reveal a similar awareness of problems of attribution, including phrases such as 'judged to be by' a given painter, or 'in the manner' of another, distinguishing the 'early' manner of a particular artist from his 'late' style or recording disagreements concerning the status of a work, whether original or copy.[31] The inventory of the paintings owned by Rubens, following his death in 1640, includes a painting 'retouched by Titian', 'A portrait judged to be by Raphael of Urbino' and a portrait of Charles V 'by Van Dyck after Titian'.[32]

Artists were regularly consulted on attributions in the seventeenth century, producing certificates (known in Italian as *perizie*), as art consultants still do, declaring that a given work was painted by a given artist. In Italy, academies of art might appoint certain artists as official assessors, as the Academy of St Luke in Rome appointed Giovanni Maria Morandi.[33] In the Netherlands, Vermeer acted as an expert witness in the Van Uylenburgh case mentioned above, while in Spain Velázquez reported to his master King Philip IV on the quality, attribution and provenance of certain paintings.[34] Another famous example of the artist as connoisseur is Gianlorenzo Bernini, who was closely observed on his visit to France in 1665 by a French amateur, the nobleman Paul Fréart de Chantelou, who accompanied him during his time in Paris. Chantelou quotes Bernini as saying that Raphael painted Leo X 'in the manner of Titian' and describes the artist in the act of examining the second series of the famous paintings of the *Seven Sacraments* by Nicolas Poussin. In this vivid record of close looking, 'Bernini remained motionless in front of the paintings for some time, and then went down on his knees and changed his spectacles in order to see better . . . He did not tire of studying them for a whole hour.'[35] Chantelou also recorded Bernini's interest in viewing Everard Jabach's collection of drawings and noted that when the artist visited the collection of the king's secretary of state, he noted several works attributed to Jacopo Bassano and declared that none of them were originals (Bernini owned a few of Bassano's paintings himself).[36]

It was at this time that attributing works of art was recorded as a collective enterprise in some circles and even as a kind of game.

In Madrid, for instance, according to the dialogues by the court artist Vicente Carducho, art lovers (*aficionados*, the equivalent of *amateurs*) discussed

> paintings, drawings, models and statues with much knowledge of all the originals by Raphael, Correggio, Titian, Tintoretto, Veronese, Palma, Bassano and other famous masters (both old and contemporary) that there are in this city . . . It was a pleasure to see this going on, with people enthusiastically, and very knowledgeably, engaging in discussion with the best artists who were there and with many other private wits, Gentlemen and Lords, who spent many a happy hour engaged in this virtuous pursuit.[37]

In London in 1637, the artist-architect Inigo Jones accompanied King Charles I to see some paintings that had been sent as a gift to the king from Rome. Charles had the labels removed in order to test the skill of Jones in the art of attribution. We learn from the papal diplomat Gregorio Panzani that 'in order to be able to study them better', Jones 'threw off his coat, put on his eyeglasses, took a candle and, together with the King, began to examine them very closely [*minutamente*]'. Panzani's verdict was that Jones was someone who really understood paintings (*molto intendente di pitture*).[38] On another occasion, Jones was described by the art agent Balthasar Gerbier while he was looking at a portrait by Titian: he 'almost went on his knees before it'.[39]

In Paris, the banker Everard Jabach (illus. 13), whose collection included works by Dürer, Holbein and Leonardo, had the reputation of a star of connoisseurship. In 1637 the painter Daniel Mytens reported to the collector Lord Arundel that 'Mr Everard' (as he called Jabach) had been to see 'a work that was said to be a Leonardo but was actually a copy after Mabuse'.[40] Jabach's disattributions impressed the Dutch scientist Christiaan Huygens, who wrote to his brother that 'You would have had unparalleled pleasure to see Jabach determine the authenticity of those pieces with a magisterial complacency; only to conclude that out of 300 drawings that were attributed to Raphael there were but two originals.'[41]

As noted earlier, concern with owning originals rather than copies was increasing at this time. When Queen Henrietta Maria sent King Philip IV portraits by Van Dyck of herself, her husband King Charles and their son, a British diplomat in Spain wrote home with the embarrassing news that the paintings 'were discovered to be no originals'. When Bernini, on his visit to Paris, was taken to see

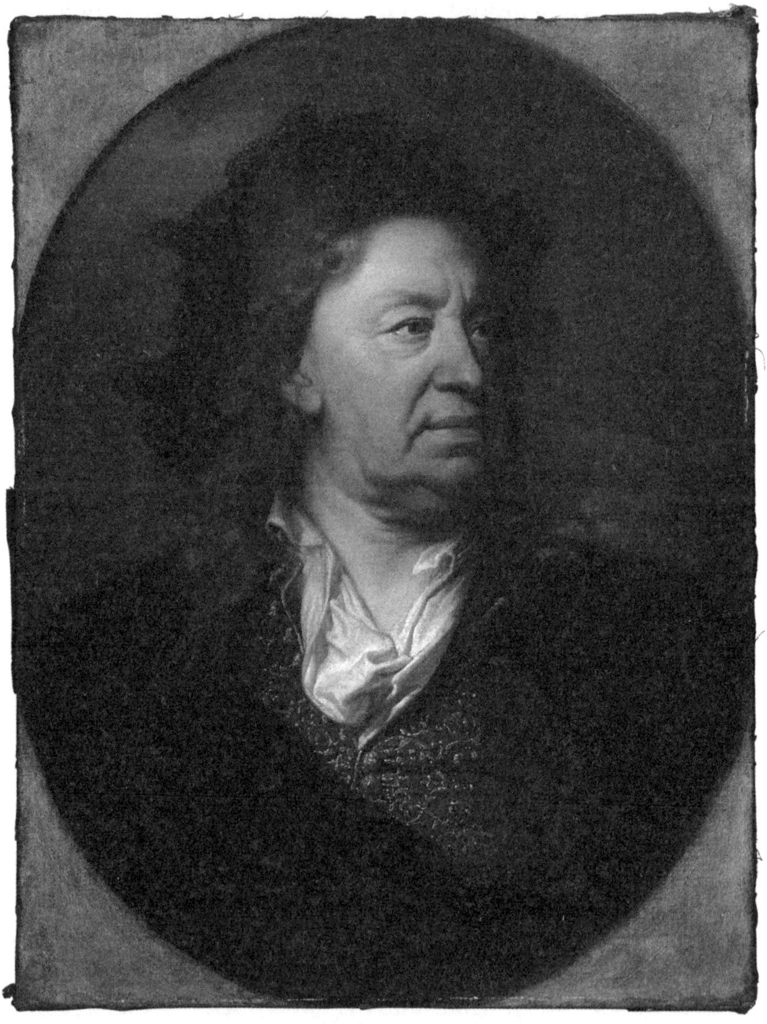

13 School of Hyacinthe Rigaud, *Everard Jabach*, *c.* 1688, oil on canvas.

a painting attributed to Raphael, he 'pointed to a hand' and remarked, 'You can always tell from the painting of these parts whether a picture is original or not.'[42] Paradoxically, this concern with originality coexisted with awareness that paintings were often the collective productions of an artist's workshop. For example, when the English diplomat Dudley Carleton wished to acquire a painting by Rubens that was 'by his hand', rather than a product of his studio, Rubens replied that the copies were 'so retouched by my own hand that it would be hard to distinguish them from originals'.[43]

The Italian Moment

Italians played a leading role in the development of connoisseurship at this time. Writers on art were often inspired by Vasari, whether to correct him, to fill the gaps that he left or to continue his work. We do not know how many connoisseurs were active in seventeenth-century Italy – or, for that matter, anywhere else. In any case, attempts to count them ignore the differences in knowledge and skill between one connoisseur and another. What can be done, though, is to describe some of the treatises on connoisseurship written at this time and to draw miniature portraits of a few of the most famous or the best documented examples of the tribe of *conoscitori*.

The earliest of the treatises was the work of Giulio Mancini, who served the art-loving Pope Urban VIII as his physician and collected paintings as a hobby, describing art as 'the delight of a gentleman' (*diletto di un gentilhuomo*). His *Considerazioni sulla pittura*, written in the years 1617–21, was not printed until 1956, but was already circulated in manuscript form in the seventeenth century. The treatise ranges widely, from the prices of paintings and instructions on how to frame and hang them to the history of art from ancient Egypt onwards and the biographies of recent artists. It also offers an early example of attempts to codify the principles and practice of what we now call 'connoisseurship'. Written for amateur collectors, Mancini's *Considerations* made explicit the 'tacit knowledge' of artists and art dealers.

In a few lines, Mancini summarized what are still considered to be the main elements of connoisseurship. He explained how to judge the quality of a painting (*dar giuditio della pittura*), how to discover the time and place in which it was made and how to distinguish originals from copies or fakes (some of which were painted on old canvases and artificially aged by smoking (a trick that Chinese forgers had discovered centuries earlier, the better to deceive the unwary buyer).

Mancini was also concerned to identify painters through their style (*modo*), recommending attention to mannerisms in the representation of details such as drapery and locks of hair as clues to attribution that are similar to individual handwriting.[44] Giovanni Morelli may have been the first to recommend looking at painted ears as a guide to attribution (as discussed in Chapter Five), but his seventeenth-century predecessors such as Mancini and Bernini had already suggested looking at hands, hair and drapery for the same reason.

Mancini also discussed drawings, noting that copies can be recognized because they lack the boldness (*fierezza*) and the vigour (*resolutione*) of the original.[45] An interest in drawings offers a criterion for distinguishing between connoisseurs and other collectors, since drawings were not displayed on the walls of grand houses as symbols of wealth or status – as paintings were – but were kept in portfolios to be taken out, examined at leisure and discussed by enthusiasts such as Sebastiano Resta and Filippo Baldinucci.

Resta, who came from Milan, was the son of an artist. He moved to Rome and became a priest in 1668 but spent much of his time with artists and fellow collectors. He planned a history of Italian art but never wrote it, although his annotations on two copies of Vasari's *Lives* reveal his preparations for this study.[46] Resta's method of attribution was to look for what he called a 'touchstone' (*pietra di paragone*), in other words a drawing or painting that was definitely by a given artist and so served as a base for attributing other works. He also carried out archival research and he supplemented his close looking at drawings and paintings by paying attention to their provenance, since, as he put it, 'pictures move around' (*girano le pitture*). Hence it is the duty of the *dilettante* (a favourite term of his) to find out where they had been and who had owned them.[47] On one occasion, Resta asked a group of his artist friends to give their opinion of a painting variously attributed to Correggio and to the Mannerist painter and architect Lelio Orsi. The participants recorded and signed their opinions.[48]

Resta's passion was the appreciation and the attribution of drawings, which he liked to discuss with his friends in a kind of salon, turning connoisseurship into a game, like the Spanish *aficionados* mentioned earlier. The reason for his focus on drawings is revealed by Resta's habit of referring to them as 'thoughts' (*pensieri*), thanks to which he 'entered into the artist's mind' and observed its changes, known in Italian as *pentimenti* (repentances). For example, he referred to Correggio's 'drawings of his first thoughts . . . his second thoughts . . . his third'. It was appropriate that Resta should have been drawn, by his friend Carlo Maratta, in the act of examining a drawing (illus. 14). Resta was honest enough to record his changes of attribution, writing on one occasion that 'I thought it was Rosso Fiorentino, but it is Baccio Bandinelli.'[49]

Resta's contemporary the Florentine Filippo Baldinucci (illus. 15) has been described as 'one of the century's greatest connoisseurs'.[50] He studied drawing, painting and engraving but emphasized (as Mancini had done) that his interest in art was simply a hobby and a pastime (*ricreazione e passatempo*). In working hours, Baldinucci was an accountant employed by the art-loving cardinal Leopoldo de' Medici. Hearing about his skill in attribution, Leopoldo challenged Baldinucci to attribute two hundred drawings to the correct artists. According to Filippo's son Francesco Saverio, Baldinucci passed this test with flying colours.[51] The result was that Leopoldo appointed the connoisseur as keeper of his collection of drawings as well as employing him to acquire works of art. Like Resta, Baldinucci planned to update Vasari's *Lives* but never published his biographies of artists (known as the *Notizie*). It was only in the eighteenth century that they appeared in print.

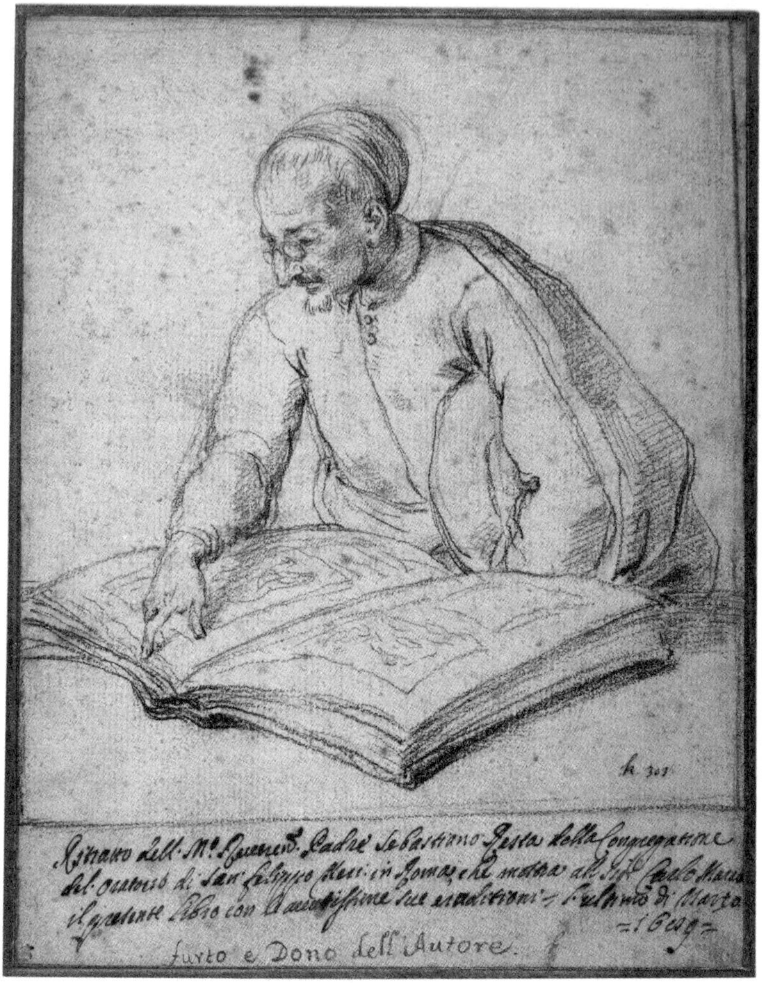

14 Carlo Maratta, *Padre Sebastiano Resta Examining a Folio of Drawings*, before 1713, red chalk on paper.

In 1681 Baldinucci wrote a letter to the Florentine patrician Vincenzo Capponi.[52] This letter might be described as a mini-treatise on connoisseurship, amplifying Mancini's brief account and adding some characteristic qualifications. The first question that Baldinucci raises is whether a correct judgement of paintings can only be made by a professional artist (*il perito professore dell'arte*) or whether there is also a role for the 'brilliant amateur' (*il dilettante ingenioso*). This debate was already an old one. Mancini, for instance, had referred to the 'right' of someone who is not a painter to pass judgement on a painting. Baldinucci's contribution was to distinguish the knowledgeable amateur from those who judge a work on the simple grounds of liking or disliking.[53]

The second question is 'whether there is a reliable rule' for telling original paintings from copies. Baldinucci distinguishes between some copies and others, noting that the ones that are most difficult to recognize are those produced by assistants in the workshop and then given a few final touches (*ritocche*) by the master. Baldinucci is also careful to distinguish between copies of paintings and copies of drawings. In the case of a sketch, he notes, like Resta, that it is particularly difficult for a copyist to reproduce the spontaneity (*franchezza*) of the original.[54]

The third question is whether attributions of works to particular artists are certain or not. Like his predecessor Mancini, Baldinucci declares that attribution is based on recognizing the individual style

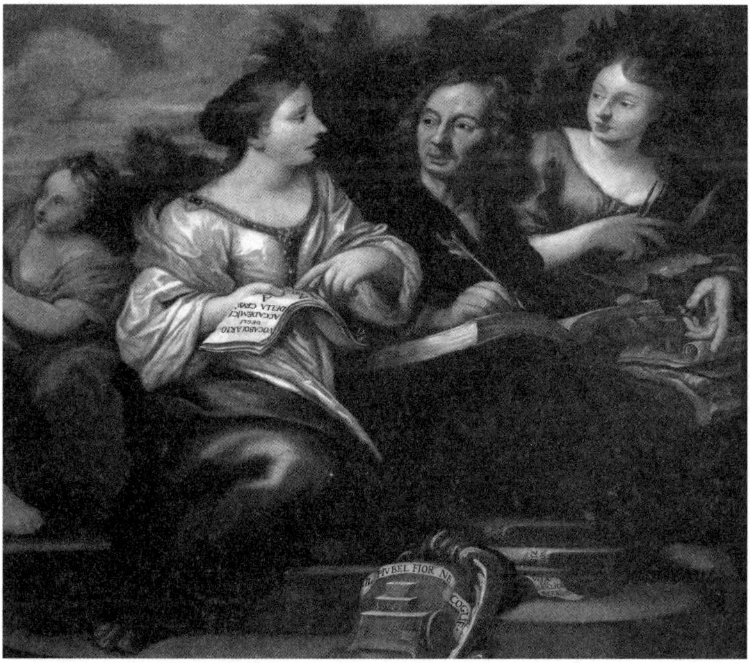

15 Detail of Pietro Dandini, *Filippo Baldinucci in the Act of Writing the Notizie*, *c.* 1691–3, oil on canvas.

(*maniera*) of the artist, his 'hand' or 'habits', as they are revealed by certain details (*minutezze*) in the hair or drapery of the figures. However, he notes with his customary caution that such judgements are never certain, since some pupils learn to imitate the style of their master, while the same painter may work in different styles in the course of a career.[55]

In the same year as the famous letter to Capponi, Baldinucci published a dictionary of artistic terms, distinguishing fourteen styles and offering about eighty terms to describe them.[56] Many more technical terms came into use at this time. The art historian Philip Sohm has collected about two hundred adjectives used in early modern Italy to describe styles. Many of them come in pairs. For example, a hard style – also known as 'dry' (*secco*), 'stony' (*statuino*) or 'wooden' (*legnoso*) – is distinguished from a soft or tender one (*morbido, tenero*). Again, a rough style (*aspro, rozzo*) is distinguished from a smooth one and a finished style from one that was deliberately unfinished (the *non finito*).[57] The expansion of vocabulary facilitated the *ekphrasis* or detailed description of paintings, which became increasingly common in the seventeenth century. Famous examples include the poet Giambattista Marino's *La galeria* (1619), mentioned earlier, and the antiquary Giovanni Pietro Bellori's description of frescos by Raphael, the *Descrizione delle immagini dipinte da Raffaelle d'Urbino* (1696). Bellori was interested in both ancient and modern works of art, ranging from Trajan's Column to the sculptures of Bernini.

It is clear that at least a few Italians had come a long way from the agent of the fifteenth-century Duke of Milan and his simple terms *aria dolce* and *aria buona*. This point is an important one since, given 'the power of language to shape what we see', a rich vocabulary for describing works of art helps viewers to notice distinctions that they might otherwise have missed.[58] Connoisseurs enriched the vocabulary of their native languages and these enrichments smoothed the path for their successors.

Reading the Signs

The attribution of paintings may be described as one practice, among others, of reading signs. As Carlo Ginzburg noted in the 1970s, the physician Mancini attributed paintings on the basis of their style in a similar way to his diagnosis of illnesses on the basis of their symptoms.[59] The increasing interest in attribution can also be linked to interest in the interpretation of signs in fields other than art and medicine.

Two Italian texts from the seventeenth century bear eloquent testimony to this interest. One was a treatise on the art of gesture by the lawyer Giovanni Bonifacio, published in 1616, a kind of encyclopaedia that includes what the book's recent editor describes as a 'theory' of its topic. It is no surprise to find a lawyer writing on this subject. Like physicians reading symptoms, investigating magistrates followed clues.[60] The second text, even closer to the art of attribution, was a treatise on letters by Camillo Baldi, a lecturer in philosophy at the University of Bologna. This treatise is mainly concerned with the traditional topic of the rhetoric of letter-writing, but it focuses, unlike its predecessors, on what writers reveal about themselves and includes a few pages on what is now known as 'graphology'.[61]

In this way, Baldi's treatise may be linked to a tradition of comparing the recognition of a painter by his style to the recognition of an individual's handwriting. According to Vasari, for instance, in the conclusion to his *Lives*, a painter, thanks to long practice, 'recognizes the various styles of artists, just as a good secretary recognizes the different ways of writing of his colleagues'. Mancini agreed, noting 'a certain experience in recognizing the painting of particular periods, just as antiquarians and librarians have for scripts', as well as recognizing the 'hands' of individual artists. The comparison between brushwork and handwriting became a commonplace, repeated by the Italian connoisseur Filippo Baldinucci, the French connoisseur Roger de Piles, the Italian art historian Luigi Lanzi, the Italian connoisseur Giovanni Morelli, his friend the British connoisseur Austen Layard, the American Bernard

Berenson and the British art dealer Joseph Duveen, who once asserted that 'the individual technique of any great painter who died centuries ago was as familiar and recognizable to him as a friend's handwriting.'[62]

The seventeenth century also marks an important period in the history of textual criticism, when leading scholars amended corrupt texts (in parallel with the restoration of paintings), dated them, and drew attention to the anachronisms that revealed forgeries, as restorers did when they recognized nineteenth-century varieties of pigment in a 'Renaissance' picture (below, Chapter Five). A famous example of the use of philology to prove forgery is Isaac Casaubon's demonstration that the *Hermetic Corpus* of ancient Greek writings believed to prophesy the coming of Christianity was in fact produced after Christ's birth.[63] Again, in 1697 the Cambridge classicist Richard Bentley disattributed the so-called Letters of Phalaris (a ruler who lived in Sicily in the sixth century BC), showing that the letters were actually written a thousand years after the tyrant's reign. Bentley's conclusion was based on the style of the text, which 'by the whole thread and colour of it betrays itself to be a thousand years younger' than its putative author.[64]

Another form of reading signs belongs to the discipline that we now call palaeography, which emerged, once again, in the seventeenth century. A debate about the authenticity of some charters issued by the Merovingian kings of France in the sixth and seventh centuries widened into a general discussion of the problem of dating documents of that period and identifying forgeries. The Jesuit Daniel Papebroch offered rules for distinguishing genuine documents from false ones, emphasizing the systematic comparison of a given charter with others that were definitely genuine. As we have seen, this was exactly the method or 'touchstone' employed by the connoisseurs of the time to attribute paintings to particular artists.[65]

In his reply, the massive and magisterial study *On Palaeography* (1681), the Benedictine Jean Mabillon criticized Papebroch as too severe, in other words as what art historians now call a minimalist. Mabillon's own rules suggested that genuine documents could be distinguished from forgeries by a study of their scripts, their legal formulae, their seals and even their ink and the material on which they were written, such as papyrus or parchment. Mabillon even claimed that he could distinguish genuine from false charters with a single glance, as an artist distinguishes 'an original painting from a copy', thus reversing the common comparison between pictorial style and handwriting.[66] In England a few years later, one of the first individuals to discuss attribution was Humfrey Wanley, who is better known as a palaeographer and an authority on Anglo-Saxon England.[67] Much later, as Carlo Ginzburg has pointed out, another great philologist, Ludwig Traube, was aware of the parallel between his method and that of Giovanni Morelli.[68]

It is intriguing that the appeal to the eye and the formulation of rules for discriminating between authentic works and forgeries in both documents and works of art should have appeared at much the same time. Both sets of rules may have been inspired by the methods of some philosophers of that period, notably Descartes, with his 'rules for the direction of the mind', and Spinoza, who described his famous *Ethics* (1677) as proving its conclusions 'in a geometrical manner'. In short, it was not only in the domain of connoisseurship that the seventeenth century was an age of codification.

Connoisseurs in France

One of the first treatises on connoisseurship listed at the opening of this chapter, the *Sentiments sur la distinction des diverses manières de peinture* (1649) was the work of the engraver Abraham Bosse. Bosse believed that only artists were able to judge works of art and made scathing remarks about the amateur connoisseurs whom he described as 'fake virtuosi' (*faux curieux*). He also criticized what he called the 'jargon' of art appreciation, listing terms such as *svelte*, *frais*, *dur*, *tendre* and *grande manière* (elegant, fresh, tender and grand style). It is difficult to decide what kind of people Bosse thought he was writing for – not the amateurs, since he is warning them to keep off the turf, and not the artists, who do not need to be told how to distinguish between styles. Nevertheless, it is likely that the amateurs, who were growing in number, actually read his book, as well as the *Idée de la perfection de la peinture* (1662) by the amateur Roland Fréart de Chambray. Like Bosse, Chambray denounced the 'jargon' of the *curieux*, such as *la Franchise du pinceau*, *les Touches hardies* (free brushwork, bold touches) and once again *la Grande Maniere*. The scholar Samuel Sorbière also criticized the jargon of the art lovers, including *bien touché*.[69]

Among the leading collectors of this period was the Italian Giulio Mazzarino, better known as Jules Mazarin, who looked after the art collection of his master Cardinal Richelieu before succeeding him as the effective ruler of France. Mazarin's interest in collecting went back to the time when he was living in Rome and employed by the art-loving Barberini family. Besides statues, tapestries and Chinese porcelain, Mazarin collected more than five hundred paintings. Most of them were by contemporary artists but the collection also included works by Correggio and Titian as well as Raphael's famous portrait of Baldassare Castiglione and Pieter Bruegel the Elder's *Four Seasons*. Mazarin's concern with attribution surfaces in a letter to his London agent, asking him to ensure that the paintings by Van Dyck that he wished to acquire were originals, not copies.[70]

Mazarin's secretary, the Count of Brienne, testified in his memoirs to his master's love of art, claiming to have heard the dying cardinal regret leaving his collection behind him: 'Goodbye, dear pictures that I have loved so much and cost me so much money!'[71] Brienne denied that Mazarin had 'a discriminating taste for painting' (*un goût fin pour la peinture*), while believing that he himself knew something about the subject (*m'y connois un peu*).[72] Whether Brienne was right or not, it is true that Mazarin relied on the advice of others, notably Jabach and the painter Pierre Mignard. On one occasion, Mazarin asked his advisers for opinions about a work attributed to Annibale Carracci. Brienne thought that it was not by his hand, while Jabach claimed that it was painted by Giovanni Lanfranco.[73]

A slightly younger amateur was André Félibien, who had lived in Rome in the 1640s as secretary to the French ambassador, became an official historian to Louis XIV and is best known today for his

Conversations on the Lives and Works of the Most Excellent Painters (1666–88), a treatise on artists and connoisseurship in the traditional form of a dialogue.[74] Félibien wrote for fellow amateurs, *les gens connoisseurs* as he calls them. His conversations take place between the master (the author himself) and the pupil, an apprentice connoisseur named Pymandre. Among the topics of the long conversation are the diversity of styles, including the contrast between the school of Raphael and the style of the North Italians, and the difficulty of distinguishing good copies from originals or the work of disciples from their masters. Pymandre asks whether artists are the best judges of paintings, and Félibien (unlike Bosse) declares that 'there are many others . . . able to judge as well as the painters themselves.'[75]

On the border of the seventeenth and eighteenth centuries we find Roger de Piles. In some respects, his career resembles that of Félibien. De Piles too was an amateur who had been trained to paint. He too was secretary to a French ambassador, in his case in Venice. In other ways, though, their careers diverge. De Piles was not only an art agent for Louis XIV, but a secret agent in the French king's service (the combination of occupations is an unusual one, but both depend on mastery of the art of observation). In 1693 De Piles was sent to spy in the Dutch Republic, assisted by a false passport and the cover story that he was buying paintings for the king of Poland. In fact, he was meeting Dutch opponents of Louis XIV's enemy, William III. When his cover was blown, De Piles spent nearly five years in prison, employing his enforced leisure to write one of his books on art.

Viewed from the angle of connoisseurship, Roger de Piles' most important book was his *Conversations on the Knowledge of Painting and the Judgements of Pictures* (1677). The *Conversations* took place, as was customary in this genre, between master and pupil, on this occasion 'Pamphile' and 'Damon'. The pupil raises the question of attribution and is told that the knowledge of 'the majority of our connoisseurs . . . goes no further than guessing the names' of the painters. Pamphile makes a comparison between handwriting and brushwork (*les touches du pinceau*) as a means of identifying individual artists, but declares that intelligence (*l'esprit*) is more important for attributions, since 'the genius of the painter' can be seen in 'the particular air that he gives to his figures'. To become a good connoisseur, according to Pamphile, also requires genius, in other words 'the eye'.[76]

Quality is the main theme of a later work by De Piles, the *Balance des peintres* (1708), with its notorious list of 57 painters who are ranged in order of merit – Leonardo is eleventh – and given marks from 0 to 18 for composition, drawing, colour and expression.[77]

While Italian connoisseurs concentrated their attention on Italian painters, the French were more eclectic. The interest in Italian art on the part of cardinals Richelieu and Mazarin has already been mentioned. When De Piles drew up his list of the best artists, they included Dürer, Holbein, Rembrandt, Murillo and Rubens. The author was a particular champion of Rubens, to whom he devoted a biography. He may be described as an early example of the connoisseur as tastemaker, encouraging French readers to appreciate this great Flemish artist. Other tastemakers will be discussed in later chapters.

Collectors and Connoisseurs in Spain

By the mid-seventeenth century, the skills of connoisseurship were spreading from Italy and France to other countries, notably to Spain, the Netherlands (North and South), Germany and Britain.

Around the year 1560, Felipe de Guevara, a second-generation collector, had already complained of ignorant amateurs who spend their money 'for some extremely bad paintings which they love so much that they would prefer you to speak ill of themselves than of their paintings'.[78] However, it was the Spanish 'Golden Age' of art and literature that marked the real beginning of connoisseurship in the peninsula. A treatise on painting, once again taking the form of a dialogue, was published in 1633 by the Italian artist Vincenzo Carducci, better known by the Spanish form of his name, 'Vicente Carducho'. In this work, Carducho discussed different styles of painting, praising the loose brushstrokes that he called *borrones*.[79] This book was soon followed by *The Art of Painting*

(1649) by the artist Francisco Pacheco, who was both the teacher and the father-in-law of Velázquez.[80]

At the Spanish court, King Philip III and his favourite the Duke of Lerma (Carducho's patron) were both collectors. Lerma, 'the major collector of the early seventeenth century', was advised by Carducho and eventually owned 1,500 paintings, including three Titians.[81] Aficionados of Titian also included the Marquis of Leganés and the Duke of Alcalà, both of them collectors on a grand scale. As we have seen, a group of connoisseurs used to meet regularly at this time in Madrid, like Sebastiano Resta's group in Rome, to discuss works by 'Raphael, Correggio, Titian' as a form of cultivated leisure.[82]

King Philip IV also took 'an extreme delight in painting', according to Rubens. He was advised on what to buy by Velázquez, who was active not only as the king's painter but as the keeper of Philip's collection, which included over 2,000 paintings.[83] The English ambassador in Madrid, Sir Arthur Hopton, described Velázquez as 'a man of great judgement' in painting, while a later writer on art, Antonio Palomino, referred to a report made for the king by Velázquez on the quality, attribution and provenance of paintings, revealing the artist's 'learning and great knowledge of art'.[84]

Later in the century, a major Spanish collector was the Marquis of Carpio, Don Gasparo de Haro. By the age of 22, he was already in possession of 331 paintings, including works by Raphael, Titian and Bruegel as well as those of his contemporaries, including Rubens. The marquis, who arrived in Rome as ambassador in 1677, was also a keen collector of drawings and soon became acquainted with Resta. Don Gasparo's collection numbered around 3,000 works at his death, among them paintings attributed to Cimabue, Giotto, Antonello da Messina, Mantegna and Leonardo (some of these works are now believed to be copies bought as originals). He also owned the famous painting by Velázquez now known as the Rokeby Venus.[85]

Charles I and His Court

In Britain there were a number of seventeenth-century collectors or 'virtuosi', to use the term, borrowed from Italian, that was current at the time to describe lovers of learning, the arts, antiquities and 'curiosities'. A few of these collectors seem to have been sufficiently discriminating to be described as connoisseurs.[86]

Among the most important of these individuals was Thomas Howard, Earl of Arundel, together with his wife Aletheia (née Talbot). The earl, who has been described as 'probably the most perceptive collector in seventeenth-century England', was best known for his collection of antiquities, the Arundel Marbles.[87] He was so proud of these statues that they appear in the background to his portrait by the Dutch artist Daniel Mytens (illus. 16). These antiquities were acquired for the earl by his chaplain and agent William Petty, who was sent to the Mediterranean on this mission in 1624. According to another agent, Thomas Roe, Petty 'was able to judge of pieces of worth'. That Arundel respected Petty's eye emerges from a letter he wrote to him in Rome, sending him a boy and adding, 'I pray you show him all of art that you can, I hope in time he will have a good guess of originals from copies.'[88]

Among Arundel's many Italian paintings were works by Correggio, Tintoretto and especially Titian, including the *Flaying of Marsyas* probably acquired through Aletheia. The earl's copy of Vasari's *Lives* is another testimony to his enthusiasm for Italian art. He was also interested in the art of the Northern Renaissance, including paintings by Dürer, Bruegel and especially Holbein. Arundel himself once referred to 'my foolish curiosity in enquiring for the pieces of Holbein'. On a diplomatic mission to Germany, Arundel wrote to Petty from Nuremberg complaining that he could not find 'one scratch of Alb: Duer painting in oil to be sold'.[89] As for Aletheia, she was a patron and collector in her own right, as well as providing most of the money for her husband's acquisitions and helping King Charles to acquire the Gonzaga collection. The two galleries in her villa, Tart Hall, included works ascribed to Titian, Bassano and Cranach.[90]

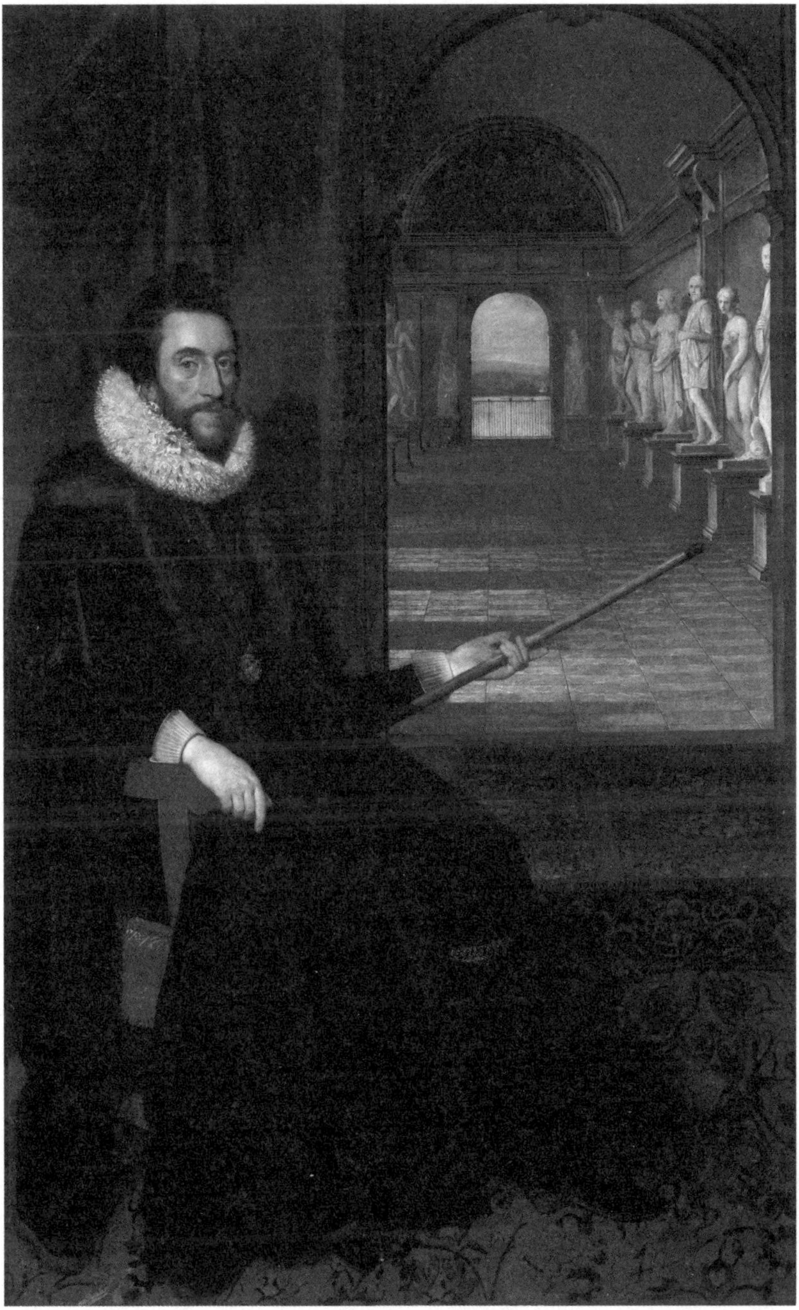

16 Daniel Mytens the Elder, *Thomas Howard, 14th Earl of Arundel*, before 1647, oil on canvas.

As we have seen, one means of deciding whether a given collector of paintings was a genuine connoisseur is to note whether he or she collected drawings. Arundel possessed an unusually rich collection of drawings, including works by Leonardo, Raphael and Michelangelo, arranged in more than two hundred albums in a cabinet in his house. That Arundel and his agents were aware of problems of attribution is revealed by his correspondence, from which we learn that the painter Daniel Mytens and the connoisseur Everard Jabach went to Amsterdam in search of paintings for Arundel, hoping to find works by Dürer and Holbein. What they found was 'a picture of Raphael which is held to be of his hand, but we hold it not so to be', and 'a woman's picture to the knee (of Andrea del Sarto, as they say, but we hold it to be of Titiano').[91]

Another leading British collector was Charles I, described by Rubens as 'the greatest lover of paintings among the princes of the world'. As Lord Arundel, who knew him well, remarked, 'His Majesty knows best what he hath gusto in.'[92] The papal diplomat Gregorio Panzani confirmed this impression, writing to Rome that Charles has 'a taste for paintings' (*gusto di Quadri*), especially old ones, and also a good nose' for quality.[93] An English monk recorded Van Dyck as telling him that Charles 'had a fine judgement of painting' (*esquisitamente intende della pittura*).[94]

Charles acquired what has been described as 'the finest collection of pictures ever assembled in this country'.[95] From the Gonzaga collection in Mantua, for instance, Charles bought works by Mantegna, Raphael, Andrea del Sarto, Giulio Romano, Correggio and Titian.[96] Whether he took advice or not, Charles was assisted by the artist Inigo Jones. Negotiations with Rubens and his collaborator Jacob Jordaens for paintings commissioned for the Queen's House at Greenwich have been described as 'dependent on Jones's ability to distinguish between their hands'.[97]

Like Charles, or thanks to him, some of his courtiers claimed to be especially fond of works by Titian. The Marquis of Hamilton owned more than 36 works by the artist as well as paintings by Giorgione, Tintoretto and Veronese. The correspondence between Hamilton and his friend and agent Basil Feilding, British ambassador in Venice, suggests that both men were semi-connoisseurs, in other words they were interested in questions of style and authenticity but reliant on expert advice. For example, Feilding writes that he is sure that Hamilton will be satisfied with some pictures he is trying to buy 'because I know by the comments of the most skillful of that art to be originals'. Hamilton is aware that he might be 'too much bewitched with those enticing things' but insists that pictures must be 'good and originals'.[98] Feilding replies describing some pictures he has bought, 'all originals', some by 'modern painters', with 'variety of several hands', but also 'an excellent piece' by Giovanni Bellini. Later, he offers Hamilton a picture by 'Old Palma the best of his hand', and a Giorgione 'of his first way and not comparable to some which I have seen of his hand'. In his turn, Hamilton expresses anxiety because 'I cannot know which are copies and which are originals you having already discovered some to be copies that was set down for originals.'[99]

Diplomats were often leading collectors, making good use of their need to travel. Dudley Carleton, for instance, was a collector in his own right as well as an agent for Lord Arundel in Venice.[100] His discernment is clear from the negotiations that he conducted with Rubens by letter; mentioned earlier.[101] In a later generation, William Aglionby was a diplomat, a physician, the translator of eleven of Vasari's *Lives* and the author of *Painting Illustrated in Three Dialogues* (1685). The dialogues, between a well-informed 'Traveller' and his less well-informed 'Friend', follow what was becoming a pattern. 'Traveller' explains the process of attribution, judging a painting by 'a constant Observation of the Manners of the Different Artists, which is acquired by viewing their works often and Conversing much amongst them'.[102] He introduces a number of terms to describe these 'manners', especially what 'the Italians call Morbidezza', glossed as 'the Softness and tender Liveliness of flesh', contrasted with the 'stiffness' of medieval art. 'Friend' also learns to describe paintings in terms of 'sweetness' and 'facility'.[103] A short dictionary of technical terms such as *chiaroscuro*, *Grotesk* and *foreshortening* is included in the book, perhaps inspired by Baldinucci's *Vocabolario*, published four years earlier.

Collecting and Connoisseurship in the Netherlands

In the Spanish Netherlands (today's Belgium), the art market, which went through difficult years during the civil wars of the late sixteenth century, made a recovery in the seventeenth. The leading connoisseur of the time was surely Rubens, who collected antiquities, 'objects of curiosity' and paintings (especially works by Titian and Bruegel).[104] Others include 'amateurs' (*liefhebbers*) such as the burgomaster of Antwerp, Nicolaas Rockox, the cloth merchant Peeter Stevens and the spice merchant Cornelis van der Geest, whose gallery was the subject of a painting in the fashionable genre of the 'cabinet picture', portraying the owner in the act of showing his collection to visitors.[105]

In the Dutch Republic, important collectors included the merchants Gerrit and Jan Reynst, to both of whom the artist Carlo Ridolfi dedicated his biographies of Venetian painters, the *Maraviglie*, published in 1648. The collection of the brothers, displayed in a cabinet in the family house on the Keizersgracht in Amsterdam, included works by Parmigianino, Titian, Lotto and Tintoretto, as well as antiquities and curiosities from the natural world. It incorporated the famous Vendramin collection of antiquities and paintings that Jan, the representative of the firm in Venice, had acquired there.[106]

Specialized art dealers made their appearance at this time, among them Hendrick van Uylenburgh, who arrived in Amsterdam in 1625.[107] He was trained as painter, became art agent for the king of Poland, moved to Amsterdam in 1625 and employed painters, Rembrandt among them, to produce pictures that he would sell. One might say that Hendrick had a gift for spotting talent among young artists, a characteristic of connoisseurs that will be discussed later in this volume.

The same is true of his son Gerrit, who was also trained as an artist and carried on the family business. However, one of his protégés, Hendrick Fromantiou, art adviser to the Elector of Brandenburg, accused him of selling fakes to the Elector. In his defence, Gerrit arranged for 35 artists (including Vermeer) to certify the authenticity of these paintings. The poet and diplomat Constantijn Huygens, who considered himself a connoisseur (writing that although others have more experience of pictures, 'I dare presume to understand a little about them'), also believed that the works were genuine. All the same, Gerrit went bankrupt.[108]

By this time the art market included auction rooms, encouraging if not driving connoisseurship. Important auctions in Amsterdam included a sale of 1639, 'mainly or entirely of works of art', from the collection of the merchant Lucas van Uffelen. The paintings included Raphael's portrait of Castiglione. Its accessibility during the sale allowed Rembrandt to make a sketch of it.[109] The portrait was also copied by Rubens.

As in Italy and France, treatises on art and artists, probably written for the amateur, were published in the Dutch Republic in the seventeenth century. They begin with Karel van Mander, the 'Dutch Vasari', whose biographies of artists were mentioned earlier in this chapter.[110] Van Mander contributed to the vocabulary of style (*handelinge*, *manier*) by his translations of terms from Vasari, including grace (*gratie*, *gracelijkheyt*), facility (*lichtveerdichey*), meticulousness (*netticheydt*) and softness (*poeslijkheyt*). An anonymous life of Van Mander, published in 1624, offered further contributions, dividing 'looseness' (*lossicheyt*) into brushwork that is *gedommelt* (scumbled) and *geglatseert* (glazed), and the finished or meticulous style into *ghetepelt* (stippled) and *opghetipt* (touched up).[111] Yet another important concept was *houding* (depth and colour harmony).[112]

German Collectors and Connoisseurs

In Germany, Joachim von Sandrart combined the roles of artist, collector, dealer and writer on art. Trained in the workshop of Gerard van Honthorst in Utrecht, he accompanied his master when Honthorst was invited to England by Charles I in 1628, spending some of his time copying the paintings by Holbein in Lord Arundel's collection. Sandrart also lived in Rome and in Amsterdam. His *Teutsche Academie* (1675–80) is a collection of biographies of German artists. Thanks to this work, a number of technical terms describing styles of painting became current in German, among them styles that are *wacke* or *tapfer* (bold), *feistlich* (festive), *glatt* (smooth) or characterized by *Gratia* (grace).[113]

A leading collector in the German-speaking world of the seventeenth century was another Habsburg, Archduke Leopold Wilhelm of Austria, Governor of the Spanish Netherlands. His gallery in Brussels is represented in a painting by its keeper the artist David Teniers the Younger (1651) and shows Flemish, Dutch and Italian paintings. Another collector, Friedrich August, Elector of Saxony (otherwise known as August II, 'the Strong', of Poland), became interested in art following his Grand Tour of Europe between 1687 and 1689 and eventually acquired 535 pictures, including the famous *Sleeping Venus* that is variously attributed to Giorgione and Titian. As in the case of Archduke Leopold Wilhelm, it is difficult to say whether or not Friedrich August was a connoisseur or simply a collector who followed expert advice, in his case that of his curator, Carl Heinrich von Heineken, whose achievements will be discussed in the following chapter.

AS WE HAVE SEEN, seventeenth-century discussions of connoisseurship include a debate about the kind of people who were qualified to judge paintings. On one side, the engraver Abraham Bosse claimed that only artists had the necessary skills. On the other side, a few writers now allowed amateurs an active role. Mancini defended the idea 'that a painting may be truly judged by any expert [*uomo perito*] who does not know how to handle a brush'. The scholar Franciscus Junius, author of a study of painting in the ancient world, supported the recognition of quality by 'laymen' (*imperiti*), while Baldinucci suggested that a few amateurs were 'just judges' of art. Nevertheless, the true age of the amateur was the eighteenth century, as the following chapter will try to demonstrate.[114]

4
The Age of the Amateurs

The division between connoisseurship in the late seventeenth and early eighteenth centuries is not a sharp one. There was a similar emphasis on the expert eye and similar discussions about quality, attributions and the way to distinguish original works from copies and forgeries. Fake Old Masters seem to have been becoming more numerous at this time, thanks to the expansion of the art market in the context of what has been described as 'the birth of a consumer society'.[1] One English connoisseur, Horace Walpole, concluded that faking Rembrandts must be 'an easy task' on the grounds of 'the numbers of men who have counterfeited that master'.[2] Eighteenth-century London also offers an early example of a trial concerned with the question of whether or not a painting was by the hand of a famous master.

The painting, representing the Virgin Mary, was bought by the French dealer Noel Joseph Desenfans, who lived in London, as a Poussin. When Desenfans learned that the painting was not by Poussin, he sued the dealer in an early example of a kind of legal case that would become increasingly common in the twentieth and twenty-first centuries.

The painter Thomas Gainsborough was called as a witness in 1787 in *Desenfans v Vandergucht* and declared that 'having had no opportunity for the study, he was no judge of the hands of the masters,' but that he found the painting 'deficient in harmony, taste, ease and elegance'. Asked in cross-examination 'whether something more than bare inspection by the eye was necessary for a judge of pictures', Gainsborough replied that 'he conceived the eye of a painter to be equal to the tongue of a lawyer.' Desenfans later wrote about the techniques of forgers, notably producing 'the appearance of age' thanks to dirt, varnish and even cooking the painting 'moderately' in an oven, to produce cracks that would otherwise have taken centuries to appear.[3]

Some scholars claim that true connoisseurship began at this time.[4] In the previous chapter, I argued that the emergence of the system took place a century earlier. Here, the eighteenth century will be presented as a period in which the methods of connoisseurship were refined and interest in the practice spread. The extension of knowledge of works of art from professionals (artists, dealers, restorers) to increasing numbers of patrons and collectors lies behind the spread of the term 'amateur' (*amatore*, *amateur*, *liefhebber*, *aficionado*) at this time.[5]

Continuities between the seventeenth and eighteenth centuries will be obvious. Knowledgeable amateurs such as Mancini, Jabach, Arundel and Mazarin already existed in the seventeenth century, as we have seen. Some treatises continued to be written in the dialogue form, among them Charles-Antoine Coypel's *Dialogue on the Knowledge of Painting* (1732). Conversations among friends discussing the attributions of paintings and drawings continued to take place. A famous example is the salon of the French collector Pierre Crozat, where aristocrats and artists met on relatively equal terms, but other instances of this form of learned sociability are not difficult to find (see illus. 19).

The art of criticism in literature and antiquities continued to move on parallel lines to the criticism of paintings. The Swiss theologian Jean Leclerc published his *Ars critica* (1696), an introduction to what would come to be known as hermeneutics, while the Italian polymath Scipione Maffei produced an equivalent for inscriptions, the *Ars critica lapidaria* (1765), soon followed by a guide, by Francesco Antonio Zaccaria, to recognizing fake inscriptions, the *Istitutione antiquario-lapidaria* (1770).

Philosophers now joined the debates about the taste for works of art. Contributions to the new field of aesthetics were made by

Alexander Baumgarten, who coined the term in his *Aesthetica* (1750); David Hume, in his essay 'Of the Standard of Taste' (1757); Edmund Burke, in *A Philosophical Enquiry into the Origin of Our Ideas of the Sublime and the Beautiful* (1757); and Immanuel Kant in his *Critique of Judgement* (1790).[6] Thanks to these debates, terms such as 'sublime' and 'picturesque' passed into everyday language.

Once again, a table of the most important texts on judging art published in this period may be useful. The number of these texts, 47 compared to the 33 listed in the previous chapter, is likely to reflect a widening interest in the topics that they discuss. The treatises responded to an increasing demand for knowledge of art, and in their turn the treatises encouraged more people to become amateurs.

1708	Roger de Piles, *Balance des peintres*
1712	Gérard de Lairesse, *Het groot schilderboek*
1718–21	Arnold Houbraken, *De groote schouburgh der Nederlantsche konstschilders*
1719	Jean Baptiste Dubos, *Réflexions critiques*
1719	Jonathan Richardson, *Two Discourses*
1729–39	Jacob Campo Weyerman, *De levens-beschryvingen der Nederlandsche konst-schilders en konst-schilderessen*
1730	Pierre-Jean Mariette, *Lettre sur Léonard de Vinci*
1732	Charles-Antoine Coypel, *Dialogue sur la connoissance de la peinture*
1741	Mariette, *Dessins*
1745	Antoine Joseph Dezallier d'Argenville, *Discours préliminaire sur la connaissance des desseins et tableaux*
1748	Anne Count of Caylus, *De l'amateur*
1749	Barthélémy Augustin Blondel d'Azincourt, *La première idée de la curiosité*
1749	Dezallier, *Voyage pittoresque de Paris*
1750	Mariette, *Catalogue Crozat*
1750	Mariette, *Traité des pierres gravées*

1751 Louis de Bachaumont, *Essai sur la peinture*
1751 Edme-François Gersaint, *Catalogue raisonné de toutes les pieces qui forment l'oeuvre de Rembrandt*
1751 Johan van Gool, *Nieuwe Schouburg der Nederlantsche Kunstschilders en Schilderessen*
1752 Jacques Lacombe, *Dictionnaire portatif des beaux-arts*
1753–63 Jean-Baptiste Descamps, *Vies des peintres flamands*
1753–7 Carl Heinrich von Heineken, *Recueil d'estampes de la galerie royale de Dresde*
1753 Marc-Antoine Laugier, *Jugement d'un amateur*
1753 Mariette, *Catalogue Coypel*
1754–73 Giovanni Bottari, *Lettere*
1755 Christian Ludwig von Hagedorn, *Lettre à un amateur*
1757 Charles-Nicholas Cochin, *Discours sur la connaissance de peinture*
1757 Antoine-Joseph Pernety, *Dictionnaire portatif de peinture*
1759–81 Denis Diderot, *Salons*
1760 Claude-Henri Watelet, *L'art de peindre*
1762 Christian Ludwig von Hagedorn, *Betrachtungen über die Malerei*
1762 Anton Raphael Mengs, *Gedanken über die Schönheit und den Geschmack in der Mahlerey*
1762 Horace Walpole, *Anecdotes of Painting in England*
1764 Johann Joachim Winckelmann, *Geschichte der Kunst des Alterthums*
1765 Scipione Maffei, *Ars critica lapidaria*
1766 Thomas Martyn, *The English Connoisseur*
1770 Matthew Pilkington, *The Gentleman's and Connoisseur's Dictionary of Painters*
1770 Francesco Antonio Zaccaria, *Istituzione antiqario-lapidaria*

1771 Carl Heinrich von Heineken, *Idée générale d'une collection complète d'estampes*
1771 Laugier, *Manière de bien juger*
1778 Pietro Edwards, *Restauro generale dei quadri*
1778 Joshua Reynolds, *Seven Discourses*
1786 Carl Heinrich von Heineken, *Neue Nachrichten von Kunstlern und Kunstsachen*
1786 François-Charles Joullain, *Réflexions sur la peinture*
1792 Le Brun, *Réflexions sur le Muséum national*
1792 Claude Watelet and Henri Levesque, *Dictionnaire des arts de peinture, sculpture et gravure*
1792–6 Jean-Baptiste Le Brun, *Galerie des peintres flamands, hollandaise et allemands*
1792–6 Luigi Lanzi, *Storia pittorica*
1797 Michel Huber and C. C. Rost, *Manuel des curieux et des amateurs d'art*

Despite continuities with the recent past, the art of judging art was gradually transformed between 1700 and 1800. Five changes were particularly important. In the first place, it was the turn of the French to dominate the world of connoisseurship in the place of the Italians. Second, the task of attribution was assisted by the reproduction of paintings in prints. Third, some dealers now played a public role in attributing paintings by printing catalogues. Fourth, the interest in connoisseurship was spreading more widely. Fifth, documents such as contracts and inventories were taken increasingly seriously as guides to dating and attributing works of art.

The French Moment

A career on the frontier between two centuries was that of the banker Pierre Crozat, who was a patron of artists (including Watteau) as well as supporting the research of Roger de Piles and

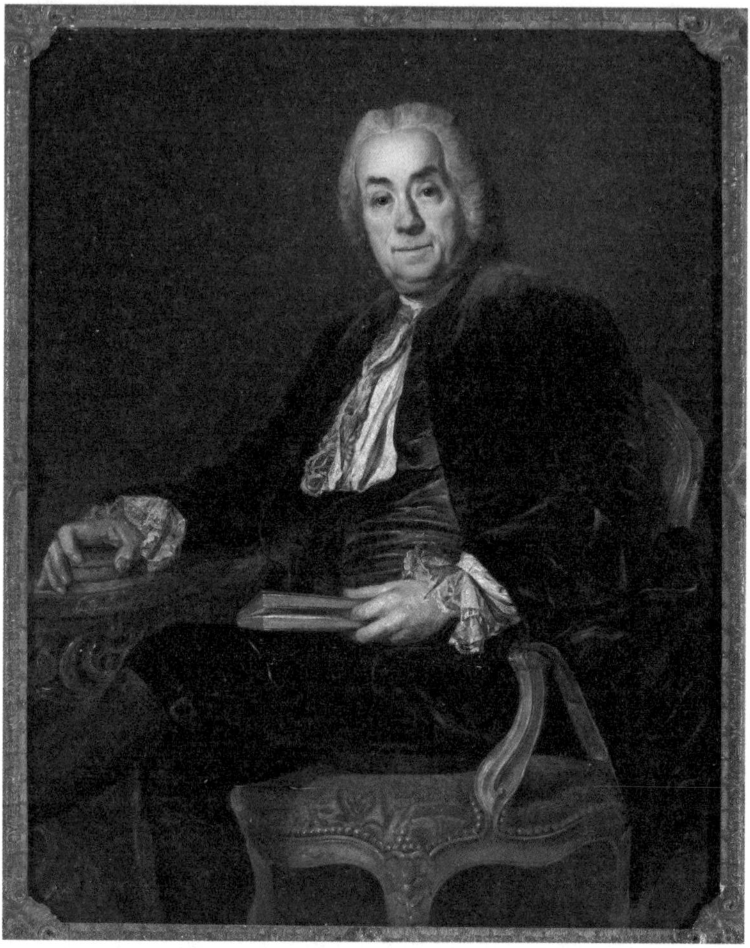

17 Alexander Roslin, *Anne Claude Philippe, Comte de Caylus*, 1752–3, oil on canvas.

collecting art on a grand scale. Among many other paintings, Crozat owned Rembrandt's *Danae* and a self-portrait by Annibale Carracci. He also collected Old Master drawings, owning more than 19,000 of them at his death.[7] Crozat's paintings, together with other important French collections, were reproduced in the *Recueil Crozat*, a two-volume work published in 1729 and 1742. In this collection of reproductions, the combination of etching and engraving achieved a greater verisimilitude than was possible in either medium alone. These volumes have been described as 'one of the most innovative and influential art books of the eighteenth century'.[8] It may have been thanks to this publicity that in 1772, when Crozat's paintings were sold to Russia's empress Catherine the Great, after the death of his heirs, concern was expressed about the loss of what we now call the 'national heritage'. The amateur Blondel d'Azincourt expressed his pleasure that the king had bought four of the best works in the collection 'so that they would not go abroad'.[9]

Drawings were a major topic of the regular conversations on art that took place on Sundays in Crozat's house on the rue de Richelieu in Paris, continuing the tradition of sociability noted in the previous chapter in the case of Resta and his friends in Rome. The members of Crozat's salon included the artists Antoine Watteau, Hyacinthe Rigaud and Rosalba Carriera, the young art dealer Pierre-Jean Mariette, the abbé Jean-Antoine de Maroulle – who was working on a French translation of Vasari – Louis de Bachaumont, who planned but did not produce a manual of connoisseurship, the Comte de Caylus, who was active both as an antiquary and a connoisseur, and the Venetian artist Anton Maria Zanetti, during his stay in Paris in 1720–21.[10]

Caylus (illus. 17) might be described as a *curieux* in the traditional manner, since he collected ancient objects and spent much of his time in their study. His most important work was his six-volume *Recueil d'antiquités* (1752–5), which included Egyptian and Etruscan antiquities alongside Greek and Roman ones. Caylus had learned the art of engraving and was adept in reproducing the styles of different artists. He also gave lectures on drawing and composition, wrote lives of Watteau and other painters and delivered and published a lecture on the idea of the *amateur*. It was the combination of the methods of the connoisseur with those of the antiquary that allowed Caylus and his friends to show that some paintings supposed to be ancient Roman were recent forgeries by the artist Giuseppe Guerra.[11]

Prints and Dealers

Prints were becoming an increasingly important part of the world of art at this time. The sixteenth century had been the age of the woodcut and the copperplate, the seventeenth century was the age of the etching and the eighteenth century the age of the mezzotint, with its subtle effects of light and shade. These media were used in original works – think of Dürer's engravings and Rembrandt's etchings – and they were collected for their own sake. The German connoisseur Carl Heinrich von Heineken published his advice on assembling a collection of prints, while some connoisseurs practised engraving themselves, among them Christian Ludwig von Hagedorn, Jean de Julienne and Barthélémy Augustin Blondel d'Azincourt.

Prints also reproduced paintings, thus allowing art lovers to become familiar for the first time with works that were otherwise inaccessible to them while held in private collections or distant countries. Despite the absence of colour, the *Recueil Crozat*, followed by a similar work reproducing paintings in Dresden, gave viewers a sense of having visited the galleries themselves. As Resta had already noted in the seventeenth century, the attribution of works of art depends on comparison. Connoisseurs were already aware of the need to travel in order to see these works, despite the problems of travel in an age of coaches and horses. Although a few of the stars had fabulous memories, it was risky to rely on memory alone. Prints offered a means of comparing paintings attributed to the same artist.[12] It seems appropriate that one of the leading connoisseurs in eighteenth-century France, Pierre-Jean Mariette, who has been described as 'the finest connoisseur there has ever been', came from a family of printsellers and carried on the family business.[13]

A few dealers in works of art have already made their appearance here, among them Daniel Nijs, the Reynst brothers and the Uylenburghs. Their practical knowledge of paintings, as well as of the market, is not in doubt. What was new in the eighteenth century, especially in France, was to find certain dealers making original contributions to scholarship by sharing their knowledge of art in catalogues and even in books. This change is linked to the rise of the art market in Paris, a new rival to older centres such as Rome, Venice, Antwerp and Amsterdam (though Rome retained its importance in this period).[14]

The first and also the supreme example of these Parisian dealer-connoisseurs was Mariette (see illus. 2). He grew up surrounded by prints because his family had been selling them for generations.[15] In 1717, when he was 23, he was sent to Vienna by his father to catalogue the extensive print collection of the famous general Prince Eugen of Savoy. In his turn, the prince sent Mariette to Italy to perfect his knowledge of art, making what might be described as a 'connoisseurial Grand Tour' that took him to Venice, Bologna, Florence, Rome and Naples. Pierre-Jean's letters to his father reveal his enthusiasm for Correggio, Titian, Veronese, the Carracci and especially Tintoretto. Replying, his father assured him that Pierre Crozat 'regards you as a future good connoisseur and art-lover' (*bon connoisseur et amateur des arts*).[16]

On his return to Paris, Mariette entered the Crozat circle and later acknowledged his debt to 'the works of the great masters which we examined there' and to the conversation of the group. His notebooks record their discussion of a drawing of Alexander the Great and Roxanne that had been attributed to Raphael. 'I had my doubts,' wrote Mariette, and 'Zanetti and the abbé de Maroulle strengthened them immensely.' 'Zanetti attributed it instead to Parmigianino.' In any case, 'in no way is this the wise and correct *manière* of Raphael.'[17]

Mariette was able to combine the knowledge of dealers such as his father with that of collectors such as Crozat and Coypel, making a major contribution to the *Recueil Crozat*. He described collecting drawings as 'my madness', diagnosing it as incurable. He repaired his drawings and pasted them into albums, mounting them with care so as to direct the attention of the viewer.[18] In his publications, Mariette 'articulated a view of drawings' current in Crozat's circle (and earlier, as we have seen, in that of Resta) 'as offering more immediate encounters with an artist's thought than finished works' and also as a 'touchstone' (*pierre de touche*) of the quality of each artist.[19]

Mariette published a collection of grotesque drawings attributed to Leonardo (though now identified as copies), discussing them in the form of a letter to Caylus in which he described the style of the drawings as 'an extreme lightness, without being dry or mannered'.[20] One of his ambitions (like his predecessors Resta and Baldinucci) was to correct Vasari's famous biographies of Italian artists, a project that he never found the time to complete, as in the case of another on the history of prints and printmaking. However, he did send many corrections to his Italian friend Giovanni Bottari, who was preparing a critical edition of Vasari's *Lives*.

Mariette was fascinated by the art of attribution, declaring that admiring beautiful works was not enough, since 'there is a sort of contentment in knowing that a given work is from a given time and by a given hand.'[21] Like other famous connoisseurs, he was assisted by a phenomenal memory. In 1763, 44 years after visiting Rome, he was able to describe to his friend Bottari the details of some sculptures in the church of San Girolamo della Carità.[22] As for Mariette's eye, it was once tested by his friend Zanetti, who sent him a print of a painting by Raphael claiming that it was the work of a sixteenth-century engraver. Mariette immediately recognized the print as a work by Zanetti himself.[23]

Mariette supplemented his eye and memory with other methods of attribution. In the case of a portrait of a middle-aged Cardinal Pole, attributed to Raphael, he argued that since the artist had died when Pole was still young, the portrait was more likely to be the work of Raphael's follower Sebastiano.[24] Mariette also concerned himself with provenance (*la filiation*, as he called it), especially in the case of paintings from the collection of Charles I that had passed to the Duc d'Orléans.

Mariette was also active as a critic, a supporter of Italian art against the fashionable French taste for Dutch paintings, and an art historian whose *Traité des pierres gravées* (1750) belongs to an antiquarian tradition. The treatise, the first part of the history of engraving that the author never completed, made use of engraved gems as evidence for the history of taste (*le goût propre à chaque nation*), which Mariette claimed to be the first to study. He praised the 'noble simplicity' of the Greeks, thus anticipating the German connoisseur Joachim Winckelmann (discussed below), who would criticize Maritette's treatise a few years later.[25]

Although his connoisseurship extended to paintings and gems, Mariette is best known for his studies of drawings and prints, recommending the latter as an aid to learning 'the character and manner of each master' (*le caractere et la manière de chaque Maistre*).[26] His training as an engraver allowed him to distinguish nuances of style in different works by the same artist. This gift may be illustrated by a minor work, Mariette's short biography of the seventeenth-century French artist Claude Mellan, whom he described as 'the inventor of a new manner of engraving'. According to Mariette, Mellan's prints are sometimes reminiscent of the work of his master Simon Vouet, sometimes of the engravings of the Fleming Aegidius Sadeler, as it is 'easy to see', and sometimes of Guercino or Agostino Carracci.[27]

A former member of the Crozat network, Mariette became the centre of a network of his own, an international 'Republic of Connoisseurs' that exchanged information like the members of the Republic of Letters. Mariette's network included Zanetti in Venice, Bottari in Rome, Heinecken in Dresden and in London both the amateur Horace Walpole and the engraver and collector Arthur Pond.

The Rise of the Dealer-Connoisseur

Mariette eventually retired from business to devote himself more fully to his passion for art. In the case of the dealer-connoisseurs who followed him, their eyes and their knowledge were used primarily to serve their business at a time of increasing demand for paintings.[28] This group included Edme-François Gersaint, Pierre Rémy, François-Charles Joullain, Alexandre-Joseph Paillet and Jean-Baptiste-Pierre Le Brun.

Gersaint, best known today as Watteau's dealer, was a pioneer in the development of auction catalogues that accompanied the list of works for sale with biographies of the artists. His list of Rembrandt's etchings, published posthumously, is regarded as the first contribution to what became a major form of connoisseurship, the *catalogue raisonné*, so-called because the attributions in such catalogues are the result of observation, study and thought.[29]

Rémy was both a dealer and an adviser to some important collectors. He was the first to distinguish in sale catalogues between certain and doubtful attributions. His 1755 catalogue claimed expertise in distinguishing originals from copies and described one lot in the sale as 'two forged Teniers, one quite well done'. His 1769 catalogue emphasized comparisons between different works, while his 1777 catalogue drew attention to provenance.[30]

Joullain too included information about the provenance of the works listed in his catalogues. So did Paillet, an auctioneer whose 'incontestable talent de connaisseur' has been noted by scholars. A specialist on Dutch painting, Paillet was one of the first to recognize the importance of Vermeer, whose works were virtually unknown at this time.[31]

Le Brun, 'the last (and possibly the greatest) in a long and distinguished line of eighteenth-century French dealer-connoisseurs' was another specialist on Dutch art. His publications included *Réflexions sur le Muséum national* (1792), which offered analyses of style. However, his most important book was the *Galerie des peintres flamands, hollandaise et allemands* (1792–6). He has been described as 'the first connoisseur to break with the prevailing habit of trying to attribute as many pictures as possible to the great and established names and to insist instead on the value of rarity and unfamiliarity'. Like Paillet, he recognized the importance of Vermeer, calling him 'a very great painter', although this judgement was not widely recognized until the nineteenth century, as we shall see.[32]

Taste and Vocabulary

The vocabulary of criticism became even more elaborate in this period than it had been in the seventeenth century. One French writer distinguished no fewer than thirteen varieties of a painter's 'touch': *légère*, *delicate*, *spirituelle*, *ferme*, *forte*, *hardie*, *fière*, *fine*, *moëlleuse*, *vigoureuse*, *trop égale*, *large* and *recherché*.[33] Sale catalogues of this period reveal the commercialization of the language of taste, in recurrent phrases such as *effet piquant*, *touche précieuse*, *touche spirituelle*, *touche vigoureuse* and so on.[34] Rémy in particular was notorious for his hyperbole.

By this time, in what might be described as a revolution in taste, at least some French connoisseurs were coming to prefer facility and grace to highly finished works not only in drawings but in paintings as well. It is surely no accident that this shift should have occurred at a time of enthusiasm for the ideas of Jean-Jacques Rousseau, especially his critique of formality. In 1759 the engraver Charles-Nicolas Cochin expressed his admiration for what he called an 'air of negligence', while Denis Diderot, reviewing an exhibition in Paris in 1767, asked 'why a fine sketch pleases us more than a beautiful picture'.

Diderot reviewed nine *Salons* altogether and in so doing established a new literary genre, that of art criticism. He was a gifted amateur, a man of letters who came late to the visual arts and often responded to paintings from a literary point of view, emphasizing the drama of the compositions, his personal response to them and their effect on the emotions of the public. Writing for readers who might not have seen a particular exhibition, Diderot evoked the paintings by means of precise, lively and sometimes lengthy descriptions of the scenes they represented, written as if he was present at the scene itself rather than a representation of it.[35]

Diderot judged the works he saw on the basis of considerable experience. 'Few critics can have spent so much time in the studios of contemporary artists.'[36] He used a precise vocabulary that included adjectives such as 'fluffy' (*cotonneux*). In the case of one of his favourite artists, the landscape painter Charles-Joseph Vernet, the critic employed terms such as *hardiesse* (boldness) and *vigueur*, as well as the more obvious *grâce* and *élégance*. Diderot trained himself to look closely in order to analyse what he called the 'magic' of Jean-Siméon Chardin, for example, 'thick touches of colour applied one above the other' (*des touches épaisses de couleur appliqués les unes sur les autres*).[37] Following Diderot's example, art criticism became increasingly important in the nineteenth century.

Collectors and Connoisseurs in Britain

It was in the eighteenth century that the term 'connoisseur' was first recorded in English (in 1714) and that connoisseurship became an important element in British culture, rather than a pastime for a few aristocrats.[38] Early in the century, the scholar Humfrey Wanley noted that 'when a painters [*sic*] hand is fixed, his manner is then limited, and so when a curious person comes into a gallery', he recognizes a work by Van Dyck or Tintoretto and can distinguish an original from a copy.[39] Once again, the rise of this form of curiosity followed the rise of an art market, this time in London, where art auctions took place regularly from the 1680s onwards and became 'the dominant method for buying and selling pictures' in the 1730s.[40]

The *Two Discourses* (1719) of the painter, dealer and collector Jonathan Richardson is a major landmark in the history of British connoisseurship. This book discusses 'the art of criticism' and 'the science of a connoisseur', what the author calls a 'NEW SCIENCE' that should (following a suggestion of his friend, the poet Matthew Prior) be known as 'Connoissance'.[41] The book was described by a leading twentieth-century connoisseur as 'the first reasoned account of the processes of connoisseurship'.[42] Indeed, Richardson claimed to have written the only book on the subject, though he admitted drawing on what he called 'ten or twelve pages' in Roger de Piles, while placing more emphasis on grace and expression.

Writing for gentlemen who were 'novice connoisseurs', Richardson focused on the main features of connoisseurship as they were discussed in the century before him, notably how to judge first, 'Of the Goodness of a Picture', second, 'Of the Hand of the Master' and third, 'Whether 'tis an Original, or a Copy'. On quality, he offers seven 'incontestable' rules for judging, concentrating in turn on composition, expression, light, draughtsmanship, colour, skill with the paintbrush and closeness to nature. In the manner of De Piles, Richardson gave each painter a score from 0 to 18.[43] The author explained how to look at a picture, first from a distance and then closely.[44] He also suggested keeping a notebook with headings such as 'handling', 'colour', 'drawing' and 'expression'.[45]

Richardson's discussion of attribution has been described as 'by far the fullest to have appeared in any language'.[46] He pointed out that details such as the folding of draperies help the viewer to recognize the work of a particular master, but also noted that it is often difficult to distinguish between masters and disciples or assistants in the workshop. In any case, he added, some artists change their style during their career, especially Raphael, who 'had three several [separate] Manners'.[47]

Richardson's son, Jonathan Richardson the younger, was also a connoisseur. In 1720 he visited Italy, as Pierre-Jean Mariette had done a year earlier, in order to improve his expertise. One result of the tour was the publication by the two Richardsons of *An Account of Some of the Statues, Bas-Reliefs, Drawings, and Pictures in Italy* (1722), a book that helped to educate the next generation of connoisseurs.

Next to the Richardsons, John Talman stands out among the British connoisseurs active in the early eighteenth century. The son of an architect, John was in Rome in 1700–1702, sketching buildings, buying architectural drawings and making the acquaintance of Sebastiano Resta. Returning to Italy in 1709, he remained there until 1716, acting as an art agent and adviser for aristocratic collectors. For example, he acted for Lord Somers in the sale of the famous collection of drawings owned by Resta, who died in 1714.[48]

A few British collectors of this period reveal connoisseurial interests, whether or not they were what Richardson called 'novices'. For example, the correspondence with his agents carried on by James Brydges, 1st Duke of Chandos, reveals the duke's enthusiasm for works of art, 'his familiarity with arguments about connoisseurship' – he was influenced by Richardson – and his concern with judging pictures on aesthetic as well as financial criteria. Chandos left a collection of 176 paintings at his death, including works by Titian and Veronese, Rembrandt and Rubens. He surely qualifies as a 'semi-connoisseur', though he has also been described as an 'unwise collector' who bought works before seeing them himself'.[49]

Among the works that Chandos coveted was Andrea del Sarto's copy of Raphael's portrait of Leo x, discussed in Chapter Two. His problem was that the painting he was offered might be a copy of that copy. Chandos told his agent that 'the very sound of a copy shocks me.' In his view, 'A picture ought to be as tenderly handled as a lady . . . the least question upon them casts a stain upon their Reputations which is hardly ever washed off.' Nevertheless, Chandos ended up buying the portrait.[50]

Another major collector of this period – to whom Chandos tried to sell some works from his collection – was Prime Minister Robert Walpole, who began buying paintings in 1720. According to his biographer J. H. Plumb, Walpole was 'one of the greatest connoisseurs of his time' and 'one of the greatest collectors in Europe'. 'After politics, his pictures and sculptures were the constant preoccupation of his life.' By the time he was sixty, in 1736, Walpole owned over four hundred paintings, including works by Poussin, Rembrandt, Rubens and Van Dyck.[51] A case might also be made for the connoisseurship of his son Horace, who made the acquaintance of Mariette when he visited Paris. Horace published a catalogue of his father's collection as well as his better-known *Anecdotes of Painting* (1762) and *A Catalogue of Engravers* (1763).

Britain could not rival the number of French expert dealers but produced at least one of the kind, Arthur Pond, who was also active as a painter, engraver, collector, restorer and agent. His training as a connoisseur went through three stages. In London, the elder Richardson was his mentor, encouraging him to do what Richardson himself had never done, that is, to visit Italy. In Rome by 1725 Pond had become acquainted with the artist-connoisseur Pier Leone Ghezzi and his circle. In Paris, on his way home to London, Pond met Mariette and continued to correspond with him after returning to England. In this way he learned the art of attribution. In England, he regularly authenticated paintings, writing 'True' on the back of a canvas together with his signature. Pond collected Old Master drawings and was described by a contemporary in anglicized Italian as 'the greatest or top Virtuosi [*sic*] in London'.[52]

Among the amateurs, Richard Payne Knight has been described as 'the most powerful gentleman connoisseur of his day'. He valued what he called 'an experienced and discriminating eye' and was asked to judge paintings attributed to Claude and Ruisdael.[53] A wealthy man, he accumulated an impressive collection that included paintings by Mantegna, Rembrandt and Claude as well as eight hundred ancient bronzes, over 1,000 Old Master drawings and more than 5,000 cameos and coins. Knight became notorious for publishing a study of *The Remains of the Worship of Priapus* (1786) as well as for his outspoken opinions. His comment on the 'false Correggios, false Titians and false Michelangelos' to be found 'swarming' in the collection of Joshua Reynolds cannot have endeared him to the president of the Royal Academy, while his dismissal of the importance of the Elgin Marbles awoke doubts about the expertise of the author of *Principles of Taste* (1805).[54]

Collectors and Connoisseurs in Germany

So far, little has been said about German connoisseurs. In the later eighteenth century, however, three stand out: Carl Heinrich von Heineken, Christian Ludwig von Hagedorn and, most famous of the three, Johann Joachim Winckelmann.

Heineken, who came from Saxony, was the son of two painters who became a scholar, curator and adviser. He was director of prints and drawings in Dresden for the Elector August III. Heineken's acquisitions for his master (besides the *Sleeping Venus* bought for August II, mentioned in the previous chapter) included the famous *Sistine Madonna* by Raphael, along with paintings by Titian, Rembrandt and Van Dyck and 50,000 engravings. Heineken's connoisseurship is revealed in his books, the *Idée générale d'une collection complète d'estampes* (1771) and the *Neue Nachrichten von Kunstlern und Kunstsachen* (News of Artists and Works of Art, 1786).

A colleague of Heineken's, Christian Ludwig von Hagedorn, came from Hamburg and was active as a diplomat, an amateur engraver, a collector, an art historian, an adviser on art to the court of Saxony and the director of the Dresden Academy of Art. He may also be described as a tastemaker, a supporter of Rembrandt at a time when neoclassical painters such as Anton Raphael Mengs were more fashionable. Hagedorn published a catalogue of his own collection as well as a *Lettre à un Amateur* (1755) and the *Betrachtungen über die Malerei* (Considerations on Painting, 1762).[55] The switch by both Heineken and Hagedorn from French, the language of the German elite, to German, thus making their work accessible to a wider readership, illustrates a reaction against what was still the 'French moment', not just in connoisseurship but in culture.

Ancient Greek sculpture was the principal interest of Johann Joachim Winckelmann and the subject of his most famous work, *The History of Ancient Art* (1764). He began his career as a librarian on an aristocratic estate near Dresden. It was there that he met Hagedorn, with whom he later corresponded. August II's collection of antiquities in Dresden inspired the young man's interest in classical art, discussed in his *Reflections on the Imitation of Greek Works of Painting and Sculpture* (1755). This publication led in turn to a stipend from the elector, giving the young man the opportunity to study in Rome.[56] Close looking and increasing experience allowed Winckelmann to discriminate between Greek originals and Roman copies. In the preface to his history, he justified his judgements by his examination of the statues themselves, in other words by his eye. Indeed, he was sometimes criticized in his own day for neglecting evidence from literary sources.[57]

Winckelmann had studied Vasari but rejected what he called a mere 'history of artists' for a history of art, 'intended', as he wrote in the preface to his *History of Ancient Art*, 'to show the origin, progress, development and fall of art, together with the different styles of nations, periods and artists'. He replaced the traditional notion of a virtually static 'classicism' with a dynamic vision of Greek art, developing over the centuries from the archaic to the Hellenistic styles.

Winckelmann was familiar with the work of earlier connoisseurs such as Filippo Baldinucci, Roger de Piles, Jonathan Richardson and Pierre-Jean Mariette. Despite his frequent criticisms of their conclusions, he followed their method, the analysis of style, as well as sharing the general admiration for the paintings of Raphael.[58] His famous distinction between the 'High or Grand Manner' of Phidias (*hoher oder grosser Stil*) and the 'Beautiful Manner' of

Praxiteles (*schöner Stil*) resembled that of connoisseurs and critics of his time. Joshua Reynolds, for instance, praised the 'Grand Manner' in the lectures he gave at the Royal Academy.

Winckelmann prided himself on his ability to distinguish authentic works from forgeries. For example, he recognized the fake antiquities of Giuseppe Guerra, since 'The painter has not demonstrated the least knowledge of the customs, dress or manners of the ancients.'[59] On a visit to Maffei's collection of antiquities in Verona, for instance, he declared that some of them were the work of 'modern impostors'.[60] However, as in the case of other famous connoisseurs, Winckelmann's judgements were not infallible. He was deceived into thinking that a fresco of Jupiter and Ganymede was an authentic ancient work, although it had just been painted by Giambattista Casanova.[61]

The Spread of Connoisseurship

Who were the connoisseurs at this time? As we have seen, they now included an increasing number of dealers, especially in France. Treatises on art continued to be published by artists, including *The Great Book on Painting* (1712) by Gerard de Lairesse, *The Great Theatre of Dutch Painters* by Arnold Houbraken, Charles-Nicolas Cochin's *Discourse on the Knowledge of Painting* (1757) and the *Discourses* of Sir Joshua Reynolds, a series of lectures delivered from 1769 onwards and first published under the title of *Seven Discourses* in 1778. Artists continued to appraise collections of paintings, a task that involved attribution as well as valuation. Appraisers included painters such as Reynolds and Charles-Antoine Coypel and the engravers George Vertue (whose notes on the history of art were the basis for Horace Walpole's *Anecdotes*) and Cochin. Like Abraham Bosse in the previous century, Cochin argued that artists are 'the only people who know how to appreciate the true qualities of paintings' (*les seuls à savoir apprécier les qualités réelles des tableaux*).[62]

By this time, however, the amateurs after whom this chapter has been named were moving towards the centre of the stage.[63] They had often been trained to draw, paint or engrave, and they knew

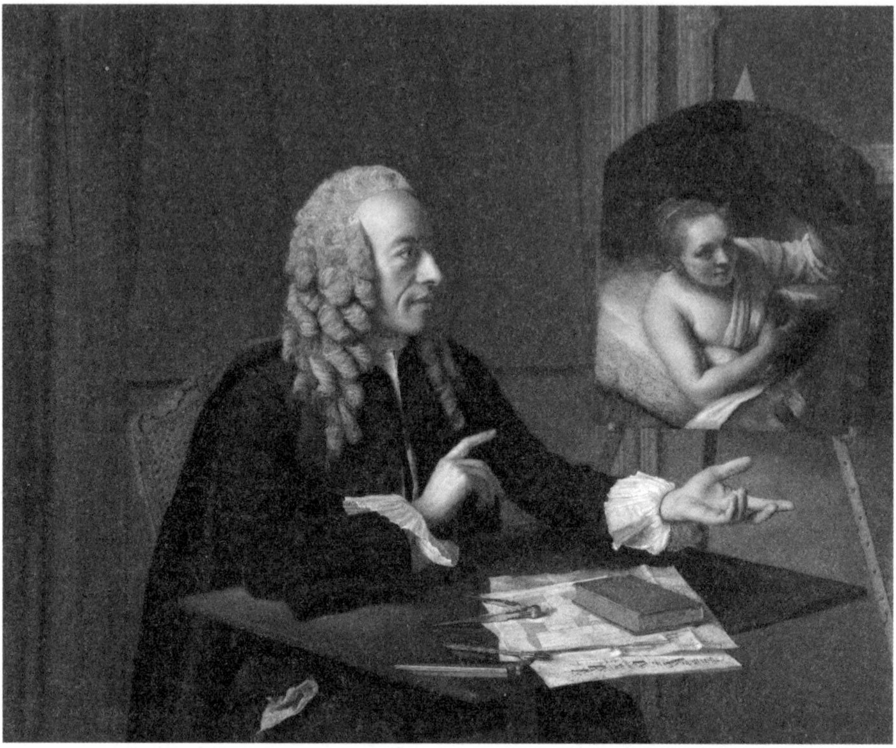

18 Jean-Étienne Lyotard, *François Tronchin*, 1757, pastel on parchment.

what they wanted to collect. In France, this group included soldiers such as the Marquis de Voyer, who was especially fond of Dutch paintings, and the Duc de Saint-Aignan, who preferred Italian art; a lawyer, Antoine-Joseph Dezallier d'Argenville; a minister, the Duc de Choiseul, another enthusiast for Dutch art; a financier, Claude-Henri Watelet, an artist himself as well as a collector of contemporary French art; a textile manufacturer, Jean de Julienne, who collected drawings; and a Jesuit, Marc-Antoine Laugier, the author of an essay that argued, against Cochin, that artists are not the only good judges of art.[64]

The banker-connoisseurs, who presumably could well afford to collect, included (besides Crozat and Watelet) François Tronchin, who lived in Geneva. Tronchin catalogued his collection according to the schools distinguished by Roger de Piles and had himself portrayed together with his favourite Rembrandt (illus. 18). His travel journal offers examples of his judgements of paintings.[65] Diplomat-connoisseurs included Charles-Maurice de Talleyrand, who was advised by Le Brun, and Count Carl-Gustaf Tessin, Swedish ambassador to Paris from 1739 to 1741, who took the opportunity of his stay to make the acquaintance of Mariette and to buy paintings and drawings.

The growing number of connoisseurs and collectors now included more women than it had in the seventeenth century. Among these female connoisseurs were Adriana de la Court, who 'had a well-trained eye', able to recognize works by Rubens and Van Dyck; Marie-Thérèse Geoffrin, best known for her salons, who owned 73 paintings and advised the king of Poland on buying French art; Madame de Bandeville, who studied drawing, left a cabinet of 138 paintings at her death and, according to Rémy, had 'a reliable eye' (*un coup d'oeil sûr*); and Anna Miller, whose *Letters from Italy* (1776) reveal her habit of close looking as well as her knowledge of technical terms.[66] There will be more to say about female connoisseurs in the following chapter.

Amateur connoisseurs were not confined to elites. In the first half of the eighteenth century an interest in art by 'middlebrow' travellers from the Netherlands, North and South, has been noted.[67] As the art market expanded in this period, so did the number of connoisseurs, not to mention *demi-connoisseurs* (a term used by Roger de Piles) or 'novice connoisseurs' (according to Richardson).[68] The Dutch artist Samuel van Hoogstraten dismissed pseudo-connoisseurs whom he described as the 'name buyers' (*naemkoopers*) attracted by the reputation of the artist rather than the quality of the painting, as well as the presumptuous connoisseurs (*warenwijze konstkenners*) who criticize artists.

The increasing number of printed catalogues of art auctions suggests a rise in late eighteenth-century France (or at least, in Paris) in the number of people interested in purchasing paintings. The suggestion is supported by the production of works that targeted would-be connoisseurs, especially in France, among them Jacques Lacombe's *Dictionnaire portatif des beaux-arts* (1752), the former monk Antoine-Joseph Pernety's *Dictionnaire portatif de peinture* (1756) and Claude-Henri Watelet's *Dictionnaire des arts* (posthumously published in 1792).

In Paris it was particularly easy to view paintings. Besides the auction rooms, there were the annual exhibitions of new pictures at the salons, from 1737 onwards, offering a new public space in which to train one's eye, while interested amateurs were often given access to private collections.[69] The salons also offered an opportunity for sociability, for discussing the works of art on view in a public space much larger than the earlier circles of Resta or Crozat.[70]

In Britain, Richardson looked forward to the time when it would be as dishonourable for a gentleman not to be a connoisseur as it was 'not to be able to read any other than his own language'. A few decades later, the English were catching up with the French, so that 'the title of connoisseur . . . is at present the safest passport into every fashionable Society.'[71] Groups of connoisseurs began to sit for collective portraits (illus. 19, 20). In London, a journal entitled *The Connoisseur* was founded in 1754. It ceased publication in 1756 but was followed by other works of popularization: Thomas Martyn's *The English Connoisseur* (1766) and Matthew Pilkington's *Gentleman's and Connoisseur's Dictionary of Painters* (1770).

Private collections were less accessible in London than they were in Paris, while in country houses they 'were few, difficult to see and badly catalogued, if at all'.[72] However, these very complaints imply a rise in interest, encouraged by the public exhibitions at the Royal Academy that became an annual event from 1769 onwards.[73] Auction rooms flourished, although London sale catalogues, unlike those in Paris, had little to say about either attribution or provenance.[74] In short, one might speak of the rise of a 'public sphere', at least in Paris and London, in the domain of art as in that of politics.[75] It was Italy that lagged behind in this respect, since the country lacked both national unity and a large capital city.

The increase in the numbers of amateur connoisseurs did not please everyone. Coypel, for instance, referred to 'a prejudiced public, a flighty public, an envious public, a public slavish to fashion'.[76] In France, the abbé Marc-Antoine Laugier wrote his guide to judging pictures 'to warn the public against the charlatanry of the

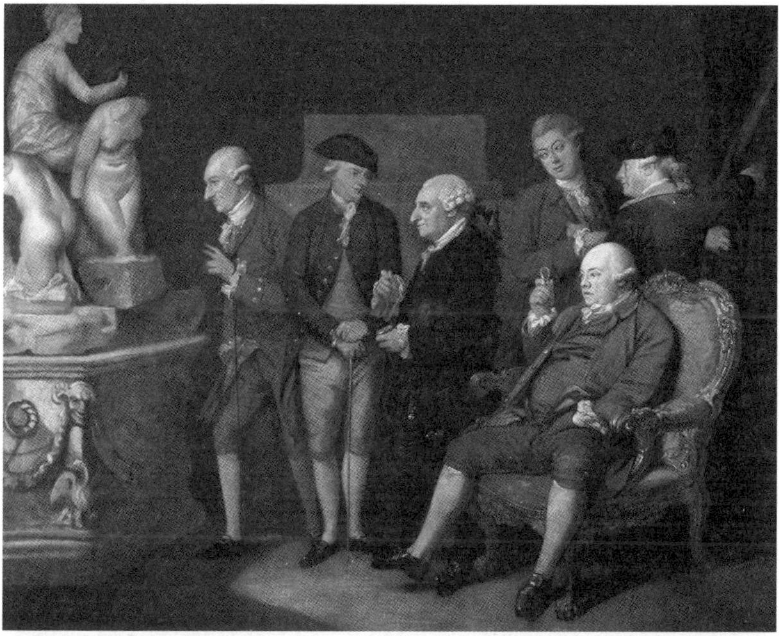

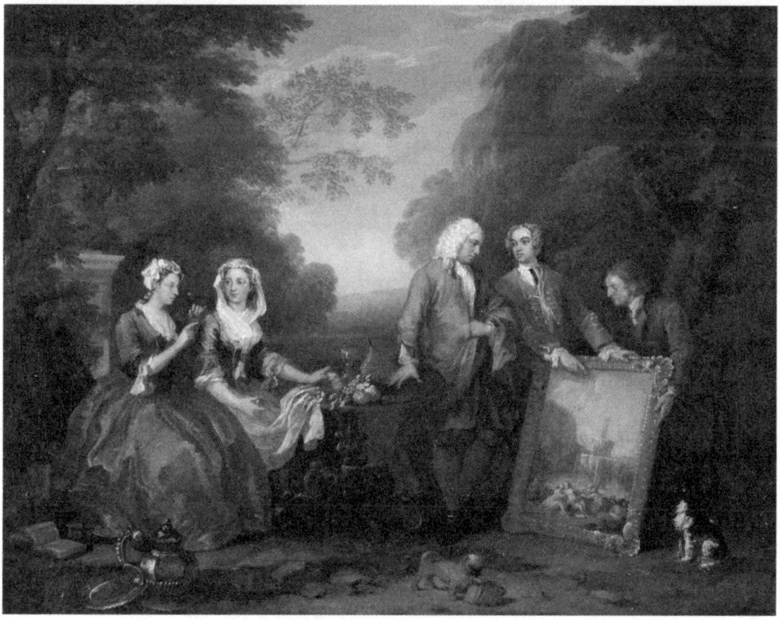

19 Richard Cosway, *Group of Connoisseurs*, 1775, oil on canvas.
20 William Hogarth, *Conversation Piece* (*Sir Andrew Fountaine with Other Men and Women*), *c.* 1730–35, oil on canvas.

pseudo-connoisseurs' (*la charlatanerie des faux connoisseurs*).[77] In England, Richardson denounced 'Low, Pretended Connoisseurs', remarking that 'Some People . . . set up for Connoisseurs without taking the Requisite Pains.'[78]

Another sign of the expansion of the group of connoisseurs or would-be connoisseurs is the increasing attention (not always favourable) that was devoted to them in literature and art. British comedies in this vein include Conolly's *The Connoisseur: or, Every Man in His Folly* (1736); Samuel Foote's *Taste* (1752), a farce that featured art dealers and their clients; and *The Two Connoisseurs* (1760) by the poet William Hayley, who was a friend of the artists John Flaxman, George Romney and William Blake.

Artists too mocked connoisseurs. The eighteenth-century English portrait painter John Opie, for instance, used the elegant oxymoron 'ignorant connoisseurs', while his colleague Benjamin Haydon called painting a profession 'cursed with connoisseurs'.[79] Caricatures included an anonymous print showing the so-called experts viewing a painting held upside down, and *A Connoisseur Admiring a Dark Night Piece*, with a completely black canvas.[80] One of the most famous English caricaturists, Thomas Rowlandson, joined in the mockery. His *Connoisseurs* (1799) shows a group of old men engrossed in a picture of a naked woman.[81] The expansion of the technical terms describing paintings was criticized as 'jargon' by (among others) the connoisseur Horace Walpole, who declared it 'almost easier to distinguish the Hands of the Masters, than to decipher the Cant of the Virtuosi'.[82]

In short, the age of the amateur offers vivid examples of both knowledge and ignorance. On one side, the would-be or pseudo-connoisseur; on the other, scholars of the calibre of Mariette and his friends, who practised connoisseurship part-time while working as dealers or occasionally, like Heineken and Hagedorn, as curators. It was only in the following century that connoisseurship become an independent profession.

5

The Age of the Professionals

> In Germany, Italy and France, connoisseurship is a profession.
>
> ELIZABETH, LADY EASTLAKE

In the eighteenth century, the major novelty in the social history of connoisseurship was the rise of the amateur. In contrast, the most important change to be discussed in this chapter, concerned with what might be called a 'long nineteenth century' from 1789 to 1914, was the appearance of new professional roles for connoisseurs, niches in which they could make a living alongside the traditional ones of artist and art dealer. These roles included the museum curator, the art historian, the art adviser and the art critic. Two other occupations that depended on close looking – restoration and forgery– were also becoming more professional at this time.[1] John Smith, who was active as a restorer as well as a dealer, claimed that the former skill was essential to a 'true connoisseur'.[2]

The separation of roles was a gradual process. In the nineteenth century, some leading connoisseurs carried on the amateur tradition, among them the noblemen Karl Friedrich von Rumohr, Athanasius Raczyński and Karl Eduard von Liphart (illus. 21). Even in the twentieth century, amateur collectors –Denis Mahon, for instance – sometimes became famous for their eye. Some individuals moved with ease between different roles, as we shall see. Nevertheless, it was in this period that professionalization became a major trend in the world of art, as it did in other social worlds of the time (engineering, for instance, or surveying and accountancy).[3]

The German Moment

Until the middle of the eighteenth century, Germans played a lesser role in connoisseurship than the Italians, French and English. The German moment began with Winckelmann and his new approach to classical sculpture. It was continued, in the case of the Old Masters, by three German scholars who were all born towards the end of the eighteenth century: Karl Friedrich von Rumohr, Johann David Passavant and Gustav Waagen. They all have an important place not only in the history of art history, which will be discussed later, but in the history of connoisseurship. All three were very much concerned with attributions, or more exactly with disattributions, reducing the number of paintings attributed to the most famous masters and restoring many of them to artists of the second rank. They were also involved with the rise of public museums

The writings of Rumohr, an aristocrat from Holstein, were described by Waagen as 'the pinnacle of critical expertise in modern painting'. Rumohr remembered that when he was a teen-ager, visiting an art gallery, 'from comparison with the Correggio I was able to infer that the painting attributed to Raphael was a considerably more recent work.'[4] At the University of Göttingen he was introduced to art history by Johann Dominicus Fiorillo, a painter who became curator of prints and paintings and finally, in 1813, professor of art history at the university.

Rumohr visited Rome in 1805–6 and his first publication on art, following in the steps of Winckelmann, was concerned with the ancient statues of the twins Castor and Pollux, displayed on the Campidoglio.[5] He also planned both to translate and – like other connoisseurs before him – to correct Vasari's famous biographies of artists. For this purpose, he spent five years in Italy, from 1816 to 1821. An article published in 1820 presented a manifesto for his approach, combining the observation of paintings with the search

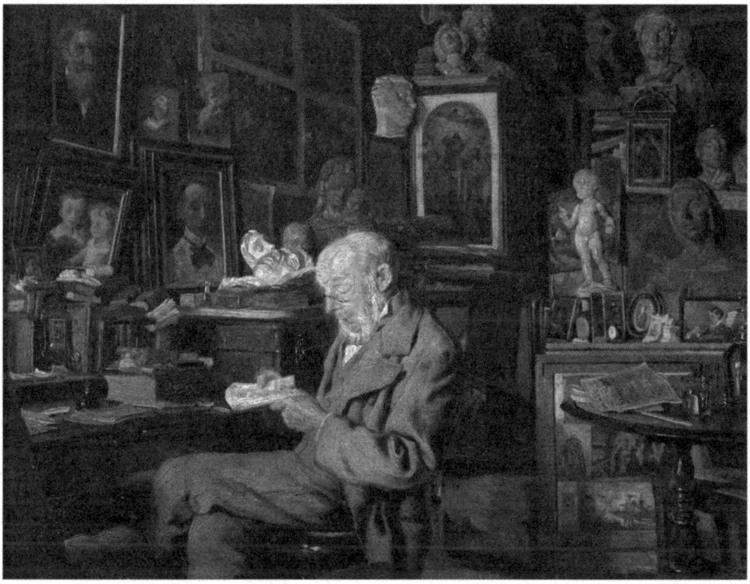

21 Ernst Friedrich von Liphart, *Karl Eduard von Liphart*, 1883, oil on canvas.

for documents about the artists.[6] The concrete results of these studies were published between 1827 and 1831 as his *Italian Researches*, revealing Rumohr's concern with precise dating as well as demonstrating that the famous critique of evidence associated with Leopold von Ranke could also be employed in the history of art.[7]

Rumohr was also a patron and a critic of art. In Rome, he supported the so-called Nazarenes, a group of German artists who preceded the English Pre-Raphaelites in adopting a neo-Renaissance style. He rediscovered neglected artists such as Moretto da Brescia, whose *Santa Giustina* and *Assumption of the Virgin* he was the first to recognize. He also 'added several early works to Leonardo's oeuvre'.[8]

Rumohr gave advice on the acquisition of Italian paintings by the Altes Museum in Berlin (recommending King Friedrich Wilhelm not to buy a certain 'Raphael'), as well as helping to plan the new picture gallery, the Gemäldegalerie.[9] He was also active as a writer on travel and cooking (a connoisseur of food), a translator of Italian short stories and the author of stories of his own, including one about the apprenticeship and travels of the young Raphael, a

Bildungsroman reminiscent of the famous novels about Wilhelm Meister by Goethe (whom Rumohr had met in 1815).

The second of the trio, Passavant (illus. 22), who came from Frankfurt, began his career as a painter, moving to Rome in 1817 and joining the circle of the Nazarenes. As his self-portrait shows, he admired the manner of fifteenth-century painters. It was in Rome that he met Rumohr, who, together with the dealer-connoisseur Samuel Woodburn, encouraged him to abandon painting for the study of art. Like Rumohr, Passavant carried out research in archives, criticized the inaccuracies of Vasari and wrote a biography of Raphael, in his case accompanied by a catalogue of the master's paintings.[10] Following the success of this book, Passavant was appointed as curator of a museum in Frankfurt, the Städelsches Kunstinstitut, where he was responsible for important acquisitions, including a Madonna by Moretto da Brescia (together with Rumohr and Waagen, Passavant was responsible for the rediscovery of Moretto in the 1830s). Thanks to his eye for significant details, Passavant also made some important re-attributions, especially of paintings by Lombard artists.[11] 'He liked to travel, and in a letter to his mother, written from Manchester in 1832, one can see an image of a train sketched by the painter,' a reminder that in the railway age, travel facilitated connoisseurship as well as contributing to the rise of an international art market. For example, the London dealer John Smith travelled as far as St Petersburg to see paintings and visit collectors.

The third member of the trio, Gustav Waagen, was the son of a painter. He was inspired to follow a career as an art historian and connoisseur by a visit to the exhibition in Paris of the paintings that had been looted by Napoleon. As in the case of Passavant, Rumohr became the young man's mentor. A visit to the Netherlands in 1819 led Waagen to write a short monograph on the Van Eyck brothers, published in 1822. This study included a catalogue of the paintings of the brothers (with detailed evidence for each attribution) and placed their art in the context of their time and place. In other words, 'he viewed art as inseparable from the artist's circumstances and historical period' and offered his readers a combination of

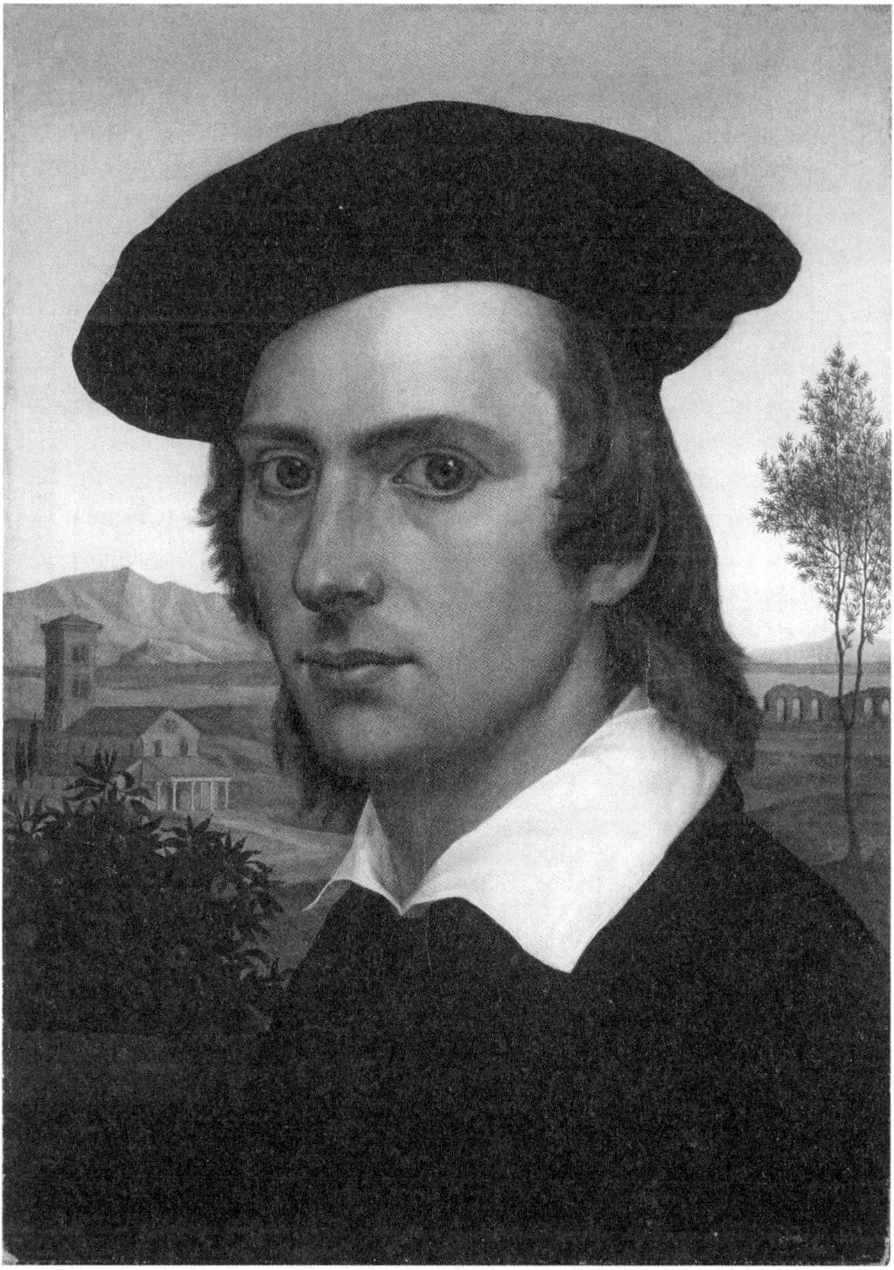

22 Johann David Passavant, *Self-Portrait with Beret in Front of a Roman Landscape*, 1818, oil on canvas.

observation with documentation, including, like Rumohr, a critique of the sources.[12]

Waagen was also involved with the foundation of the Berlin picture gallery and became its director, in 1830, as well as professor of art history in Berlin in 1844. He is said to have been Prince Albert's choice as director of the National Gallery in London, although it was an Englishman, Charles Eastlake, who was appointed. Nevertheless, Waagen's British career became as important as his German one, thanks to frequent visits to Britain and good relations with that country's collectors and curators.[13] Waagen's activities in Britain included helping to organize a major exhibition in Manchester and appearing before select parliamentary committees concerned with the arts. As a connoisseur, he is remembered not only for his pioneering work on the Van Eycks, but for his comments on Old Masters in British private collections, described in his *Treasures of Art in Great Britain* (1854) and *Galleries and Cabinets of Art in Great Britain* (1857). The famous exhibition of Old Masters ('Art Treasures') in Manchester in 1857 was inspired by his books.[14]

The comments in those books reveal the author in the act of judging art and demonstrate his frequent scepticism, symbolized by question marks, of traditional attributions of many paintings. On Lord Methuen's 'Jan van Eyck', for instance, he wrote 'A very beautiful picture by some Netherlandish painter . . . about sixty years after the death of Jan van Eyck'. Methuen's 'Michelangelo' was judged to be 'as little the work of Michael Angelo as any other repetition I have seen'. In the Duke of Northumberland's collection, Waagen noted that a portrait of the young Edward VI was attributed to Mabuse, although he died five years before Edward was born (the portrait was re-attributed to Holbein). In Lord Folkestone's collection, he re-attributed a *St Sebastian* supposedly by Sebastiano del Piombo to the minor master Jan Sanders van Hemessen and commented, 'Only the rapidity with which I was compelled to view this collection on a former visit can excuse my having allowed the name of Sebastiano del Piombo to pass unquestioned.'[15] Waagen also purged the canon of Leonardo's works from some over-optimistic attributions. For example, he reattributed some works to Giovanni Antonio Boltraffio, a lesser painter in Leonardo's circle.[16] His positive attributions include assigning the 'Manchester Madonna' to Michelangelo, the *Portrait of a Collector* (now in the National Gallery in London) to Parmigianino and the *Holy Family* (now in the J. Paul Getty Museum in Los Angeles) to Giulio Romano.[17]

The Chronological Turn

In what ways did the practice of the German scholars discussed in the previous section differ from their predecessors? In the case of their contribution to art history, it was by their more critical attitude to the sources. In the case of connoisseurship, it was by making what might be described as a 'chronological turn', emphasizing both the development of individual artists and the development of art. These trends are visible not only in the writings of these scholars but in the rearrangement of paintings in galleries in the chronological order of different 'schools' of artists.

An early example of this rearrangement, which would later seem natural, was the Uffizi collection, reorganized by its curator Luigi Lanzi and described in his catalogue (1782). Another is the imperial gallery in Vienna, which, according to the catalogue published in 1783, presented 'a visible history of art'.[18] Lanzi has been praised, along with his German colleagues, for the critical approach to sources in his *Pictorial History of Italy* (1792–6).[19] In the nineteenth century, organization by chronology became a general trend. For example, John Smith's catalogue of Rembrandt's paintings, published in 1836, was arranged in chronological order.[20] The paintings in the Berlin Museum were arranged in chronological order on the advice of Rumohr, while the collection in the National Gallery in London was rearranged in similar fashion on the advice of Waagen. The Louvre followed suit.

This concern with chronology should be placed in a wider context. In the history of historical thought, an interest in dating goes back to the ancient world, while some early modern antiquaries were interested in the chronology of styles. In the seventeenth century the English antiquary John Aubrey, for instance, made, for his own use, chronologies of changes in costume and in architecture, paying particular attention to the sequence of Gothic styles, especially in window tracery.[21] What was new in the nineteenth century was the attention paid to chronology as part of a deeper sense of the past which German scholars, who have been so prominent in the movement, call 'Historismus'. Historicism, as it is generally known in English, may be described as 'the discovery of time'.[22] Changes over the long term were now emphasized in studies of geology, zoology and linguistics. The historicist approach was even extended to astronomy, as scientists became interested in the formation and the collapse of stars. Closer to connoisseurship, a concern with development became visible in biography and archaeology.

Earlier biographers, from Plutarch and Suetonius to Vasari and beyond, had been concerned to describe the character and achievements of individuals without much concern for chronological order, let alone precise dates. In contrast, nineteenth-century biographers focused on their subject's 'evolution' or 'development' (*développement* in French, *Entwicklung* in German, *sviluppo* in Italian), another keyword of the time. The word gradually changed its meaning from a literal 'unfolding' of what was already there to the appearance of something new, especially within individual personalities.[23] Historicism affected the way in which connoisseurs looked at paintings. As Denis Mahon, a leading twentieth-century connoisseur, observed, the art historian needs to see a work of art 'as nearly as possible in the way in which its creator saw it'.[24]

Another new trend in this period was the rise of systematic archaeology, the study of the remote past based on the chronology of artefacts such as stone axe-heads and iron swords. For example, at the Museum of Northern Antiquities, which opened in Copenhagen in 1819, its curator, Christian Thomsen, decided to organize the museum's collection in a chronological manner. Thomsen was concerned with precise dating, based not only on the form of each object but on the types that were found together in graves or hoards. From this evidence he concluded that a Stone Age had been followed by a Bronze Age and that by an Iron Age. He organized the objects exhibited in the museum according to these three epochs and wrote a guide to them in which he presented his conclusions.[25]

The archaeologist may be described as a kind of connoisseur, concerned with the attribution of objects to a particular place and time. Conversely, connoisseurs may be described as a species of archaeologist, concerned with styles and their development.[26] We should not be surprised to find that Winckelmann was an inspiration to Thomsen, who was interested in paintings as well as in swords and axe-heads.

Studies of individual artists now paid more attention than before to their development. In 1836, for instance, the dealer-connoisseur John Smith's *catalogue raisonné* of Rembrandt's paintings broke with tradition by adopting a chronological order, on the grounds that

> This method will enable the admirers of his works to judge in some measure of his gradual progress; commencing from a system of laborious finishing, and thence gradually attaining a rich, free, and what may be termed a scientific style, which at length terminated in a broad and luxuriant dexterity of handling.[27]

Smith was also the first to gather evidence to support the attribution of paintings to Johannes Vermeer, although he only dedicated half a page to that artist.[28] The rise of enthusiasm for Vermeer will be discussed later in this chapter.

It may be no accident that both Rumohr and Passavant focused their attention on Raphael. Not only was he viewed as one of the greatest of the Old Masters, but, as Vasari had already noted, Raphael's style changed several times as he successively encountered the works of Perugino, Leonardo and Michelangelo, took something from each but made it his own. In similar fashion, later in the century, Cavalcaselle would study the development of Titian's painting over the artist's long working life.

Nineteenth-century connoisseurs and art historians focused more sharply on individuality than their predecessors. In earlier centuries, the practice of attribution revealed an interest in differences between individual artists, but this interest was now taken much further. In his *Handbook of the History of Painting* (1837), for instance, Franz Kugler emphasized what he called 'artistic personality' (*künstlerischen Persönlichkeit*).[29] The 'primacy of the artist's individuality' encouraged an emphasis on a single master rather than a collective workshop and even attempted to link style to character, as in the case of Waagen's study of the Van Eycks and of Waagen's friend Lady Eastlake, who described the art of Michelangelo as 'the expression of the grandest and most energetic individuality the world has ever known'.[30]

Waagen was also a friend of the Swiss historian Jacob Burckhardt and wrote to him praising the chapter on 'the development of the individual' in the *Civilization of the Renaissance in Italy* (1860).[31] A year after Burckhardt, the French curator Charles Clément published a study of the Renaissance as the first era of individual 'genius', a concept that had been launched by the Enlightenment philosopher Lord Shaftesbury and that was taken up with enthusiasm by the Romantic movement.[32] This emphasis was an expression of an age in which a group of German Romantics participated in what has been described as the invention of the self. Burckhardt himself once declared his wish to be 'a good private individual'.[33] Hence he 'stands accused of projecting back onto the Renaissance an anachronistic, post-Enlightenment, post-Romantic conception of selfhood'.[34]

Biographies of single artists multiplied at this time. Famous artists were celebrated alongside religious, military and political heroes in historical paintings and sculptures. Jean-Auguste-Dominique Ingres, for instance, painted *The Death of Leonardo* and also *Raphael and La Fornarina* (the painter's mistress). Monuments were erected to artists in their native cities, beginning with Dürer in Nuremberg and Rubens in Antwerp (both in 1840) and followed by Rembrandt in Amsterdam, Velázquez in Seville, Delacroix in Paris and so on (in England, though, Reynolds had to wait until 1931 for his statue in London). This view of the artist as hero naturally had an impact on the art market, raising the prices of works by the famous names.

The Market for Old Masters

As in earlier periods, connoisseurship was shaped if not driven by the art market, while the market was now driven in its turn by the enormous redistribution of works of art from the French Revolution onwards. In 1792 the famous collection assembled in the early eighteenth century by the Duke of Orléans was sold by his great-grandson to a Belgian banker and quickly sold again, in part to a consortium of British aristocrats.[35] In 1796 the French Directory asked Napoleon to send back paintings from Italy, 'liberating them', in the words of the revolutionary priest Henri Grégoire. Napoleon's armies also looted paintings from Spain, the Netherlands and Germany.

By this time, the main rival to Paris as a market for art was London, where dynasties of dealers combined their commercial eyes with a sense of quality.[36] At Thomas Agnew & Sons (founded in 1817), William Agnew had an 'unrivalled eye for a profitable picture' and 'often bought ahead of the taste of his day'.[37] Christie's included James Christie the younger, a scholar as well as an auctioneer, who 'raised the business that he followed' (in the words of the *Gentleman's Magazine*) 'to the dignity of a profession'.[38] Colnaghi's included Dominic Colnaghi, who was active not only as a dealer but as an adviser to collectors and a patron of painters such as John Constable and Samuel Palmer, while the connoisseur Otto Gutekunst joined the firm in 1894.[39]

British dealer-connoisseurs at work in this milieu also included Samuel Woodburn and John Smith. Woodburn, who specialized in prints, has been described as 'the most prestigious and successful English dealer of his day', as well as 'one of the most interesting pioneers in the collecting of early Italian art'.[40] Woodburn's colleague Smith, founder of another dynasty of dealers in art, produced *catalogues raisonnés* of artists in nine volumes (1829–42) in order 'to ascertain the genuine works of the Dutch and Flemish painters from the spurious'. Unlike the catalogues of earlier dealers, Smith's were not confined to his own stock.[41] Waagen described him as 'a refined connoisseur', though he also suggested (in a recurrent example of a scholar's prejudice against dealers) that Smith's attributions of paintings were biased by his desire not to antagonize their owners.[42]

The increase in the demand for Italian paintings on the part of the growing number of British collectors and galleries was matched for a time by an increase in the supply. Italian paintings imported to Britain rose from 415 in 1821 to a peak of 4,057 in 1841 and remained high until the unification of Italy in 1861. The paintings came from the collections of impecunious Italian aristocrats such as Count Vittore Pisani (the former owner of Veronese's *Alexander*, now to be seen in the National Gallery in London) or from churches and convents that had recently been dissolved. Italian art-lovers could only look on in helpless dismay at these losses. The novelist Alessandro Manzoni, for instance, declared himself to be 'heartbroken' by what he called the 'exile' of the *Alexander*.[43]

A growing centre of the international market for Old Masters was Florence, thanks to increasing demand at a time when there was a fashion for the Italian Renaissance, expressed in collecting as well as in the neo-Renaissance style in architecture, furniture, ceramics and women's clothing.[44] The growing numbers of foreign tourists included would-be connoisseurs who wished to buy as well as to look at Renaissance art. One of the leading art dealers in Florence was Stefano Bardini, who began his career as an artist, then became a restorer and finally a dealer, specializing in the art of the Renaissance. 'He built an enormous and robust enterprise in Florence, as well as a vast and complex national and international professional network.' Bardini also advised curators at the South Kensington Museum and the State Museum in Berlin, identifying' fake sculptures of the Renaissance – although he has been suspected of selling fakes himself, as well as smuggling works of art out of Italy.[45]

American and Russian collectors also joined the raid on Italian Renaissance art. In the USA, the buying of Old Masters by millionaires was at its height between 1880 and 1914. Leading figures in the race to acquire these paintings, whether or not these buyers should be described as connoisseurs, included Isabella Stewart

Gardner (whose husband's family owned a shipping company), Henry Clay Frick (whose business was in coke and steel), Henry Gurdon Marquand (whose wealth came from building railroads) and Louisine Havemeyer (whose husband's fortune came from sugar). They relied on expert advisers and middlemen, who included Bernard Berenson, the appropriately named Otto Gutekunst and the Impressionist painter Mary Cassatt, the last of whom took the Havemeyers to Spain to search for works by El Greco.[46]

In Russia, Dmitri Shchukin, born into a family of wealthy textile merchants, studied abroad and went to lectures by Wilhelm Bode. This experience encouraged Dmitri to collect paintings from the Dutch Golden Age. He once remarked that 'Every collector must have an eye. But we Shchukin brothers have something extra: we have noses ... In my own case this faculty was focused on Old Masters.'[47]

Museums and Curators

The rise in prices of Old Masters was a result of increasing demand, not only from private collectors such as the ones described above but from the directors of the new public galleries and museums. Curatorship became a profession. Part-time curators of private collections could be found in early modern Europe, among them the artist David Teniers the Younger and the scholar Carl Heinrich von Heineken. What was new in the nineteenth century was the rise of the professional curator together with that of the public museum.[48] Early examples of the latter include:

1753 the British Museum (moved to Great Russell St, 1852)
1793 the Louvre, Paris, opened to the public
1798 the Rijksmuseum, the Netherlands
1801 Musée des Beaux-Arts, Bordeaux
1803 Musée des Beaux-Arts, Brussels
1809 the Brera, Milan
1809 the National Museum, Copenhagen
1819 the Prado, Madrid

1820 Hessisches Landesmuseum, Darmstadt
1824 National Gallery, London (to Trafalgar Square, 1838)
1830 Gemäldegalerie, Berlin
1836 Alte Pinakothek, Munich
1852 Hermitage Museum, St Petersburg, opened to the public
1852 South Kensington Museum (later the Victoria and Albert Museum)
c. 1855 Dresden, Gemäldegalerie, opened to the public
1861 National Gallery of Victoria, Melbourne
1870 Boston Museum of Fine Arts
1872 Metropolitan Museum of Art, New York
1876 Philadelphia Museum of Art
1879 Art Institute of Chicago
1883 Manchester City Art Gallery
1885 Birmingham Museum and Art Gallery
1891 Kunsthistorisches Museum, Vienna

Museums required a professional staff to acquire, display and catalogue the holdings, as well as to clean, conserve and, where necessary, to restore them. All these tasks required a hands-on knowledge of works of art, in other words, connoisseurship.

In many private collections, paintings had been hung in the most convenient spaces in the collector's house in apparently random fashion. In contrast, the curators of museums and galleries wished to educate the public in the history of art and so, following the chronological turn, began to arrange paintings in the order of the successive regional or national 'schools' to which they belonged.

Curators were also concerned to catalogue their collections, a task that required the works to be attributed to particular artists. In 1843, for instance, the director of the Prado, Pedro Madrazo, began publishing a catalogue of its paintings that took him many years to complete. In Britain, Ralph Wornum published his *Descriptive and Historical Catalogue of the Pictures in the National Gallery* in 1847 (he would become Keeper of the Gallery in 1855). In France, Frédéric Villot, the recently appointed curator of paintings in the

Louvre, published a catalogue of the collection in 1849. He probably did his work too quickly. At any rate, Otto Mündler, a German theologian, art dealer and disciple of Waagen who would become a leading connoisseur in his turn, published a critique of the attributions in Villot's catalogue a year later.[49] Mündler went on to make similar criticisms of a catalogue of the Alte Pinakothek in Munich published in 1866.

A major role for curators of public museums and galleries at this time was to acquire more and more paintings, especially works of the Old Masters. This role was performed with particular vigour by Charles Eastlake and Wilhelm Bode.

Charles Eastlake

The former, later 'Sir Charles', was trained and practised as a painter and became president of the Royal Academy in 1850. However, he had become interested in the history of art when he had, like Waagen, visited the exhibition, shown in Paris in 1814–15, of the paintings looted by Napoleon during his campaigns. In 1830 he visited North Italy and copied a number of Renaissance paintings. Eastlake was appointed keeper at the National Gallery in 1843 and director in 1855, giving him the power and the money to acquire masterpieces for the collection.

That Eastlake was a connoisseur himself is evident from his surviving notes on the paintings he had seen as well as in his *Director's Report to the Trustees of the National Gallery* (1857).[50] The report discusses the quality, attribution, provenance and condition of works he had viewed and includes remarks such as 'I could not satisfy myself that it is by Hubert van Eyck' (on a Madonna in Cologne) or the claim that 'a picture ascribed to Piero della Francesca' in Volterra is really by Ghirlandaio.[51] Eastlake was also the author of an essay entitled 'How to Observe'.[52] He was prepared to take advice of others. One of his advisers was Otto Mündler, whom he appointed as his 'travelling agent', searching for acquisitions as well as accompanying the director on his 'picture hunt'.[53] Thanks to the two of them, the National Gallery acquired 137 Italian Renaissance

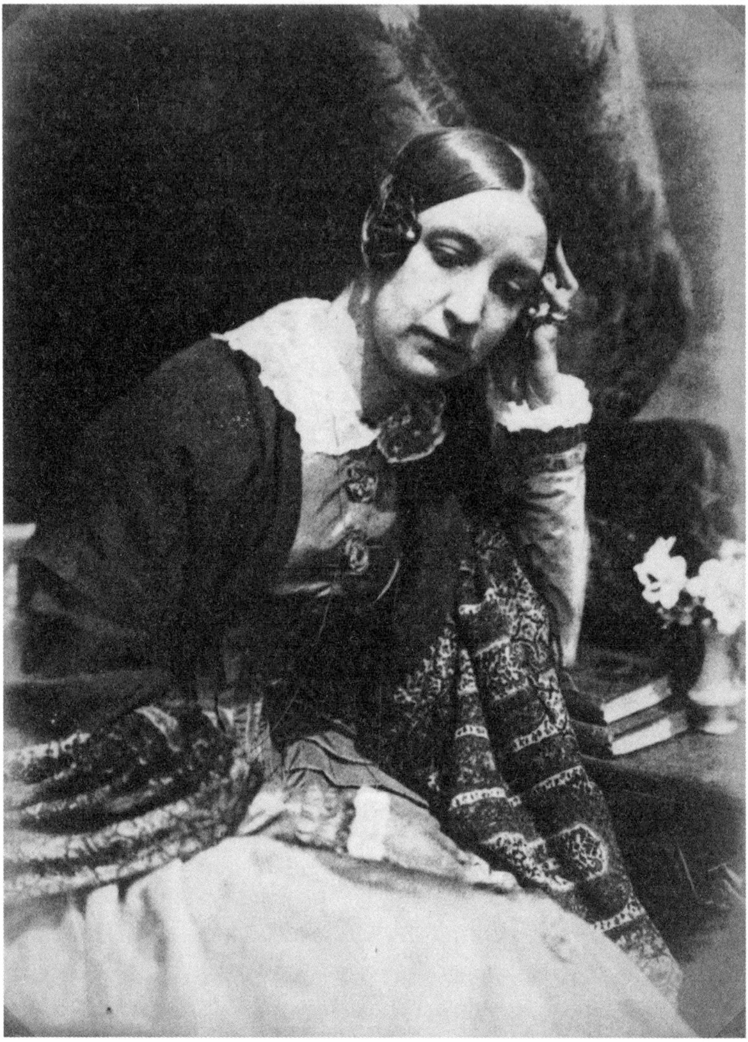

23 Hill & Adamson, *Elizabeth Rigby* (*Lady Eastlake*), 1843–7, photograph.

paintings between 1855 and 1865. The acquisitions, some of them still to be seen on the walls of the Gallery, included *The Martyrdom of St Sebastian* (1475) by the Pollaiuolo brothers, Uccello's *Battle of San Romano* (*c.* 1440), Moroni's *Tailor* (*c.* 1570), Veronese's *Alexander and the Family of Darius before Alexander* (1565–7) and Piero della Francesca's *Baptism of Christ* (*c.* 1437–45), which Eastlake himself had owned for a time.[54]

Another adviser to Eastlake was his wife Elizabeth, who was already a connoisseur when they met but became an admirer of Charles's gift for attribution and 'the way in which he smashes a false name'.[55] Elizabeth Rigby, later Lady Eastlake (illus. 23), was taught to draw, paint watercolours and make etchings. She became a friend of Passavant and Waagen, and translated their books into English. After marrying Charles, she travelled with him to search for and purchase Old Masters. By her husband's death in 1865 she could claim an 'exceptional education in connoisseurship'.[56] She later became acquainted with Giovanni Morelli and wrote an article about him in the *Quarterly Review*, a journal to which she was a regular contributor.

Wilhelm Bode

Wilhelm Bode, later 'von Bode' (illus. 24), was even more aggressive and successful than Eastlake in acquiring works of art. He offers a leading example of a scholar whose success in making attributions, as he said himself, was due to his opportunity as a curator in a leading gallery for repeated looking and comparison and thus for establishing a sense of artistic personality.[57] However, Bode also believed that attributions should be based on documents, not simply on the expert eye.[58]

Despite his frequent illnesses, Bode's abundant energies allowed him to devote himself to a campaign for acquisitions and the enlargement of the museum complex in Berlin (of which he was appointed general director in 1905), not to mention his 'almost incessant travel from the late 1860s to the late 1910s', including visits to Scandinavia, Hungary and Russia.[59] Bode complained that administration and travel together left him no time for research, but this did not prevent him from publishing a great number and variety of books and articles that included monographs on Italian sculptors of the Renaissance, oriental rugs and even the life of Goethe.[60]

Bode was trained as a specialist on Dutch painting of the seventeenth century, writing a doctoral thesis on Frans Hals (1870), followed by essays on Dutch painting (1883) and culminating in an eight-volume catalogue of Rembrandt (1897–1905). He has been described as 'an essential figure' (along with Thoré, discussed below) in the discovery and appreciation of Vermeer, in other words, a tastemaker, though he accepted some fakes as genuine works of the master.[61]

As a connoisseur, Bode, like Eastlake, was influenced by Otto Mündler, whom he met in 1868, asking him, 'do I have a reasonably correct or educated eye for art?', and soon winning the older man's respect.[62] Another mentor of Bode's was the Baltic aristocrat Karl Eduard von Liphart (see illus. 21), whom he met in Florence on his first visit to Italy in 1871. Liphart was described by Crowe and Cavalcaselle as 'an acute connoisseur', though his importance in the history of connoisseurship has not been sufficiently appreciated. He was, like Morelli, trained in medicine but gave up this profession to concentrate on collecting drawings and paintings of the Italian Renaissance.[63] He moved to Florence in 1862, where his house became a salon in which works of art were discussed, carrying on what was by now a long tradition. The day after he met the young Bode, Liphart took him to the Uffizi to test his eye. According to Bode himself, as soon as he recognized that a painting attributed to Rembrandt was actually the work of Hercules Seghers, 'I had hardly spoken the name when the old gentleman embraced me in public.'[64]

That Bode was a fine connoisseur is also attested by the historian Jacob Burckhardt, who visited galleries with him in 1875, remarking that 'It is quite astonishing, what a good eye he has.' Burckhardt gave Bode a free hand to revise the *Cicerone*, his famous guide to Italian art. Bode's eye was also recognized by two leading connoisseurs, his former assistant Max Friedländer and the British curator John Pope-Hennessy, who noted Bode's 'almost unfailing sense for quality'.[65] It should be added that Bode thought little of the art of his own time, including the paintings of Cézanne, Van Gogh, Gauguin, Matisse and the Cubists and Futurists.[66] His eye was essentially an early modern one.

Friedländer, on the other hand, admired the paintings of Manet, Cézanne and Munch, although his main area of expertise was in paintings from the Netherlands from Van Eyck to Bruegel, a topic to which he devoted a monumental study in fourteen volumes. He

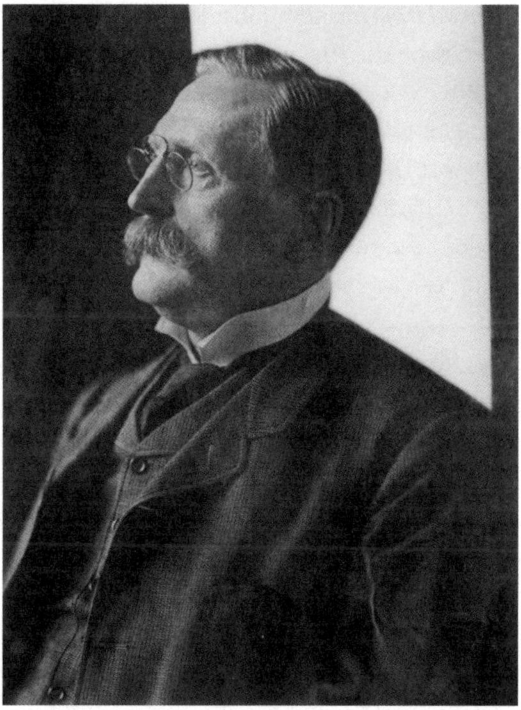

24 Wilhelm Bode, *c.* 1909.

was equally famous for his eye and his wit, as his books *Genuine and Counterfeit* (1929) and *Art and Connoisseurship* (1939) both testify. These books also reveal his ambivalence to Morelli and Berenson, both of whom he described as gifted but also as 'charlatans'.[67]

Bode's attributions, presented in peremptory fashion without explanation (like those of Berenson a little later), were often controversial, but the ones that are generally accepted include his recognition of the portrait of Ginevra de' Benci (now to be seen in the National Gallery, Washington) as a Leonardo, along with the *Annunciation* that is now in the Uffizi. A third Italian example of Bode's sharp eye is his attribution to Leonardo's master, Andrea del Verrocchio, of a painting of a *Madonna with a Seated Child.*[68] On another occasion, Bode recognized a portrait of a woman as a work by Dürer and bought it for the Berlin Museum. When the frame was removed, it was revealed that Dürer had signed it. Bode was also the first to attribute a painting of *Tobit and the Angel* to Rembrandt. Although Bode's attribution to Rembrandt alone of the *Man with a Gold Helmet* is now considered doubtful, the painting is certainly worthy of the master.[69] Bode also recognized that a statue of a *Virgin and Child* in the Victoria and Albert Museum, attributed to Donatello, was a nineteenth-century fake.

As might have been expected, however, a number of Bode's confident attributions, some of them following the opinions of the dealer Stefano Bardini, provoked criticism.[70] His attributions to Botticelli, for instance, were rejected by Berenson, while other attributions of paintings of the Italian Renaissance were denied by Morelli and his disciple Gustavo Frizzoni. In old age, Bode certified two paintings, a *Lacemaker* and a *Smiling Girl*, as the work of Vermeer, but they are now thought to be the work of the notorious Dutch forger Han van Meegeren.[71] Worst of all for Bode's reputation in his own time was his attribution of a wax bust of the Roman goddess Flora (which he bought in London for £8,000) to Leonardo da Vinci. The bust was declared to be a forgery by an English restorer who claimed to have made it himself, creating a scandal that was discussed in the newspapers in England and France as well as in Germany. Today, some connoisseurs think it possible that the bust is a much-restored example of a work from Leonardo's circle.[72]

Disagreements with Bode often turned into personal conflicts, fuelled by competition. As Friedländer remarked, Bode saw things as 'black or white, good or bad', and people as 'friends or foes', without any middle position.[73] For example, Bode and Berenson 'each sought to discredit works that the other had certified'.[74] As for Morelli, Bode called him a 'quack doctor' and dismissed his famous method as a simplification that made him blind to the quality of the works that he described.[75]

Like his younger rival Berenson, Bode worked closely with a dealer in art, in his case Charles Sedelmeyer, the publisher of his sumptuous Rembrandt catalogue. The catalogue was denounced by an Austrian art critic as an example of 'harmonious collaboration between French business speculation and German pseudo-research' and a corruption of Rembrandt scholarship.[76] Bode, who wrote many certificates of authenticity, eventually admitted that he had been under pressure from the dealer to declare some paintings owned by Sedelmeyer to be Rembrandts, although he himself did not agree with the attribution. He was also involved with the dealer Joseph Duveen, but in Bode's case (unlike Berenson's, as we shall see) he refused money for his advice, only accepting gifts of paintings to his museum.[77]

Restorers and Conservators

One of the duties of curators of museums was and is to ensure the conservation and, if necessary, the restoration of the paintings in their custody. This task of restoration was left to artists until the later eighteenth century, when the first specialists are found, including the families of the Picaults and the Hacquins in Paris. Robert Picault invented a way of transferring paintings from a wooden panel to canvas, as in the case of Andrea del Sarto's *Charity*. François-Toussaint Hacquin transposed Raphael's *Santa Cecilia* onto canvas when it arrived in Paris in 1797.[78] Both families guarded their secrets. In Venice, Pietro Edwards, who was appointed official restorer of paintings in public hands, studied chemistry and tried to make restoration a science, shared his techniques in his *Restauro generale dei quadri* (1778).[79] In the nineteenth century, what some restorers knew was summarized for a wider public in a manual by Morelli's friend Giovanni Secco Suardo. There were many later editions of this handbook, a milestone in the textualization of practical knowledge that was first published in 1866.[80]

At this time a number of restorers saw their task as not simply cleaning paintings but 'improving' them. Giuseppe Molteni, for instance, a painter who became director of the Brera in Milan, was described by his friend Morelli in 1865 as 'a truly incomparable restorer', 'with a fine sensibility for art' (*un sentiment très fin pour l'art*).[81] He made his studio at the Brera 'a kind of salon or rendez-vous for collectors and dealers'.[82] However, like Eugène Viollet-le-Duc and other restorers of Gothic buildings, Molteni used his gifts to adapt the works he was restoring to the taste of his own time. For this reason, his cleaning of Raphael's *Marriage of the Virgin* (1504) was much criticized. In contrast to Molteni's free approach was the work of 'minimalists', as we may call them, such as his former pupil Luigi Cavenaghi and the art historian Giovanni Battista Cavalcaselle, whose restorations included the Giotto frescos in Assisi and the Mantegna frescos in Padua.[83]

It is scarcely surprising to find that the restoration of paintings was extremely controversial at this time, with disputes about over-cleaning taking centre stage. The painter, dealer and connoisseur William Spence, giving evidence to a Select Committee of the House of Commons in 1853, probably shocked his listeners when he noted the use of a penknife in Italy to remove dirt from pictures, though he added that in Florence and Rome it was considered 'the safest of all modes of cleaning'.[84] The committee had been appointed to investigate after Charles Eastlake had ordered the restoration of a number of famous paintings, including Titian's *Bacchus and Ariadne* (1520–23). The restoration was strongly criticized in the press, notably by the critic John Ruskin, who claimed in a letter to *The Times* that the Titian had been 'scraped raw'.[85] Despite the development of a science of 'conservation' (replacing the over-ambitious term 'restoration' and emphasizing the need for the reversibility of any changes), controversies of this kind have continued until our own time.

Forgeries

The frontier between restoration and forgery may be difficult to define, but some individuals clearly transgressed it. At a time of increasing demand, especially by foreigners, for works by the big names of the Italian Renaissance, the temptation to increase the supply of these works was great, and at least a few artists and dealers succumbed to it. Some of the sculptures that they sold ended up in the Louvre, the State Museum in Berlin and the South Kensington Museum. For connoisseurs, the detection of these fakes was part of the 'attribution game'. Some forgers also appear to have seen their activity as a kind of game, a means of outwitting critics and connoisseurs as well as a source of easy money.

It is difficult to estimate the number of fakes at this period, owing to the 'dark figure' of works that remain undiscovered. What we do know is that several gifted artists produced fakes at this time, notably two Italians, the sculptor Giovanni Bastianini and the painter Icilio Federico Joni.

Bastianini has been described as 'a genius among forgers', 'the greatest forger who has ever lived' or, more precisely, 'the most infamous and gifted nineteenth-century imitator of Italian Renaissance sculpture'.[86] He made busts of some of his contemporaries but is better known for works in a Renaissance style that deceived leading connoisseurs, whether or not he intended to do so. His relief of a *Virgin and Child* was bought for the South Kensington Museum by the curator John Charles Robinson under the impression that it was a work by the Renaissance sculptor Antonio Rossellino. His bust of Lucrezia Donati was attributed by Cavalcaselle to the Renaissance sculptor Mino da Fiesole. A bust of an unidentified lady was authenticated by Berenson as a work by a third Renaissance sculptor, Luca della Robbia. A bust in wood, entitled *Giovanna degli Albizzi*, was accepted by the National Gallery in Washington as a work by a fourth Renaissance sculptor, Desiderio da Settignano.

Yet another of Bastianini's busts, made in 1863 and representing the Florentine poet Girolamo Benivieni, was sold to the Louvre three years later as a Renaissance work. On this occasion, the sale provoked the sculptor to claim authorship. This gesture suggests that Bastianini may have been engaged in pastiche rather than forgery. He worked for nearly twenty years for Giovanni Freppa, known as 'the king of the dealers', 'perhaps the most ruthless and unscrupulous purveyor of forged works of art among the Florentine dealers of his time'.[87] However, Bastianini was paid relatively little for his sculptures. For a bust of Savonarola, for instance, he was paid about 500 lire, although the work was soon resold for 10,000 lire. This discrepancy suggests that deception may only have begun after the sculptures had left Bastianini's workshop, moving along a chain of more or less scrupulous individuals as the price increased.[88]

One day in June 1899, when the couple was in Venice, Mary Costelloe (who was not yet Mrs Berenson) wrote in her diary that 'We called on the Antiquario beside St Mark's and found more excellent Sienese forgeries, which gave us doubts about – most of

Bernhard's pictures!' In October the same year she reported that 'We have run our forger to earth.' 'He' turned out to be 'They', a group of young men in Siena. 'Their chief is Federigo Ioni.' This incident may have inspired Mary's lecture on 'How to Tell a Forgery', given in Chicago in 1904.[89]

In his lively autobiography, Ioni (or Joni) described himself as 'a painter of old pictures' rather than a forger, though he certainly intended to deceive. The methods he used to make his paintings appear to be antiques included the use of genuine old panels, thus blurring the distinction between forgery and what might be described as creative restoration. Ioni was trained as an artist and began his career as a restorer and a decorator of book-bindings, but gradually became more ambitious. His memoir describes commissions to copy works by Vincenzo Foppa and Ghirlandaio as well as to restore a Renaissance painting of St Catherine of which the head was missing – the artist was asked to ensure that the head's replacement was not 'too Ionesque' (*troppo Ionesca*), suggesting that he was already well known for his pastiches.[90] Ioni prided himself on painting in a Renaissance style but in a manner that differed from all the masters of the period (*che non assomigliava a nessuno di quei maestri*). He also claimed that Berenson refused to believe that Ioni's painting of a *Virgin and Child* was a modern work.[91]

Art Historians

Another new profession for connoisseurs was that of art historian. The nineteenth century was the age of the rise of art history, especially in the German-speaking world. Art history differed from the tradition of artists' biographies by including not only monographs on particular artists but studies of the collective enterprise of art, its practices and institutions. Major publications before 1850 included the following:

1764 Johann Joachim Winckelmann, *Geschichte der Kunst des Altertums*
1792–6 Luigi Lanzi, *Storia pittorica della Italia*

1813–18	Emmanuele Antonio Cicogna, *Storia della scultura*
1815–20	Johan Dominicus Fiorillo, *Geschichte der zeichnenden Kunst*
1823	Seroux d'Agincourt, *Histoire de l'art par les monumens*
1827–31	Karl Friedrich von Rumohr, *Italienische Forschungen*
1836	Maria Graham, *Essays towards the History of Painting*
1837	Franz Theodor Kugler, *Handbuch der Geschichte der Malerei*
1841–2	Kugler, *Handbuch der Kunstgeschichte*
1841	Atanazy Raczynski, *Geschichte der neueren Deutscher Kunst*
1842	Heinrich Gustav Hotho, *Geschichte der deutschen und niederländischen Malerei*
1843–	Karl Schnaase, *Geschichte der bildenden Künste*
1845	Anna Jameson, *Memoirs of the Italian Painters*
1847	Charles Eastlake, *Materials for a History of Oil Painting*
1849–69	Charles Blanc, *Histoire des peintres des tous les écoles*

The authors of these works were extremely diverse. Lanzi was a priest and, like Eastlake, a keeper of an art gallery. Fiorillo and Kugler were professors. Emmanuele Cicogna, Carl Friedrich von Rumohr, Maria Graham and Anna Jameson were private scholars. Charles Blanc worked for the Ministry of the Interior and founded the *Gazette des Beaux-Arts*.

In contrast, in the second half of the nineteenth century, art history would be written mainly by professionals, whether they were located in museums or universities. A new form of sociability or collective connoisseurship, the academic seminar, was added to the tradition of the salon.

Retrospectively, one might describe connoisseurs such as Mariette as – among other things – art historians, though the phrase only came into general use with the establishment of the discipline in universities, especially, once again, in the German-speaking world. Indeed, chairs in the subject were for a time a virtual monopoly of universities in that world, as the following table of their foundation shows.[92]

1830	Koenigsberg
1844	Berlin
1852	Vienna
1855	Jena
1855	Zurich
1860	Bonn
1873	Leipzig
1886	Basel

The first international congress of art historians, held in Vienna in 1873, marked another step in the institutionalization and professionalization of art history.

Connoisseurship in a United Italy

Two of the most famous nineteenth-century connoisseurs, Giovanni Battista Cavalcaselle (see illus. 3) and Giovanni Morelli (see illus. 4) were active at the time that Italy was united and themselves contributed to the process of unification. Both men were also active in stemming or at least limiting the flow of works of art out of Italy, a flow that was increasingly viewed as the loss of the national heritage.

Cavalcaselle was originally trained as an artist but dropped out of the Academy of Art in Venice, preferring to tour Europe to look at paintings. In exile after the failure of the revolution of 1848, he took the opportunity to visit museums in Spain, France, Belgium and Germany. He lived in England for a time, where he began his famous collaboration with an Englishman, Joseph Crowe. Crowe was a many-sided man. Having studied to be an artist in Paris in the studio of Paul Delaroche, he became a reporter for the *Daily*

News and then a foreign correspondent for the *Illustrated London News* and *The Times*, covering both the Crimean War (1853–6) and what was known at the time as the 'Indian Mutiny' (1857). In his spare time, he studied the history of art.

In London, Crowe and Cavalcaselle began to produce a series of books, of which the most famous is the three-volume *History of Painting in Italy* (1864–6). The text reveals a sensitivity to the condition of the paintings that is surely the result of Cavalcaselle's experience as a restorer. Describing Piero della Francesca's famous *Baptism of Christ*, for instance, the text notes that 'A serious drawback to the enjoyment of this picture is the abrasion of its colour,' while 'the insight it gives into Piero's mode of painting in the Florentine method of oil is most interesting.'[93]

The *History of Painting* also reveals a keen eye, or two pairs of eyes, for differences between originals and copies, as in the case of Andrea del Sarto's copy of Raphael's famous portrait of Pope Leo x. Unlike Giulio Romano, who had mistaken the copy for the original, Crowe and Cavalcaselle were aware of

> the perfect keeping, ease, grandeur, modelling and relief of form; the peculiar flavour of art which distinguish Sanzio [Raphael] from Del Sarto . . . The peculiarity of their schooling produces distinct modes of handling. Andrea did not place tones over each other and fuse them together by glaze and half glaze, according to the process which Raphael had learnt from Leonardo and Perugino. His is a more immediate and rapid system, which has frequently the disadvantage of giving an air of emptiness to his works in oil.[94]

Cavalcaselle later served as Inspector of Fine Arts in the Italian Ministry of Education.[95] His attitude to the drain of Italian art abroad is summed up in his description of the British artist and dealer William Spence (who bought Piero's *Baptism of Christ* from the canons of San Sepolcro for £400) as 'looting the country's works of art' (*spogliando il paese degli oggetti d'arte*).[96] He called for an inventory of the Italian artistic patrimony, a listing essential to the task of defending that patrimony from spoliation. As a first step in this direction, the Italian prime minister, Count Cavour, invited both Cavalcaselle and Morelli to catalogue the works of art belonging to the former convents of Umbria and the Marches.

For his part, Giovanni Morelli, who was probably the most influential connoisseur of this whole period, followed a varied career. He was trained in comparative anatomy and in medicine but did not practise as a doctor. On a visit to Berlin in 1838 he met Rumohr, Waagen and Bode's mentor Karl Eduard von Liphart. In Paris a year later he met the dealer Otto Mündler, who seems to have converted him, like Bode, to connoisseurship. Like Cavalcaselle, as noted in Chapter One, Morelli participated in the Italian revolutions of 1848. He became a deputy and a senator after the unification of Italy in 1861.

In parliament, Morelli criticized the export of works of art from Italy. Although he advised English collectors such as his friend the archaeologist Austen Layard, he only informed them about minor works by Italian artists so that the real masterpieces would remain in the country in which they had been painted. He tried, without success, to prevent Eastlake from buying the *Madonna of the Swallow* by Carlo Crivelli, going to see the minister of education and 'begging him not to allow the picture to leave Italy'.[97] When Bode tried to buy Giorgione's famous *Tempest*, Morelli persuaded him that the asking price was too high.[98] Eastlake's successor as director of the National Gallery, William Boxall, wrote in 1866 that 'Morelli and Cavalcaselle I find are both enemies to our carrying off pictures and I cannot tell you how impossible these acquisitions are become throughout the country.'[99]

Morelli was notorious for his critique of his predecessors, including the friend who had introduced him to connoisseurship, Otto Mündler, whom he described as having 'pursued no method in his studies but was wont to be guided solely by the general impression produced upon him by a picture'.[100] Even Cavalcaselle was criticized by Morelli for failing to appreciate the 'inner life of art', despite the latter's admission, in a letter to Layard, that his rival's eye is 'well practised, indeed one of the most practised that I know' (*son oeil est très exercé, de plus exercés même que je connaisse*). 'Messrs Crowe and Cavalcaselle', as Morelli called them, though they were often praised for attributions, were also criticized for 'erroneous views' of Giorgione and for the attribution to Palma himself of 'an admirable work of Palma's pupil, assistant and imitator, Giovanni Cariani', failing to see that 'the form of the ear . . . is wholly unlike Palma'.[101] Morelli's gift for satire was often exercised at the expense of his colleagues, whom he described as 'the crowd of so-called experts and connoisseurs of art' (*il volgo dei cosidetti intelligenti e conoscitori di belle arti*).[102]

Morelli was a particularly aggressive critic of Bode. For example, the claim that a Madonna in the gallery in Berlin was an early work by Palma elicited the comment: 'Had Dr Bode . . . examined this picture with a critical eye, instead of only observing the label, he would have seen that it could not be the work of a beginner.' Again, the paintings and drawings that Bode 'so lavishly' ascribes to Verrocchio were described by Morelli as 'for the most part the work of other contemporary and inferior Florentine hands'.[103] Morelli even used the index of his book as a weapon: the entry for Bode includes 'mistakes work by M. de Verona for one by Carpaccio . . . wrongly ascribes works at Bologna to Costa . . . mistakes an original by Bonifacio for a copy . . . erroneous views with regard to Leonardo'.

Morelli's positive ideas on connoisseurship were developed in the 1850s, published in German as articles in the 1870s and in book form in 1890 in three volumes of *Studies in Art Criticism* (*Kunstkritische Studien*). The studies, published under a pseudonym ('Lermolieff', more or less an anagram of 'Morelli'), include sections taking the traditional form of a dialogue between a connoisseur and a student, while making more of its dramatic possibilities than Félibien, say, or Boschini had done. Morelli had himself written plays, one of which, *The Artists*, was staged in Milan in 1860.[104]

Morelli was an *enfant terrible* who loved to shock his readers. As the preface to his book on the galleries of Munich and Dresden points out, he had radical views on 'the question of the authorship of a great number of paintings in public and private collections', being convinced that 'although they pass for works by Italian masters, they are in reality for the most part imitations by Northern and principally by Flemish painters.' Even the style of Morelli's essays was controversial, since

> it has been said that my writings lacked that grave and learned tone which is alone calculated to impress the reader and which distinguishes a serious student of art from a superficial dilettante . . . but in this world many persons say the most foolish things with an air of the greatest solemnity.[105]

Morelli has become famous, or infamous, for his emphasis on details, noting the significance of the apparently insignificant, especially the representation of hands, ears or eyes as clues to the author of a given work of art. In paintings by Sodoma, for instance, 'the hands have tapering fingers, the knuckles being often only indicated by a kind of dimple,' while almond-shaped eyes are 'met with in all Sodoma's pictures'. There was, as we have seen, a tradition of focusing on details as a means to attribution, a custom well-enough known to be satirized in the *Gentleman's Magazine* in 1735 as paying attention to 'some little Corner, the Touch of a Plant, the Tip of a Cloud'.[106] However, Morelli transformed this negative view into a positive one.

Although he was an independent scholar, Morelli viewed himself as a professional, opposed to what he called 'dilettantism' (*Kunstdilettantismus*). He wrote about his 'experimental methods' and compared them to the methods of Galileo and Darwin. However, Carlo Ginzburg, using Morelli's method to study Morelli himself, has noted changes in the way he described it between the 1870s and 1890.[107] Indeed, Morelli once described his famous method not as a way to make an attribution but simply a means 'to control the judgement which subjective impressions might lead us to pronounce'.[108] His fate has been to be identified with the use of small clues, whereas he was also concerned with what he called the 'total impression' (*Totaleindruck*) given by a painting.

Whether intuitive or not, the similarity between Morelli's form of connoisseurship and medical diagnosis has been noted more than once. One might say that when he turned to connoisseurship, Morelli took with him the intellectual habits formed by his earlier training. Similarities between his method and the approach to clues of Sherlock Holmes (who explained to Watson why he was careful to observe ears) have been noted. So have parallels with the method of Sigmund Freud, especially in the latter's *Psychopathology of Everyday Life* (1901), with its reading of small unconscious actions such as slips of the tongue. Indeed, it was Freud himself who pointed out that Morelli's method was 'closely related to the technique of psychoanalysis'.[109]

In any case, Morelli had a remarkable eye for paintings. One of his best-known successes was his attribution to Giorgione of the painting of the *Sleeping Venus* in the gallery at Dresden, where it had been assigned to the seventeenth-century painter Giovanni Battista da Sassoferrato. Today, it is generally agreed to be a work by Giorgione, although some scholars believe that it was completed by Titian.

A major difference between Morelli and Bode was their influence on the following generation of connoisseurs. Bode's followers were relatively few, though they included Max Friedländer, Wilhelm Valentiner (a Rembrandt specialist who became a museum curator in the USA) and Frida Schottmüller (an expert on Donatello), all of whom began their careers as his assistants, as well as the Dutch connoisseur Abraham Bredius.

Following the advice of Bode, whom he met in 1878, Bredius specialized in Dutch art of the seventeenth century, especially the paintings of Jan Steen, Rembrandt and Vermeer. Like Bode, he combined connoisseurship with the search for documents, spending long hours in cold archives, 'often wrapped in his fur coat'. He published seven volumes of early inventories of works of art.[110] However, Bredius made his name through his criticism of accepted attributions. In his catalogue of Rembrandts, for instance, he reduced their number to 630 or fewer. Bredius also seemed to have a good nose for forgeries. A painting of a cottage that the French connoisseur

Théophile Thoré had attributed to Vermeer was re-attributed by Bredius, when still a young man, to a minor eighteenth-century painter, Dirk Jan van der Laen. Bredius also claimed that a famous painting of *Christ and the Woman Taken in Adultery*, attributed to Rembrandt, was in fact 'one of those very clever forgeries from the first half of the eighteenth century'.[111] It is both ironic and tragic that Bredius is often remembered today not as a discoverer but as a victim of forgery, accepting fake Vermeers as genuine, as we shall see in the following chapter.

Morelli's Followers

Morelli's style of connoisseurship appealed to a younger generation, the 'Morelli-ites', as the English critic Roger Fry called them, although some of them moved away from his approach later. The list of members of what we might describe as the 'school' of Morelli begins with his friend Layard, better known as a British diplomat and as the archaeologist who excavated the Assyrian palace of Nineveh. Layard was also a collector of Italian Renaissance art, owning works by Cosimo Tura, Gentile Bellini and Vittore Carpaccio as well as by Morelli's favourites, Giovanni Battista Morone and Moretto da Brescia (whom he described in a letter to Layard as 'one of the most noble and one of the most original painters of the sixteenth century'). Layard had grown up in Florence, where he was given lessons in drawing. In his *Autobiography* he noted with pride that when he was a boy, his father 'was much pleased by my readiness in attributing to the right masters the pictures he pointed out to me, or the school to which they belonged'. Morelli later became his mentor in connoisseurship. In his turn, Layard financed the translation of Morelli's books and wrote a memoir of his friend.[112]

Most followers of Morelli came from the next generation. Gustavo Frizzoni, for instance, was the son of one of Morelli's friends. He became both a connoisseur and an art historian, assisting Morelli and carrying on his master's work in a series of books that centred on the art of the Italian Renaissance.[113] Jean Paul

Richter, best known for his studies of Leonardo's notebooks, was another disciple. Bernard Berenson began his career as a follower of Morelli and continued to refer him as 'my revered master' as well as to 'us Morellians'. In a later generation, Kenneth Clark, who became Berenson's assistant, once confessed that 'I am quite glad of my Morellian training.'[114]

Three leading female connoisseurs were disciples of Morelli: Maud Cruttwell, Mary Logan Smith (later Mary Costelloe and finally, Mary Berenson) and Constance Ffoulkes. Cruttwell, a friend of the Berensons, learned about Renaissance art from them and published a series of monographs on Italian artists, from Signorelli (1899) to Donatello (1911).[115] Mary Berenson, who will be discussed together with Bernard, was a connoisseur in her own right. As for Ffoulkes, she was a student and later a translator of Morelli, who introduced her to both Layard and Lady Eastlake in 1887. She is best known for a monograph on Vincenzo Foppa, published in 1909, which made use of Morelli's notes on the artist and was written

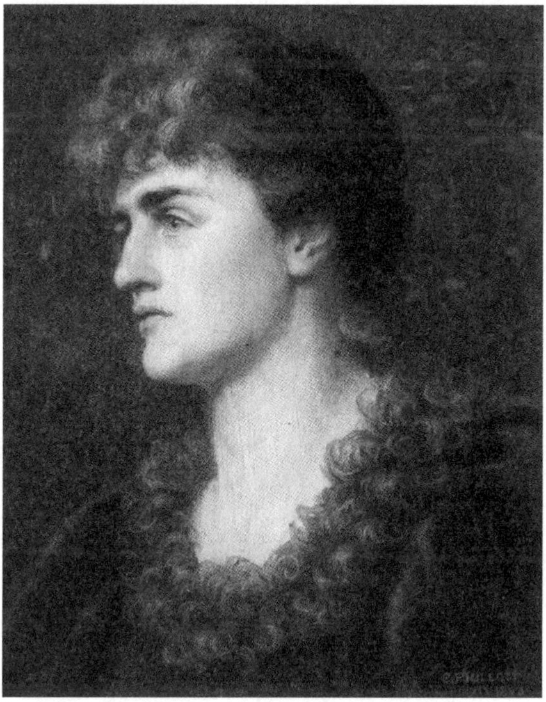

25 Constance Phillott, *Eugenie Sellers Strong*, 1890, oil on canvas.

together with an Italian historian, Monsignor Rodolfo Maiocchi. The introduction to this book confessed that 'whatever we may have learned in this wide field is due to his [Morelli's] writings, and to his personal teaching and direction.' The influence of Morelli is apparent in the authors' use of details such as hair and hands in attributing to Foppa the charming fresco of a child reading Cicero. Another debt was their use of the Brera altarpiece, which Morelli was the first to attribute to Foppa, as the 'criterion' for further attributions. The double dedication of the book to both Morelli and the scholar Gustav Ludwig, known for his research in Venetian archives, symbolized the double approach of the monograph, which combined close looking with documents from the archives.[116]

Morelli's influence was not limited to specialists on the Italian Renaissance. For example, the German scholar Wilhelm Vöge approached medieval French sculpture in a Morellian manner.[117] The Austrian art historian Franz Wickhoff, who became famous for his study of ancient Roman art, met Morelli in 1879, when he was 26, and was converted to his method. Wickhoff and his Viennese colleagues will be discussed further below.[118]

Between the sixteenth and eighteenth centuries, as we have seen, the study of antiquities influenced the study of paintings. In the late nineteenth century, the process was reversed. Two leading British students of ancient Greek and Roman art were inspired by Morelli's method. The British scholar Eugénie Sellers (later, Eugénie Strong, illus. 25) learned from both Morelli and the German classicist Adolf Furtwängler, with whom she studied, to make attributions of ancient Roman statues on the basis of stylistic analysis. She had discovered Morelli by 1893, when her friend Violet Paget (better known as 'Vernon Lee') wrote to her mother that 'Miss Sellers . . . is applying to ancient sculpture the method lately invented by Morelli for painting,' distinguishing between Polykleitos and Myron, for instance, by the way in which they represent hair.[119]

John Beazley, a professor of classical archaeology at Oxford whose field was the study of ancient Greek red-figure and black-figure vases, has been described as 'the greatest ever practitioner of the Morellian method', who stands out for 'the sheer quantity and subsequent acceptance of his attributions'.[120] Beazley, who was well acquainted with the art of the Italian Renaissance and even used the term 'Mannerist' to refer to some of his vases, used stylistic analysis along the lines of Morelli (of whose work he was probably aware, though he did not cite it) to attribute paintings to various masters whose names were unknown but whose styles or 'systems of forms' he distinguished, most famously the 'Berlin Painter', so christened after an amphora in the Staatlichen Museen in that city.

A later generation has become more critical of Beazley's method than his contemporaries had been, though it is worth noting that he did not claim that the systems of forms that he distinguished were always the work of a single hand. On the contrary, he recognized that they might include pupils and copyists.[121] He may still be criticized for an anachronistic emphasis on individual artists.

Art Historians versus Connoisseurs

Some scholars see no problem in combining the eye of the connoisseur with the research of a historian. Nevertheless, the relation between art history and connoisseurship (or more exactly, between certain practitioners of these two disciplines) has sometimes been a difficult one.

Art historians have not always taken attribution seriously. Even Jacob Burckhardt, who cared about the quality of works of art and had a good eye for it, scoffed at what he called 'attributology' (*Attribuzlerei*). In similar fashion, Aby Warburg, who described himself as a historian of images, dismissed what he called 'the whole nosey tribe' of 'connoisseurs and attributionists . . . only inspired by the temperament of a gourmand'.[122] Some art historians viewed connoisseurs as doing nothing more than providing raw material for their own more ambitious works. For example, in 1881 the German art historian Anton Springer published an article, 'Kunstkenner und Kunsthistoriker', in which he claimed that 'connoisseurship always remains an activity of merely preparatory nature.'[123]

Morelli was perhaps thinking of Springer when he remarked, in a book published nine years later, that 'Connoisseurs say of art historians that they write about what they do not understand; art historians, on their side, disparage the connoisseurs and only look upon them as drudges who collect materials for them.'[124] On one side, we see a passionate belief in the power and the reliability of the trained eye in attributing paintings and detecting forgeries. On the other, an equally passionate belief in the evidence of documents. On one side, *connaissance*; on the other, *savoir*.

The problem of incompatibility between the two sources of knowledge was a relatively new one. It is only in this age of professionalization and specialization that we find a tension between the partners, a strain in the marriage between them. In this crowded marriage we should not forget the curator. Wilhelm Bode claimed that connoisseurship should be left to the professionals (meaning curators) and criticized Morelli as a dilettante and a 'quack doctor'.[125] Lady Eastlake, herself an amateur connoisseur, noted that 'In Germany, Italy and France, connoisseurship is a profession,' one that required 'the astuteness of the lawyer, the diagnosis of the physician, and the research of the antiquary and historian'.[126]

By the middle of the twentieth century, it was time to speak of separation between the partners, if not of divorce. Among Warburg's followers, Erwin Panofsky defined the connoisseur as 'a laconic art historian', surely a gibe at Bernard Berenson and his famous lists of names, while Edgar Wind criticized connoisseurship in his lectures on *Art and Anarchy*.[127] On the other side, the primacy of the eye was defended by Berenson, whose 'persistent indifference to documents' has been noted; by Pietro Toesca, whose watchword was 'first the connoisseurs, then the historians' (*prima conoscitori, poi storici*); and later by Toesca's student Roberto Longhi, to whom the same remark is attributed.

Fortunately, some scholars combined the skills of the connoisseur and the art historian, including members of the Vienna School of art history, a remarkable group active in the cultural golden age of the Austro-Hungarian Empire in the years before the First World War and led by Franz Wickhoff and Alois Riegl. Links between the practices of art history and plain or general history were particularly close in Vienna, where the Institut für Österreichische Geschichtsforschung, which was founded in 1854, included art history on its curriculum. The art historian Julius von Schlosser, a former student of Wickhoff's, edited literary sources for art history.[128] Another student of Wickhoff's, Max Dvořák, wrote a dissertation on the falsification of documents by a fifteenth-century imperial chancellor before turning to art history, which he came to view as a form of cultural history (*Geistesgeschichte*).[129] Given this concern with documents, it is no surprise to see that in Vienna the study of illuminated manuscripts received particular emphasis, notably in Wickhoff's famous study, *Die Wiener Genesis* (1895), of a sixth-century Greek text, and also in Dvořák's studies of Byzantine influence on fourteenth-century miniatures and on manuscripts from Avignon.[130]

In the second place, the complementary opposite of the first, the Vienna tradition emphasized the primacy of the object, implying the primacy of the eye. For this reason, successive professors – Rudolf von Eitelberger, Franz Wickhoff, Alois Riegl and Julius von Schlosser – did not give their lectures at the university but in the Museum für Kunst und Industrie, next to the objects that they discussed. Indeed, Riegl remained active as a curator as well as a lecturer until he became a full professor.[131]

The collective belief in the primacy of the eye was linked with admiration for Morelli. Eitelberger's former student Moriz Thausing was a follower of Morelli and introduced his own students, including Riegl and Wickhoff, to the master. Wickhoff later expressed his debt to Morelli for his 'personal instruction' (*persönliche Unterweisung*).[132] His Morellian approach is visible not so much in his *Wiener Genesis* as in his catalogue of Italian drawings in the Albertina.[133] Morelli praised Wickhoff for his 'feine Blick', as well as criticized him for trying to run before he could walk. In return, Wickhoff criticized Morelli for his failure to use documentary evidence.[134] Hans Tietze, who was a student of Riegl and Wickhoff (to both of whom he dedicated his book on method), expressed criticisms of Morelli's focus on ears and hands, describing it as 'stylistic analysis as Bertillonage' (*ein Bertillonage der Stilkritik*), a reference to the French policeman Alphonse Bertillon and his once famous method of identifying individuals by means of precise physical measurements.[135] However, Tietze did employ the Morelli method himself in his studies of Dürer and of Venetian drawings. Another Austrian, Fritz Saxl, 'always defended Morelli against his detractors and I think the manner had become such a part of his makeup that he used it quite unashamedly'.[136]

In short, at a time of increasing distance between connoisseurs and art historians, the Vienna School was able to combine the *savoir* and the *connaissance* of art and, with more difficulty, the careers of art historian and curator.

Photography

In the later nineteenth century, connoisseurship and art history were increasingly assisted by photography. Indeed, for a long time, it was impossible to imagine lectures on art history that were not illustrated by images from a slide projector, preferably presented on two screens to enable comparison. Comparison had long been advocated, as we have seen, as a means of attribution, but this was no easy task, given the dispersal of the works of many Old Masters. By the eighteenth century, connoisseurs such as Mariette were making use of engraved reproductions of paintings to help in the attribution process. The problem raised by this method was that even the most faithful engravings are mixtures. They superimpose two hands, that of the painter and that of the engraver.

The invention of photography offered a solution to this problem. Some professional photographers were already specializing in the reproduction of works of art by the mid-nineteenth century. The brothers Alinari, for example, founded their firm in Florence in 1854, issued their first catalogue two years later and were given permission to reproduce paintings in the Uffizi Gallery from 1860 onwards. By 1869, if not before, photography was being used to establish an attribution, in this case the attribution to Michelangelo of the *Entombment of Christ* that is now in the National Gallery in

London.[137] A year later, the English connoisseur John Charles Robinson suggested that many of the 'errors' in Passavant's study of Raphael might have been avoided if photographs had been available in his time.[138] Looking back at his *Cicerone*, first published in 1855, Jacob Burckhardt remembered that it was written 'at a time when there were few railways, inadequate guides and no photography'. No wonder that the connoisseur Roberto Longhi once declared that 'as a means for the rapid diffusion of artistic knowledge, the invention of photography had a cultural significance little less important than the invention of printing was for literary texts.'[139]

Some connoisseurs, such as Philippe Burty (discussed below), thought that photographs were inferior to prints, but others made increasing use of this new aid. Morelli, who collected many photographs, emphasized the opportunity they offered 'to study the forms' of paintings 'without being misled by the colouring'.[140] By the end of the nineteenth century, museums were establishing photo archives. The archive of the South Kensington Museum, for example, contained 100,000 photos by 1897. The British collectors Robert Witt and his wife Mary began to acquire photos of works of art in 1899 and ended up with 750,000 of them, bequeathed to the Courtauld Institute in London.

Critical voices could also be heard, expressing fears that looking at photographs of a work of art might become a substitute for close looking at the original. Bernard Berenson, for instance, was ambivalent about the new medium. In 1893 he welcomed it as an aid to 'really accurate connoisseurship'.[141] However, when asked in 1896 to decide whether a certain painting was or was not by Velázquez, Bernard wrote to his future wife Mary that 'I do not like to deal in such big game without autopsy.' Twelve years later, in 1908, he wrote to his patron Isabella Stewart Gardner about a painting that she was considering buying that 'Agnew [the art dealers] is sending you a photo but don't think it gives you anything like an idea of the picture.' In later life, on the other hand, Berenson welcomed photography again.[142]

Tastemakers: The Rise of the Art Critic

As already noted, a new role or niche for nineteenth-century connoisseurs was to practise as an art critic. In a broad sense, art criticism was what earlier connoisseurs had practised when they made judgements of quality. However, a distinction needs to be made between judgements of quality that were made in passing, in the course of attributing paintings or writing the biographies of artists, and what might be called art criticism as a literary genre or even an institution with an important role in the formation of taste.

The rise of art criticism in this more precise sense began in the late eighteenth century. It took place in two contexts. One of these was the rise of exhibitions, especially the annual exhibitions of new paintings in the famous salons in Paris, which widened the public interest in contemporary art in France, and the similar annual exhibitions at the Royal Academy in London.[143] Diderot's art criticism took the form of responses to nine of the Paris salons.

However, Diderot's responses were available only to a small number of subscribers to Grimm's journal, which circulated in manuscript. The second condition for the rise of art criticism was the proliferation of printed journals in the early nineteenth century, especially in France. Some of these journals were mainly concerned with other topics, but included a regular section on art, among them the monthly *Revue des Deux Mondes*. The writers included leading men of letters such as Stendhal, Baudelaire and Zola.[144] In similar fashion, in Britain, *Blackwoods Magazine* (a monthly) and the *Quarterly* and *Fortnightly Reviews* offered space for art critics and connoisseurs, Elizabeth Rigby among them.

These journals offered an arena for debates such as the battle in the 1820s for and against romanticism in general and the paintings of Delacroix in particular.[145] Debates of this kind often made the reputation of artists, critics and connoisseurs (along with some art dealers) as spotters of new talent and also (along with some artists) as arbiters of public taste, or at least as what have become known in the digital age as 'influencers' on these attitudes.[146]

As we have seen, Rumohr, Passavant and Waagen influenced the rediscovery of the paintings of Moretto da Brescia. Charles Eastlake may have been thinking of this example when he noted the role of the connoisseur in changing taste.[147] For further examples of discovery and rediscovery we may turn to the writings of two individuals, one French and one British: Thoré and John Ruskin.

Thoré was a many-sided man. Involved in politics, he was present at the barricades in Paris during the revolution of 1830 but became disillusioned with the regime of Louis Philippe that followed and (like Cavalcaselle in Italy) supported the revolution of 1848. Like Cavalcaselle, Thoré was forced into exile, in his case in Brussels. Since his writings were banned in France, he wrote under a pseudonym, 'William Bürger' (in other words, 'Citizen').[148]

Thoré's writings on art were in tune with his politics. Writing on contemporary art for *Le Constitutionnel* in the 1840s, he favoured Delacroix, and in the 1860s, on his return to Paris, he praised Courbet. His taste for art of the Dutch Golden Age may reflect his critique of industrial society. He viewed smooth finish as reactionary and a sketchy style as progressive. He claimed that the art of the Golden Age was insufficiently appreciated, treated as a minor art (*petite peinture*), and that he would rescue it.[149] As a social historian of art, Thoré noted that Dutch art became original around the year 1600, at exactly the time of independence and the transition to a republic.

Thoré argued that to understand paintings, it was necessary to know the manners and customs of the people in the place where they were produced, and that 'One only knows a painter really well after owning his pictures, so as to look at them in all kinds of light and under different impressions.'[150] An enthusiastic collector, he confessed to his 'picture mania', complaining to a friend that 'I am cluttered up. I have no more space. And I buy all the time.'[151] Among the paintings that he owned were Vermeer's *Concert*, his *Woman Standing at a Virginal*, his *Woman with a Pearl Necklace* and the *Goldfinch* of Carel Fabritius (which he wished to look at one more time when he was dying).

Thoré was an occasional dealer in paintings, an adviser to collectors and curators (including Charles Eastlake), a cataloguer for auctions and a reviser of many attributions in his principal field, as well as contributing to the rediscovery of Velázquez. His catalogue of the works of Vermeer, published in 1866, re-attributed paintings to the master that had previously been ascribed to Pieter de Hooch. He published two volumes describing the paintings in Dutch museums, a work that Wilhelm Bode 'almost knew by heart'. Thoré remains most famous for his successful campaign for recognition of the importance of Vermeer, a campaign that was still necessary in his time, despite the treatment of the artist as a major figure by some earlier connoisseurs such as Paillet and Le Brun (discussed in Chapter Four). If the need to rediscover Vermeer now seems odd, it is worth remembering that as late as 1860 the connoisseur Gustav Waagen knew of only six works by the artist, compared to the 34 or so attributed to him today.[152]

Still more famous is the Englishman John Ruskin, who learned to draw at the age of twelve and became a champion of Joseph Turner at the age of seventeen, defending his art from a hostile review in *Blackwoods Magazine* and calling him 'Shakespearian'.[153] He went on to champion John Millais, whose *Christ in the Carpenter's Shop* (1849–50), denounced by many critics (including Charles Dickens), he defended in letters to *The Times*, and to support Edward Burne-Jones, whom he described as 'a great dramatic master'.

Turning to the art of the past, the second volume of Ruskin's *Modern Painters* (1843–60) was important in stimulating the taste for the works of Giotto, Fra Angelico and Giovanni Bellini. As his biographer Tim Hilton remarks, 'Ruskin was neither the first nor the sole discoverer of early Italian art,' but 'he was by far the most persuasive.' 'Some of Ruskin's attributions were wrong, and remained wrong,' but this feature of his connoisseurship was unimportant if set beside his influence on taste, that of his contemporaries and that of posterity.[154] Less predictably, Ruskin's great discovery in Italy in 1845 was Tintoretto, by whom he was 'overwhelmed'. 'I never was so utterly crushed to the earth before any human intellect as I was today, before Tintoret', whose *Crucifixion* he copied at this time. 'As for *painting*, I think I didn't know what it meant until today.'[155] Ruskin later championed Veronese, whom he discovered in 1858;

Carpaccio, whom he described as 'a new world to me' in 1869; and Botticelli, whom he came to appreciate in the 1870s.[156]

Ruskin collected paintings as well as writing about them. He bought works by Turner, whom he knew personally, owning more than three hundred of his drawings and watercolours. He owned a splendid fifteenth-century painting of a *Madonna and Child*, sometimes attributed to Verrocchio. Ruskin also collected medieval manuscripts, especially Bibles and Books of Hours, mainly for their illuminations. From around the year 1850, 'the collecting and study of illuminated manuscripts became one of the greatest of his pleasures and the most constant of his pursuits.'[157]

The Rediscovery of Eighteenth-Century France

Two major changes in European taste in the late nineteenth century, the rediscovery of the art of eighteenth-century France and the discovery of the art of Japan, were led by three French connoisseurs. Their names were Edmond de Goncourt, his brother Jules and Edmond's friend Philippe Burty. Surprise has sometimes been expressed at the simultaneous rise of enthusiasm for these two forms of art, although both are characterized by elegance and delicacy.

The French Revolution had been followed by a reaction against the art of the old regime, especially the work of Watteau, Boucher and Fragonard, their paintings symbolizing the aristocratic world that the Revolution had destroyed. In early nineteenth-century France the major conflict of taste was that between the classicism of David and Ingres and the romanticism of Delacroix. Revolutions are never complete, whether in taste or in politics, and minor artists continued to imitate Watteau and Boucher as late as the 1830s and '40s. We might therefore speak of a 'survival' of interest in eighteenth-century art, merging with the revival of that interest in the second half of the nineteenth century. This revival was exemplified by the connoisseur Louis La Caze, who took pride in a collection that included important works by Watteau, Fragonard and Chardin.[158]

In his efforts for the rehabilitation of eighteenth-century French art, Goncourt was assisted by his friend Burty, a collector, connoisseur and critic with interests that ranged from etchings to tapestries, from ceramics to photography and from Delacroix to the Impressionists.[159]

In other words, when Edmond de Goncourt claimed that he and his brother Jules had 'initiated' what he called 'the resurrection of the art of the eighteenth century' he was exaggerating their achievement. Nevertheless, the Goncourt brothers did play a significant role in what we might call – in a word that would surely have shocked them – the 'popularization' of the taste for eighteenth-century art. The brothers published a study, *L'art du XVIIIe siècle* (1859–76), together with a series of books on the history of the period, including *La Femme au XVIIIe siècle* (1862). They were also collectors of eighteenth-century drawings, furniture and porcelain. Edmond, who once remarked that 'learning to see is the longest form of learning in all the arts,' established his credentials as a connoisseur by publishing a *catalogue raisonné* of Watteau.[160]

The interest in collecting eighteenth-century French art soon spread to the British, led by an eccentric bachelor, the fourth Marquess of Hertford, who lived in Paris but passed on his paintings and his enthusiasm to his illegitimate son Richard Wallace, who bequeathed his pictures and his name to the Wallace Collection in London, which opened in 1897.[161] Soon afterwards the art historian Emilia Strong (no relation of Eugénie Strong), who had been advised by Ruskin to study at the South Kensington Art School, published *French Painters of the Eighteenth Century* (1899).

The Spread of Connoisseurship

During what is described here as the 'age of the professionals', the numbers of amateur connoisseurs or would-be connoisseurs continued to expand, especially at the turn of the century. In France, two journals with the name *Le Connaisseur* were founded at the beginning of the twentieth century, one in 1901 and the other in 1907. In Britain, too, two new art journals were founded at this time: *The Connoisseur* (the fourth journal with that name) in 1901, and the *Burlington Magazine for Connoisseurs* (1903). The latter was managed by a committee that included Bernard Berenson and Roger Fry, the painter, critic and collector who played an important role in the reception of 'Post-Impressionism' (as he was the first to call it) in Britain, thanks to an exhibition that he organized in London in 1910 with Clive Bell. It was followed in 1912 by a second post-Impressionist exhibition. Fry's interest in connoisseurship is revealed not only in his sense of quality but in his critique of a catalogue of Old Master drawings that included 'one or two really obvious howlers in the matter of attributions'.[162]

For these journals to succeed – and *The Connoisseur* survived until 1992, while the *Burlington Magazine* still exists – there must have been a sufficient number of subscribers, informed lovers of the decorative arts if not necessarily of paintings. Like the growing number of exhibitions, the journals both catered for and amplified these interests. They encouraged new forms of sociability in the tradition of the earlier salons. The Burlington Fine Arts Club, for example, founded in 1866, became a centre for the discussion of problems of connoisseurship. So did some commercial galleries in London, notably the Goupil Gallery (opened in 1857) and the Grosvenor Gallery (founded 1877), which hosted Fry's Post-Impressionist Exhibition.[163] It is in this context that we should place Morelli's complaint about 'the mass of so-called appreciators and connoisseurs of the arts [*il volgo dei cosidetti intelligenti e conoscitori di belle arti*], from whom God deliver us'.[164]

Collecting Modern Art

While Dmitri Shchukin, discussed earlier, collected Old Masters, his brother Sergei preferred modern art, discovering Impressionism in Paris in 1897 and going on to buy works by Cézanne, Gauguin, Picasso and Matisse. At the end of the period described in this chapter, thanks to individuals such as Sergei, modern art became a serious rival to Old Masters in the eyes of collectors, while Paris became the capital of the market for it. The leading auction room there was the Hôtel Drouot, founded in 1852.[165] Drouot's coexisted with individual dealers, including three who deserve to be described as connoisseurs because they combined what a former dealer turned author, Philip Hook, calls 'a commercial eye' with a talent for spotting talent, betting on young artists who would later become famous.[166] The three, all of them active before the First World War, were Paul Durand-Ruel, Ambroise Vollard and Daniel-Henry Kahnweiler.

Paul Durand-Ruel (illus. 26), who took over the family business in 1867, originally bought, sold and collected Old Masters. He also spotted the talent of Corot and the Barbizon School of landscape painters. Still more important was his discovery of the Impressionists, whose work he both supported and exhibited – he was a pioneer of the solo exhibition – at a time when this was still a bold move.[167]

In similar fashion, Ambroise Vollard, who opened a gallery in Paris in 1893, specialized in contemporary artists. Following his discovery of Cézanne, he showed and sold works by Gauguin, Van Gogh, Derain and Bonnard. He later exhibited Matisse and Picasso, who painted his (Cubist) portrait.[168] Like Durand-Ruel, Vollard supported his artists before they were recognized by a wider public.

Daniel-Henry Kahnweiler was, like Sedelmeyer and Jacques Seligmann, a German who moved to Paris, where he opened his gallery in 1907. He once referred to Durand-Ruel and Vollard as his 'masters'. Kahnweiler specialized in the paintings of the Cubists (Georges Braque, Pablo Picasso and Juan Gris) and the Fauves (especially André Derain, Maurice de Vlaminck and Kees van Dongen) at a time when they were all virtually unknown. Kahnweiler once described the functions of an art dealer as to help artists, 'to be an intermediary between them and the public' and 'to spare them financial anxieties'. He did not simply praise these artists but told them when he thought they were improving or not doing their best work.[169] Kahnweiler also published a study of Cubism (in German), in 1920.

In Berlin, where an art market was emerging, a similar role to the three Paris dealers was played by Paul Cassirer, who opened a gallery there in 1898, and held exhibitions of Impressionists (Manet,

Monet, Renoir), Post-Impressionists (Cézanne, Van Gogh) and leading modern German painters such as Lovis Corinth and Ernst Ludwig Kirchner. His exhibition of works by Van Gogh played an important role in spreading the artist's reputation as a modern master.

By the late nineteenth century the art market in New York also extended to the work of modern masters. Thanks to the advice of her friend Mary Cassatt, Louisine Havemeyer became one of the first American collectors of works by Degas, Manet, Monet and Renoir. Durand-Ruel was saved from bankruptcy when he

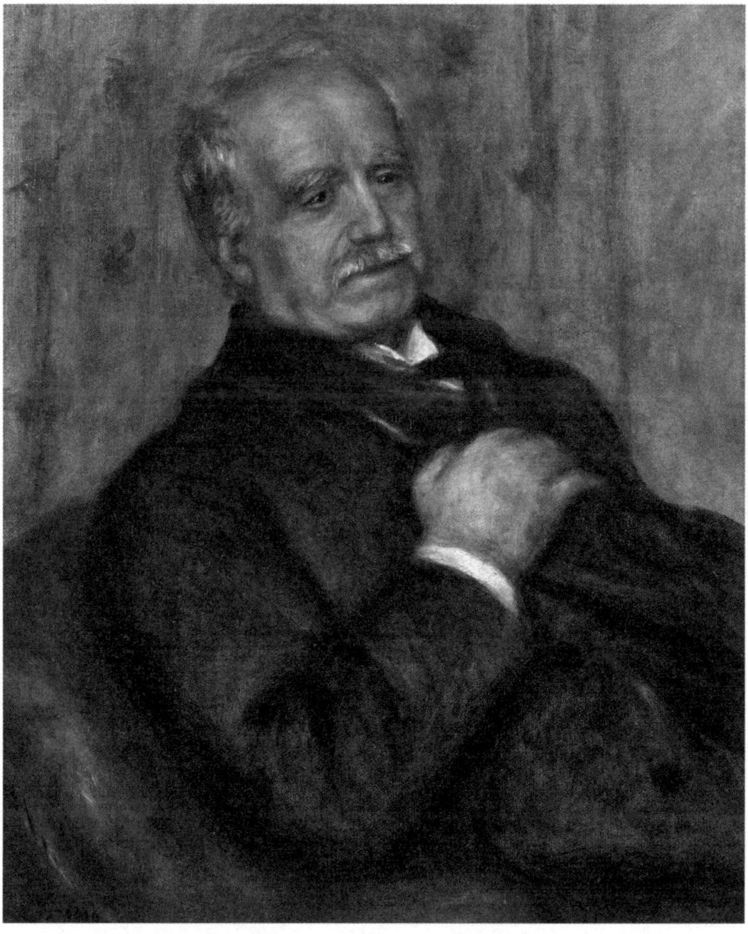

26 Pierre-Auguste Renoir, *Paul Durand-Ruel*, 1910, oil on canvas.

exhibited Impressionist paintings in a show organized by the American Art Association in Madison Square in 1885. Cubist paintings exhibited by Kahnweiler at the famous Armory Show in New York in 1913 helped to launch the movement internationally. In the twentieth century, the market for modern and contemporary continued to grow at the expense of the Old Masters, as we shall see in the following chapter.

The Connoisseur in Literature

The expansion of the group of connoisseurs, semi-connoisseurs and would-be connoisseurs was accompanied, as in the late eighteenth century, by a proliferation of images of figures appreciating or failing to appreciate works of art. For example, Albert Hahn's cartoon 'To Two Rembrandt Connoisseurs' (illus. 27) shows two men with magnifying glasses crawling around a painting, a vivid illustration of both literal and metaphorical myopia.

In literature, novels that featured connoisseurs began with Balzac's *Cousin Pons* (1846). Balzac was himself a collector of paintings and owned works attributed to Holbein and Bronzino. His protagonist, Pons, described as a 'ferocious collector' of bric-à-brac and a 'picture maniac' (*tableaumane*), is a connoisseur who recognized works by masters such as Giorgione, Dürer and Van Eyck, buying them cheaply because no one else recognized them. In one chapter, 'the connoisseurs of painting', Balzac describes a Jewish dealer, armed with the usual magnifying glass.

Philippe Burty's *Grave Imprudence* (1880), a novel that includes characters reminiscent of Manet and Monet, also introduced a connoisseur who is not unlike the author. Marcel Proust expressed interest in judgements by the eye, wished he could have met Berenson and portrayed Charles Swann as a connoisseur with a special love of Vermeer in the first volume of his *In Search of Lost Time* (1913).[170]

In Italy, Carlo Placci, a friend of Berenson, published *Un furto* (1891), a novel in which the hero steals a Botticelli in order to prove a contested attribution. The novel also includes a character who

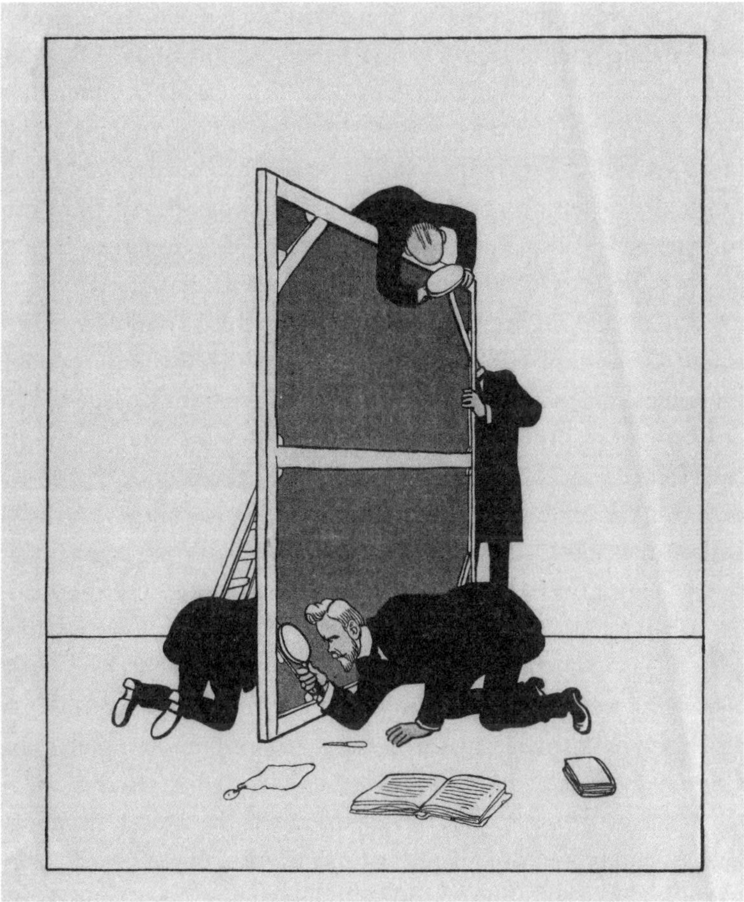

27 Albert Hahn, 'To Two Rembrandt Connoisseurs', woodcut from *Het Land van Rembrandt* (1906).

resembles Morelli and expresses similar views on connoisseurship.[171] Anglophone literature also offers portraits of connoisseurs at this time, beginning with Henry Merritt's *Robert Dalby and His World of Troubles: Being the Early Days of a Connoisseur* (1865) and ending with John Galsworthy's *In Chancery* (1920), in which Soames Forsyte is the connoisseur.

The novelist in whose work connoisseurs appear most frequently is Henry James. In *The Portrait of a Lady* (1882) the lady's unpleasant husband, Gilbert Osmond, owns 'a dozen or two of early masters' and some sixteenth-century drawings, including a sketch by

Correggio. Osmond seems to think 'that life was a matter of connoisseurship' and that his wife Isabel should 'figure in his collection of choice objects'.[172] Again, in *The Golden Bowl* (1904), in which that beautiful object is at once the title, the symbol and in a sense the protagonist of the story, the wealthy Adam Verver is not only a collector, the owner of a painting by Luini, but has 'the spirit of the connoisseur'. When Adam and his daughter Maggie add an Italian prince to their collection, the consequences are unexpected.[173]

The novel (not one of James's best) in which connoisseurship is most important is *The Outcry* (1911), in which the author chose the topical theme of the drain of Old Masters from Europe to the United States, inspired by the Duke of Norfolk's attempt to sell his Holbein to a foreign buyer in 1907.[174] The plot of the novel turns on the attribution of an Old Master – possibly a Moretto – and on the public outcry, fanned by the newspapers, against the owner's attempt to sell this 'national treasure' to an American, described as one of a 'conquering horde' of barbarians 'armed now with huge chequebooks instead of with spears and battle-axes'. A leading figure in the novel, Hugh Crimble, a young man 'working, tooth and nail, at what he called the wonderful modern science of Connoisseurship', appears to be based on the young Berenson.[175]

It seems fitting to end this chapter with Berenson, the most famous connoisseur of all, at least in the Anglophone world, and with his wife Mary, who became a connoisseur in her own right as well as an assistant to her husband.[176] Like Charles and Elizabeth Eastlake, Bernard and Mary offer a famous example of conjugal connoisseurship. Bernard trained Mary, who published a *Guide to the Italian Pictures at Hampton Court* (1894) and other works and lectured on Renaissance art, notably in the United States in 1904. She travelled with Bernard to look at paintings, took care of his notes, typed his manuscripts, improved his prose, encouraged his work and argued with him over attributions. As a connoisseur, it has been argued, she 'is deserving of a large measure of his glory'.[177]

Which of the pair contributed most to Bernard's first book, *Venetian Painters* (1894), remains a controversial question. Since this is a problem of attribution, it seems reasonable to approach it, as in the case of paintings, by comparing the style of the text with that of the three later books in the famous quartet, which dealt in turn with Florentine, Central Italian and North Italian painters. Unlike the later books, *Venetian Painters* spends much of its space on the historical context, discussing the 'spirit of the Renaissance' in a Burckhardtian manner, notably 'the awakening to the sense of personality' and 'the longing for the perpetuation of one's fame'. This historical approach suggests that much of the book was written by Mary, although passages such as the praise of Crivelli and the comparison of his work to 'the freedom and spirit of Japanese design' were surely written by Bernard.[178]

In contrast, *Florentine Painters* (1896) focuses on critical concepts such as 'tactile values' in Giotto, 'a sense of movement' in Pollaiuolo and 'life-enhancement' in Botticelli.[179] Again, *Central Italian Painters* (1897) notes that Piero della Francesca 'is hardly inferior to Giotto and Masaccio in feeling for tactile values', and praises Raphael for his 'feeling for space'.[180] As for *North Italian Painters* (1907), Mary not only typed the manuscript and encouraged the author when he was depressed about it, but 'changed a lot here and there, little things ... and then some serious things too, about which we grappled for half an hour when I had finished'.[181] She later complained that 'B. B. does not recognize that I had any share in building up his career, though without me in the beginning he wd have drifted and never written a line.' Bernard later admitted, in 1938, that 'she pounces on my manuscript as she used to do in her past and most ferocious years' and 'in the course of demolition displays a mental energy, acumen and subtlety, simply amazing'.[182]

Berenson is the first American to be discussed here, although he was born in Lithuania at a time when it was still part of the Russian Empire. His Jewish family emigrated to the United States when he was ten years old, in 1875, just before the rise of American millionaire collectors.[183] Berenson also stands out in this chapter because he was an outsider. He was neither a professional artist, art historian nor curator, despite devoting much of his life to what he and his wife called 'conoshing'. He made his living as a freelance adviser to collectors and also to dealers, from Otto Gutekunst at Colnaghi's to

Joseph Duveen, with whom he had a long and profitable partnership. He was also active as a critic (opposed to the new forms of non-representational art), as a philosopher of art and as a collector who owned over a hundred Italian Renaissance paintings at his death, together with some fine examples of oriental art.[184]

Berenson first visited Italy in 1888 at the age of 23. He met Cavalcaselle in Rome and Morelli in Milan in 1890, the year in which he remembered telling his friend Enrico Costa that 'nobody before us has dedicated his entire activity, his entire life, to connoisseurship' with 'no thought of reward' (that came later!).[185] As a connoisseur, Berenson began as a follower of Morelli but gradually moved away from his approach. In his essay 'Rudiments of Connoisseurship' (published in 1902 but written about eight years earlier) he discussed 'morphology' as a method of attribution, including the shapes of hair, noses and ears. By 1905 he was calling his earlier approach 'crassly Morellian'.[186]

What particularly interested Berenson at this point was the reconstruction of artistic personalities such as Lorenzo Lotto, not only adding several paintings to the canon of Lotto's work but attempting to follow what he called 'the moods and oscillations in the mind of an artist'. A more controversial example was Berenson's claim to have discovered an unknown artist whom he christened 'Amico di Sandro' because his style resembled that of Botticelli, yet with a perceptible difference. He described this friend as 'a distinct artistic personality' with 'a gayer, more easy-going temperament' than Botticelli's.[187]

Berenson became famous for his attributions. This activity took the form of lists, appended to his four volumes on Italian painters but frequently revised. He made these attributions on the basis of his 'eye', or on what he called his 'sixth sense', in other words a 'sense of quality' that is 'God's gift' but also requires 'arduous training'.[188] Like other leading connoisseurs, Berenson combined close looking with a good memory for what he saw. He had an unusual ability to immerse himself in a painting. In front of the *Surrender of Breda* by Velázquez, for instance, he wrote that his eyes 'sank' into the painting and that he almost 'disappeared into it'. Or again (as noted in

Chapter One), 'We must look and look and look till we live the painting and for a fleeting moment become identified with it.'[189]

Berenson freely admitted that his attributions were based on his feelings. Of a painting of St Sebastian that he attributed to Antonello da Messina, for example, he wrote, 'I felt that it could not be other than Antonello.' However, the brief but vivid descriptions of paintings in the four volumes on Italian painters allow us to see what it was about particular paintings that most impressed him. After praising Pollaiuolo for his sense of movement, for instance, Berenson describes *Hercules Strangling Antaeus*:

> the suction of Hercules' grip on the earth, the swelling of his calves with the pressure that falls on them, the violent throwing back of his chest, the stifling force of his embrace . . . the supreme effort of Antaeus, with one hand crushing down upon the head and the other tearing at the arm of Hercules.[190]

The famous lists were presented as pure assertion, without attempts at justification, and this oracular quality may even have contributed to their fame as well as provoked criticism. In contrast, in later life, in articles published in the *Gazette des Beaux-Arts* and elsewhere, Berenson did offer explanations for attributions. He admitted to past mistakes, writing, 'I shall try to explain how I have been led to abandon my former attribution and how I reached my present view.' He also referred to details that prompted a given attribution. In the case of a painting he thought was by Filippo Lippi, Berenson noted 'the profiles of buildings and furniture', 'the attitudes of the figures . . . the folds of the draperies', and in the case of a portrait of a lady, 'the shark-like mouth'.[191] In other words, he continued to follow Morelli's method alongside relying on his feelings.

Berenson claimed that 'without connoisseurship a history of art is impossible' but denied that connoisseurship might be assisted by history. He had little time for documentary evidence, especially when he was young, writing of 'petty documentation' and declaring that art should be studied 'as independently of all documents as is the world's fauna or the world's flora'.[192] He criticized what he called 'a mania for provenance' and dismissed the contribution of science and technology to attribution, writing on one occasion of 'the sibylline equivocation of X-ray photographs'.[193] He also dismissed the study of iconography and on one occasion went so far as to call Erwin Panofsky 'the Hitler of art study', a dramatic example of the recurrent conflict between connoisseurs and art historians.[194]

Berenson began as a minimalist, notorious for his disattributions. In a review of an exhibition of Venetian painting in London in 1895, he remarked that of 33 paintings in the show that were attributed to Titian by what he called 'superannuated connoisseurship', only one 'is actually by the master'.[195] He later reduced the number of known Titians from 1,000 or so to 133, to the discomfiture of a number of owners. In later life, however, Berenson moved in the opposite direction. For example, he was too quick to attribute a profile portrait of a lady, the 'Minghetti Leonardo', to the master and came to regret his decision. Nonetheless, his correspondence with Duveen shows him still insisting that an 'Andrea del Sarto' is not by Andrea, that a 'Raphael' is not by Raphael and that a 'Pintoricchio' was actually painted by 'an assistant of that master's'.[196]

Berenson came to regret the time he had spent on attribution, regarding it as a trivial pursuit while finding it impossible to abandon. He preferred to view himself as a critic and a philosopher of art. He admired the Victorian critics Walter Pater, whose book on the Renaissance he claimed to know 'almost by heart', and John Ruskin, whose voice can be heard in his writing from time to time. Where Ruskin had compared Turner to Shakespeare, Berenson did the same for Titian, as well as writing of Lotto's *Cingoli Madonna* that it had 'a sublimity which is rare elsewhere in painting and which I can compare to Milton only'.[197] As a young critic, Berenson displayed a self-confidence that some might call brashness. His idea of art criticism included a strongly negative side, even in the case of the 'masters'. Masolino's figures are described as 'childish', Ghirlandaio 'had not a spark of genius', Correggio is subject to 'frequent failures' and Michelangelo 'failed in his conception' of the *Last Judgement*.[198]

The tension between the excitement of attribution and the sense of time wasted persisted for much of Berenson's life. As early as 1895, he wrote that 'I no longer care a smart farthing who painted anything,' although he continued to labour on his most scholarly work, a *catalogue raisonée* of the *Drawings of the Florentine Painters*, finished in 1897 though not published until 1903. In 1901 he claimed that 'determining who painted or carved or built whatsoever it be' is 'worthless ... in the life of the spirit'. In 1908 he admitted to 'a sinking feeling of how wasteful it was to bother about the who-is-whos-ity of such small fry'.[199]

Nevertheless, Berenson had become an addict, unable to give up the excitement of the chase, even for minor artists. In 1911 he confessed that 'I ... enjoy the tracking of infinitesimal painters like foxes to their lairs.' Again, 'the quarry may not be worth the pains expended in pursuit' but 'I, for one, love the sport.'[200] That sport, which had begun, as he once told Costa, with 'no thought of reward', paid for the Berensons' expensive lifestyle and especially for I Tatti, the Tuscan villa that they first rented and then bought, restored, extended and maintained. As an adviser to collectors, Berenson began modestly. His first fee, in 1893, was $100. Three years later, though, he was boasting that he had earned $10,000 that year.[201]

Working with the German connoisseur Otto Gutekunst, Berenson persuaded Isabella Stewart Gardner, who saw herself as a latter-day version of Isabella d'Este, to buy Italian Renaissance paintings, including several by Botticelli and a famous work by Titian, *The Rape of Europa*, for which she paid £20,000 in 1896, at that time a large sum for a painting.[202] They did indeed, as Gutekunst put it, 'make hay while Mrs G shines'.

Berenson's rich clients also included the newspaper mogul William Randolph Hearst, the banker Andrew W. Mellon, the steel magnate Henry C. Frick and the financier John Pierpont Morgan. Hence famous museums such as the Isabella Stewart Gardner Museum in Boston and the Frick Collection in New York are, among other things, documents of Berenson's judgement as a connoisseur. Berenson also became an adviser to dealers, notably Joseph Duveen. He worked closely with Duveen for three decades, during which he received at least $100,000 per year. In 1912 the dealer agreed to pay Berenson a quarter of the net profit from the sale of every picture acquired on his advice.[203] Such rewards gave the connoisseur the means to pay not only for his villa but for his art collection, which included 125 Renaissance paintings, together with some fine specimens of oriental art.

One might say that Berenson was in the right place at the right time for someone with his gifts, since his early career coincided with the moment that rich Americans began to spend big money on paintings. However, his financial rewards came at a moral price that has been called a 'Faustian bargain'.[204] Berenson was subject to pressure. 'They are continually at him', Mary once complained, 'to make him say pictures are different from what he thinks.'[205] Sometimes he resisted the pressure, sometimes not. Berenson's commercial activities harmed his reputation for connoisseurship and illustrate another of the challenges to the practice at the time of the dizzy rise in the prices of Old Masters. As he grew older, his duties as an adviser and his increasingly wide network of acquaintances, ranging from politicians to musicians, left Berenson less time for research.

In the course of his long career, Berenson acquired followers of his own, Berensonites in the manner of Morellians. As a schoolboy, the British art historian and connoisseur Ellis Waterhouse chose books by Berenson 'for all his school prizes'.[206] One of Berenson's former assistants was Kenneth Clark, who became director of the National Gallery in London and a well-known writer and lecturer on art. Remembering Berenson, Clark once declared, 'I owe him more than I can say and probably more than I know.'[207] Another former assistant was Yashiro Yukio, a Japanese scholar who wrote a major study of Botticelli. A third was Luisa Vertova, who would become a specialist on Old Masters at Christie's and publish a number of books on Italian Renaissance painting. Like a Renaissance master, Berenson presided over a workshop.

As his fame increased, Berenson was visited by a number of young men who later became distinguished connoisseurs or art historians. Osvald Sirén arrived in 1902, Roberto Longhi in 1912, Meyer Schapiro in 1927, Philip Pouncey in 1930 and both Sydney

Freedberg and Benedict Nicolson in 1937. Berenson enjoyed putting them to the test of attributing objects in his collection. Their names will recur in the following chapter.

6
Globalization and Science

In the age of professionalization, described in the previous chapter, one important element of the process was still lacking: formal training. Like art dealers, restorers and conservators often learned their skills in the family, as they had done in the past. Connoisseurs developed their eye by means of practice, at home and abroad (the importance of travel for Bode, among others, has already been emphasized). Apprentice connoisseurs might be helped in the early stages of learning to look by advice from a mentor. Gustavo Frizzoni, for example, was taught by Morelli, who was a friend of the family. Kenneth Clark was taught by Berenson and in his turn acted as a mentor to another two distinguished 'eyes', Denis Mahon and John Pope-Hennessy.

Only in the twentieth century was a more formal system of training established. An early example is the course at Harvard for future curators, 'Museum Work and Museum Problems', established in 1921 and taught by Paul Sachs until 1948. Sachs trained students to improve their visual memories and introduced them to the practice of attribution.[1] Again, at Barnard College, Columbia University, a course on connoisseurship was regularly given by Julius Held, who taught at the college for more than thirty years, from 1937 to 1970. In France, curators were trained at the École du Louvre. Michel Laclotte, a later director of the Louvre, remembered that when he took the course, around 1950, 'there were only six or seven of us each year'. Sylvie Béguin, a specialist on the Renaissance, also took the course and later taught it. Her students included Philippe

Costamagna, who has noted her 'exceptional eye'.[2] In Italy, Roberto Longhi founded a course on connoisseurship at the University of Florence, held in his home and making use of his collection of photographs. The course was continued by his former student Mina Gregori.[3] In twenty-first-century Britain, short courses on connoisseurship for art lovers have been taking place regularly at the Royal Academy and the National Gallery, while an MA in Fine and Decorative Art that includes connoisseurship has been established at Sotheby's Institute of Art in London.[4]

Meanwhile, the system of connoisseurship has continued to evolve. Two changes have been particularly important, globalization and what German scholars call 'scientification' (*Verwissenschaftlichung*). Both are responses to problems that are generating more problems in their turn.

Discoveries and Rediscoveries: Eighteenth-Century Japan

The Western discovery of Japanese art began immediately after the opening of Japan in 1868 under the new Meiji regime. In this case too, Edmond de Goncourt exaggerated the role of himself and his brother in what he called 'the victory of Japonisme'.

In fact, they shared the discovery with a number of others, including the collector-critics Théodore Duret, who visited Japan in 1871 to escape the Franco-Prussian War, Louis Gonze, director of the *Gazette des Beaux-Arts*, and Charles Ephrussi, owner of the *Gazette*, whose collection of netsuke has been immortalized by his descendant Edmund de Waal.[5] An important role was also played by art dealers such as Philippe Sichel, who visited Japan in 1874 and 'sent 45 crates with 5,000 objects back from Yokohama'. Conversely, two Japanese dealers, Wakai Kenzaburō and Hayashi Tadamasa, settled in Paris.

Edmond's friend Philippe Burty played an important role in the discovery of Japan as in the rediscovery of eighteenth-century France. His interest was probably awakened by exhibitions devoted to it in Paris in 1867 and 1869. It was he who coined the term

'Japonisme' to describe an enthusiasm that he, like Goncourt, did his best to spread. He collected Japanese prints, ceramics and other objects – more than he could afford – from the specialist dealers Sichel and Samuel Bing, took an interest in Japanese literature and even tried to learn the language.[6]

On the other hand, Burty published little on Japanese art, while Goncourt, who also amassed a considerable collection, published studies of two masters of the Japanese print, *Utamaro* (1891) and *Hokusai* (1896).[7] The first of these studies is essentially a catalogue with descriptions of Utamaro's prints, offering relatively few remarks on style but emphasizing elegance, delicacy and 'the graceful lengthening of the oval of his faces of women'.[8] The second, more ambitious study hailed Hokusai as 'one of the most original artists in the world', 'the founder of the Popular School' and the artist who 'victoriously released the painting of his country from Persian and Chinese influences . . . rejuvenated it, renewed it and made it truly and completely Japanese'.[9]

The enthusiasm for Japan was greatest, or at least most obvious, in France, but extended to Britain, the United States (including the expatriate American artist James Whistler, who decorated his studio in Chelsea with prints by Hiroshige), Spain (notably the painter-designer Mariano Fortuny) and Italy (where the fashion was spread by the critic Vittorio Pica).

IN OUR AGE OF GLOBALIZATION, the living artists who are best known internationally include a Chinese (Ai Weiwei), a Japanese (Yayoi Kusama), an Indian (Anish Kapoor) and a Nigerian (Yinka Shonibare). The art market is shifting away from the Old Masters and towards modern, contemporary and non-Western art. This situation offers opportunities to both dealers and connoisseurs, enlarging the number of collectors who need advice from experts. It also offers challenges, as major changes always do, making some old knowledge obsolete and requiring new forms of expertise.

The second major change is the increasing impact of science and technology on the world of art. It ranges from the employment of the chemical analysis of paint to assist the identification of forgeries to the recent use of artificial intelligence to attribute works of art. The balance between personal acquaintance with works of art (*connaître*) and scientific methods (*savoir*) is changing in favour of the latter, but the old debate about the reliability of the connoisseur's eye continues to reverberate.

Globalization

Works of art have been circulating more and more widely since the late nineteenth century, when American collectors discovered European art and Western collectors discovered the art of Japan. Exhibitions of art produced outside Europe spread awareness of alternatives to the Western tradition:

1867	Exhibition of Japanese art at Exposition universelle, Paris
1890	Japanese Exhibition, Paris
1903	Exposition des arts musulmans, Paris
1910	Meisterwerke Muhammedanischer Kunst, Munich
1935	Exhibition of Chinese Art, Royal Academy London

Some connoisseurs of Western art also collected works from other cultures. Bode, for instance, wrote about oriental rugs and was praised at his memorial service in 1929 because he had 'made Islamic and East Asian art museum-worthy'. Berenson became interested in Islamic art after visiting the famous Munich exhibition in 1910. He later travelled in the Middle East.[10]

Japanese interest in Western art developed at the same time as the Western discovery of Japanese art, in other words following the opening of the country to foreigners after 1868. A few Japanese artists began to paint in the Western style, some of them learning from Western artists who taught at the Technical Art School in Tokyo (founded in 1876) while others studied in Paris.[11] This interest was encouraged by the mediation of the connoisseur Yukio Yashiro (illus. 28), a former assistant of Bernard Berenson and a specialist in fifteenth-century Italian art, when he returned to Japan. Some Japanese began to collect Western art. Matsukata Kōjirō, for instance, was the head of a shipbuilding firm who had studied in the USA and lived in England from 1916 to 1918. Among his favourite artists were Auguste Rodin, Claude Monet and Frank Brangwyn. In 1959 the National Museum of Western Art, which included Matsukata's collection, opened in Tokyo. The attraction of later Japanese collectors to the paintings of Renoir and Van Gogh offers a striking example of circularity, since both artists were admirers of Japanese art. Van Gogh's *Sunflowers* was sold for just under £25 million to a Japanese buyer in 1987, while three years later the businessman Ryoei Saito, president of a paper company, spent $160 million on Van Gogh's *Portrait of Dr Gachet* and Renoir's *Bal du moulin de la galette* (the small version).[12]

In the case of China, Western interest in traditional painting grew more slowly than the interest in traditional porcelain. An

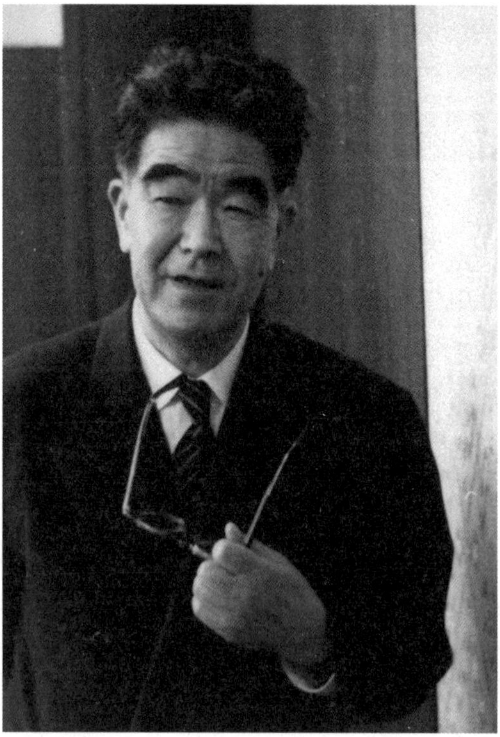

28 Yukio Yashiro, 1960s.

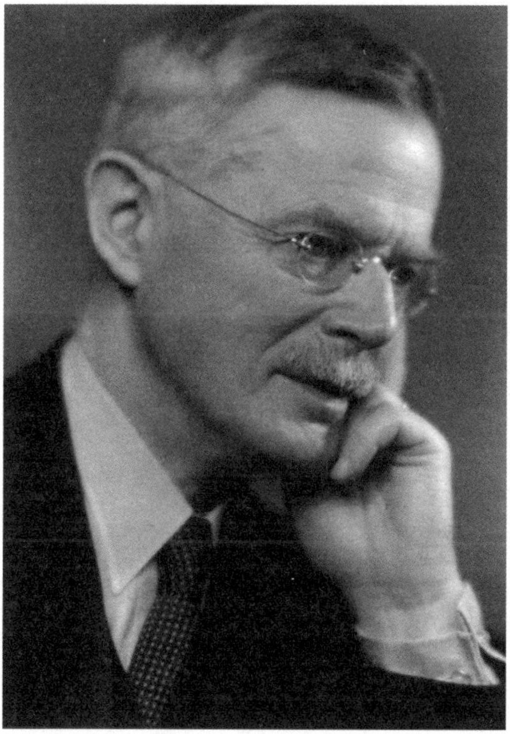

29 Osvald Sirén, 1950–66.

important figure in the story was a Swedish connoisseur, Osvald Sirén (illus. 29). Like Yashiro, Sirén began his career by studying Italian Renaissance art. His interest in theosophy led him to Buddhism and also to Chinese painting and sculpture, on which he wrote a series of studies.[13] The International Exhibition of Chinese Art at the Royal Academy in London in 1935 both expressed and encouraged a growing interest in Britain, where an Oriental Ceramic Society had been founded in 1921. British connoisseurs of Chinese porcelain included Robert Hobson, a curator at the British Museum from 1897 to 1938, and the collectors Percival David and his wife Sheila Yorke-Hardy.

Conversely, some eight decades later, rich Chinese collectors were switching to Western art – to Impressionists, for instance, and to works by Picasso and Edvard Munch.[14] Today, 'The new emerging markets for western art are China, Southeast Asia, India, the Middle East, Russia and Brazil.'[15] To meet increasing demand,

Sotheby's has established fourteen departments of non-Western art.[16] It has opened branches in Hong Kong and Tokyo, while Christie's has opened in Hong Kong and Shanghai. The British dealer Jay Jopling, founder of the gallery White Cube in London, opened branches in both Hong Kong and São Paulo in 2012. However, Chinese auction rooms are competing with the two big British firms with increasing success. Hong Kong, Beijing and Shanghai are now major centres of the market in works of art, while the rise of a market for contemporary Indian art is visible in India, with M. F. Husain and F. N. Souza among the most sought-after artists.[17]

A World Market

A major change in the system is the increasing importance of art as investment or speculation. The idea is not a new one. In the seventeenth century, dealers and collectors such as Mancini waited for prices to rise before selling particular works.[18] In 1786 the Paris dealer François-Charles Joullain was already criticizing 'amateurs' with what he called 'the spirit of speculation', buying works of art only to them sell again at a profit.[19] However, investment and speculation – not to mention money laundering – took off in the late twentieth century. In the 1970s, for instance, the pension fund of British Railways (as it then was) invested in paintings, including Picasso's *Blue Boy*.[20] From the late 1980s the trend became stronger, fuelled at least in part by a decline in interest rates that led to a boom in the art market. The boom was and is particularly strong in the case of contemporary art, as was revealed in dramatic fashion in 2022 when Inigo Philbrick, a former protégé of Jay Jopling, was convicted of fraud. The profits – and the risks – are particularly high in this sector of the market, which has been described as 'wildly unstable', with artistic reputations much more dependent on the taste of a few influencers than in the case of the market for Old or even Modern Masters.[21]

Exhibitions of art have become increasingly global both in their scope and in their location. The famous Biennale of Venice was founded in 1895 in order to show works from different parts of the world. Since then, a number of rival biennials have been founded, including the following.

1951 São Paulo
1957 Paris
1973 Sydney
1984 Havana
1987 Istanbul
1990 Dakar
1995 Gwangju (South Korea)
1995 Johannesburg
1996 Shanghai[22]

From one point of view, this trend may be described as a declaration of independence from the old European regime. From another point of view, the development of an art market and biennial exhibitions outside Europe and the USA reveals the increasing importance of a Western model.

East Asian millionaires who collect Western art now have rivals in the Middle East. Sheikha al-Mayassa, sister of the emir of Qatar and chair of Qatar Museums, concentrates on contemporary American art (Koons, Lichtenstein, Rothko, Warhol). Since her annual budget for buying art is $1 billion, her purchases have had a significant impact on the art market. She paid $250 million for a Cézanne in 2012, and $300 million for a Gauguin in 2015.[23] An even more spectacular spend was Mohammed bin Salman's acquisition in 2017 of a painting of Christ as *Salvator Mundi*, attributed to Leonardo, for no less than $450 million.

Globalization has affected careers as well as prices. Many living artists have moved from their native country to Europe or the United States. Some are exiles fleeing from persecution at home, while others are expatriates in search of new opportunities to make a name for themselves. Ai Weiwei is a bit of both. He studied in the USA in the 1980s, discovering the work of Andy Warhol and Jasper Johns, returned to China in the 1990s and left the country again, this time as a political exile, in 2015, living between Berlin, Cambridge and Montemor-o-Novo in Portugal.

Pictorial styles have also been affected by globalization. Once associated with a particular region or nation, usually in the West, they have become international, available to artists in many parts of the world, whether they have learned about these styles from personal inspection or from reproductions. Surrealism, for instance, has spread widely from Paris, as an exhibition at the Tate Modern in 2022, 'Surrealism Beyond Borders', made very clear. Among other artists who had been more or less unknown to the British art-loving public, it featured paintings by Remedios Varo, a Catalan who discovered Surrealism while living in Paris and ended her career in Mexico.

Borrowings have led to lively debates among both artists and critics, focusing on the question whether modernism in its various forms is a simple imitation of the West or can be adapted to other cultures. In Japan, for instance, this question was already being discussed in the 1920s. The artist and writer Murayama Tomoyoshi discovered modernism when he was studying in Berlin at this time. He criticized Japanese artists who imitated Western styles, telling them to 'stop acting like monkeys'. In similar fashion, after the Second World War, the work of the avant-garde Gutai group was criticized in Japan as 'rehashed Dada'.[24] In contemporary China, according to the art historian Gao Minglu, artists still face a dilemma, a choice between a strategy of 'emphasizing nationalistic cultural characteristics' or one of 'de-emphasizing their cultural identity'.[25]

Paradoxically, the critics may themselves be criticized for Eurocentrism, for assuming that modernism is a Western monopoly and ignoring what have been called the distinctive 'non-metropolitan modernisms' to be found elsewhere, thus 'decentering modernism' and 'provincializing Europe'.[26] One answer to Gao's dilemma has been hybridization. In the 1920s the Bengali painter Jamini Roy, for instance, was a modernist who also drew on the popular art of the region, especially scroll paintings.[27] In post-war Japan, a group of artists, Bokujinkai, founded in Kyoto in 1952, drew on modern abstract art in order to renew the Japanese tradition of calligraphy.[28] It is also worth remembering that borrowing has not been a one-way process. What the Impressionists and Post-Impressionists, not to mention Whistler, learned from the art of Japan is well known. More recently, some of David Hockney's iPad views of Yosemite National Park evoke memories of Chinese scrolls, as the artist himself is the first to admit.[29]

Viewers from many parts of today's world have become more familiar than ever before with some masterpieces, thanks to both reproductions and exhibitions. Hokusai's *Great Wave*, for instance, has joined Van Gogh's *Sunflowers* and Leonardo's *Mona Lisa* as a global icon. The *Mona Lisa* itself has been exhibited outside Europe, in New York in 1963 and in Tokyo in 1974. Like paintings, art historians and curators are increasingly mobile. Today, Gao Minglu holds chairs in both Tianjin and Pittsburgh. Gerardo Mosquera, a Cuban who organized the first Biennial in Havana, was also adjunct curator at the New Museum of Contemporary Art in New York from 1995 to 2009 – while continuing to live in Cuba. The Mexican Cuauhtémoc Medina was appointed associate curator of Latin American Art at the Tate Gallery in 2002, before returning to Mexico as chief curator of the Museo Universitario de Arte *Contemporáneo*. The careers of both Mosquera and Medina offer reminders of the rise or at least the international recognition of connoisseurship in Latin America.

Latin America

Pre-Colombian art was already being collected in Mexico in the early nineteenth century, encouraged by the increasing interest in Aztec culture that followed the independence of the country from Spain in 1821. In the twenty-first century, interest in Latin American art and its history has been increasing in both the USA and Europe, driven by enthusiasm for modern and contemporary art but extending to art in the colonial period. In the region itself, it is not difficult to point to historians and critics of art such as the Mexican Martha Zamora, or collectors such as the Venezuelan

Patricia Phelps de Cisneros and the Brazilian Bernardo Paz (the founder of the outdoor art museum Inhotim), or to conservators such as the Brazilian Edson Motta. Motta, who has been described as 'the father of restoration in Brazil', was trained in the USA but adapted the techniques of conservation that he had learned there to the tropical climate of his homeland.[30]

More difficult to find until quite recently were individuals concerned with all three of the main elements of connoisseurship: quality, authorship and authenticity. It is now possible to identify such individuals, although – like some of their European counterparts – they often dislike the old-fashioned term 'connoisseur' and prefer to call themselves art 'advisers', 'consultants' or 'experts'.

Why was it so difficult to find Latin American connoisseurs in the past? One reason was the existence of serious obstacles in the way of anyone who might have chosen to move in this direction but lacked access to works of art and in particular to the European Old Masters with whose paintings Western connoisseurs were traditionally concerned. In contrast with the situation in Europe and the United States, Latin American museums still contain only a few examples of paintings by Old Masters (in MASP in São Paulo, for instance, and in the Museo Nacional de Arte in Mexico City). To make connoisseurship of colonial art still more difficult, written sources such as treatises and letters are lacking, while the physical condition of most paintings from that period is not good enough to allow reliable conclusions to be drawn from the close observation on which traditional connoisseurship is based.

Since the paradigm of connoisseurship in Europe and North America was based on the Old Masters, the scarcity of their works in Latin America was an obstacle to the development of connoisseurial skills. Latin America also lacks first-class Old Masters of its own, although masters of the second rank were active in the seventeenth century, among them Cristóbal de Villalpando and Juan Correa. Both artists were followers of Rubens but knew his work only from engraved reproductions. Prints of paintings by Rubens were often copied freely by local artists, and the copies might be copied again, leading scholars such as Barbara Mundy and Aaron Hyman to conclude that colonial Latin American art requires a new form of connoisseurship, 'a different way of looking' that Hyman calls 'looking between', focused on the chain of transmission rather than on single works.[31]

The case of sculpture is different, and it is no accident that one colonial Latin American sculptor has been recognized as an equivalent to a leading Old Master: Antônio Francisco Lisboa, known as Aleijadinho ('little cripple', thanks to an unknown disease that made it increasingly difficult for him to work). Little is known about his life, apart from his activity in the Brazilian state of Minas Gerais, in which he was born in the 1730s and died in 1814. His style of sculpture was a powerful and original form of baroque.

In spite of the personal style of Aleijadinho's most famous works, notably the statues on the Via Sacra in the city of Congonhas, the attribution of statues to the master and even to his workshop is extremely controversial, as a review of an exhibition in São Paulo in 2018 made very clear. Jorge Coli, professor of art history at the University of Campinas, remarked that 'it is not necessary to be a great specialist to notice right away that not all the sculptures in this exhibition come from the same hand or even from the same workshop,' given the great differences in both their quality and their styles.[32]

The new paradigm of connoisseurship, which places more emphasis on contemporary art, offers opportunities to Latin Americans that did not exist earlier. Modern 'masters' include Frida Kahlo, whose attraction for collectors is proved by the number of forgeries of her works. In 2020 an American dealer who specializes in Latin American art told an interviewer that 'I am offered at least one false Frida Kahlo a month,' while a German curator declared, 'There are thousands of Frida Kahlo fakes. She is possibly the artist who has painted more dead than in life.'[33] This tribute to her work is evidence of her popularity outside as well as inside Latin America. The world of faking in Buenos Aires is evoked in a recent novel set in that city, describing a connoisseur who issues false certificates of authenticity for forgeries of leading Latin American painters. Maria

Gainza, the author of this novel, entitled *La luz negra* (The Black Light), is herself an art critic.

The more fakes there are, the more detectives are needed. The higher the price of paintings, the more advisers are required, whether by clients or auctioneers. Art 'consultants', as some of them prefer to call themselves, now include a number of Latin Americans, mainly women, who are also active as scholars and as organizers of exhibitions. They include the Brazilian Kiki Mazzucchelli, the Venezuelan Valentina Tintori and the Mexican Lassla Esquivel, who describes herself as operating 'between two strands: one producing commercial and curatorial projects; and another more academic oriented, doing research and teaching'.[34]

Rediscoveries of Old Masters

In the twentieth century, as in the nineteenth, some neglected Old Masters were rediscovered, thanks in part to the efforts of connoisseurs. Famous rediscoveries have included El Greco, Piero della Francesca and Caravaggio.

In the case of El Greco, artists and writers as well as connoisseurs were the pioneers. In Spain, the rise of nationalism encouraged interest in this painter, who was born in Crete and trained there but was described by the critic Manuel Cossío as more Spanish than the Spaniards themselves. Interest in the work of El Greco was not confined to Spain. A number of modernist artists and critics, including Édouard Manet, viewed Greco as a forerunner of their movement. Mary Cassatt, whose activity as an art adviser was noted in the previous chapter, was an early enthusiast for the work of El Greco, describing him as 'two centuries ahead of his time'. Again, the German painter Franz Marc saw the appreciation of Greco as 'closely tied to the evolution of our new perceptions on art' – that is, Expressionism. Roger Fry noted that Greco is 'not merely modern but actually appears a good many steps ahead of us'.[35] Fry was described by a fellow connoisseur, Kenneth Clark, as 'incomparably the greatest influence on taste since Ruskin ... In so far as taste can be changed by one man, it was changed by Roger Fry.'[36]

Just as the rise of Expressionism raised the reputation of El Greco, a growing interest in Cézanne lay behind the rediscovery of the paintings of Piero della Francesca, first by artists (including Matisse) and then by the rival connoisseurs Bernard Berenson and Roberto Longhi (though his work had already been appreciated by Charles Eastlake).[37] Berenson, who declared Piero to be in the same class as Giotto and Masaccio, told a friend that 'it is since Cézanne that Piero has been considered great,' while Longhi wrote that 'Piero was rediscovered by Cézanne and Seurat,' and in his playful way imagined Piero as echoing Cézanne by saying to a friend that 'everything in nature is spherical or cylindrical.'[38] Longhi also played a major role in the rehabilitation of Caravaggio, though some of the credit should also go to the English connoisseur Denis Mahon, who was already collecting seventeenth-century Italian paintings in the 1930s.[39]

Contemporary and Modern Art

All art was contemporary once, but as we saw in Chapter Three, the taste for old paintings only began to spread from the late sixteenth century onwards. What is new in the age of globalization is the gradual displacement of the Old Masters from their central position in the history of collecting, at least in the West.

As desirable objects for collectors, Old Masters are falling behind their rivals the Impressionists, Post-Impressionists, Moderns and Post-Moderns. 'Today', as a former dealer has remarked, 'the number of people who collect old master paintings is small by comparison with those who buy contemporary art.'[40]

The list of auction prices below illustrates the overtaking of Old Masters by modern ones, except in the case of Leonardo, where prices have been driven up by the rarity of his paintings as well as by his special place in the collective imagination.[41]

Old Masters

2002 Rubens, *Massacre of the Innocents*, £49 million

2007 Poussin, *Fuite en Egypte* (Flight into Egypt), €17 million

2015 Rembrandt, *Maerten Soolmans and Oopjen Coppit*, €160 million
2016 Rubens, *Lot and His Daughters*, £45 million
2017 Leonardo, *Salvator*, $450 million
2019 Caravaggio, *Judith*, $170 million
2020 Tiepolo, *Madonna of the Rosary*, $17 million

Modern Masters

2006 Klimt, *Adele Bloch-Bauer*, $135 million
2006 Pollock, *No. 5, 1948*, $140 million
2011 Cézanne, *Card Players*, $250 million
2012 Munch, *Scream*, $120 million
2013 Warhol, *Silver Car Crash*, £105 million
2013 Bacon, *Lucian Freud*, £142 million
2017 Basquiat, *Untitled* (Skull), $110 million
2018 Hockney, *Pool with Two Figures*, £71 million
2023 Klimt, *Dame mit Fächer* (Lady With a Fan), £85.3 million
2025 Klimt, *Elisabeth Lederer*, $180 million

The increasing interest in contemporary art has affected the study of art history. By 2010, according to a survey published at that time, 'A clear majority of applicants to graduate schools of art history intend to make contemporary art their major research field and their future professional specialization.'[42] In general history, too, there is a visible shift towards the study of the last few decades.

The rise in the demand for contemporary art has made spotting new talent increasingly important. One example of a dealer with this gift is Jean Boghici, a Romanian who emigrated to Brazil, arriving without any money. His rise to wealth and fame began when he appeared on a television quiz programme and successfully answered questions about Van Gogh. Boghici used his winnings to open a gallery in Copacabana, Rio de Janeiro, in 1961. Among the talented young Brazilian artists whose gifts he recognized was Hélio Oiticica, a participant in the Neo-Concrete movement who is now world-famous.

The Science of Art

The second major change in the system of connoisseurship in this period has been the increasing importance of science and technology in a number of domains: the conservation of paintings, the detection of forgeries and even the attribution of authentic works to their creators. For these purposes, the first important aid was photography, as we saw in Chapter Five, followed in turn by chemical analysis, the use of X-rays, infrared and ultraviolet light and finally, in our own time, artificial intelligence. All these methods were resisted by some connoisseurs when they were first employed, but all of them except the most recent, AI, have become essential aids to the study of works of art.

Photography played an increasing role in connoisseurship in the twentieth century. Despite his doubts, noted earlier, Berenson went on to make great use of photos. In his old age, he confessed that 'Nowadays I hesitate to come to a conclusion about a work of art without submitting it to the leisurely scrutiny of photographs,' which he could examine from his armchair or bed.[43] He eventually collected around 300,000 photos himself. This may seem a large number for a private individual, but it was surpassed by another star connoisseur, Federico Zeri, who had accumulated 500,000 at his death in 1998.[44]

Doubts continued to be expressed. Max Friedländer, for instance, warned his readers of the dangers of relying on photographs. So did Edgar Wind, who became the first professor of art history at Oxford in 1955. As a student at Oxford a few years later, I attended Wind's seminar on Renaissance medals. He began by telling us not to trust photographs, which were mere 'shadows', and encouraged us to place the medals on the palms of our hands, thus viewing them as they were originally viewed (since the seminars took place in the Ashmolean Museum, we were allowed to touch objects from which the public is separated by a glass case).

When the authenticity of a painting attributed to Caravaggio came to trial in London in 2015, the American connoisseur Richard Spear was asked in court whether a photograph was an inadequate means of attribution. His answer was 'twenty, thirty years ago, yes, inadequate. Today, with high-resolution digital photography and with good, high-resolution photography that you can zoom in on, you can see a very great deal about brushwork etc.'[45] When making their attributions, connoisseurs are no longer dependent on the naked eye, the magnifying glass or a collection of prints.

The Uses of Chemistry

A major change in the art of conservation in the twentieth century was the increasing use of scientific methods, leading to the establishment of a new profession, 'conservation scientist'. These methods included the chemical analysis of small fragments of paint in order to reveal later additions to a picture or to unmask forgeries. This method was already being employed in the later nineteenth century, when Arthur Church was appointed the first professor of chemistry at the Royal Academy, in 1879. Church later published *The Chemistry of Paints and Paintings* (1890).

The use of chemical evidence met with resistance from some connoisseurs. In a dispute with the French dealer Charles Sedelmeyer in 1912 over the attribution to Rembrandt of a painting sold by Sedelmeyer to a rich American, the Dutch connoisseur Abraham Bredius claimed that the painting was a forgery. When Bredius suggested that chemical analysis might decide the question, Sedelmeyer described this suggestion as an 'astounding proposition' that 'proclaims the bankruptcy of expertise!'[46] The Dutch connoisseur Cornelis Hofstede de Groot reacted in similar fashion in 1925, in the case of a dispute about the authenticity of a painting, the *Merry Cavalier* (not the famous *Laughing Cavalier*) that Hofstede believed to be by Frans Hals. When chemical analysis showed that the paints employed included artificial ultramarine, first produced in 1826, the connoisseur responded with an aggressive pamphlet in defence of his eye.[47]

When the Dutch chemist Martin de Wild, who came from a family of picture restorers, published his doctoral dissertation on scientific research into paintings in 1928, it must have looked like a reply to Hofstede. De Wild, who became a restorer himself, gave evidence in the Wacker trial of 1932, in which the Berlin dealer Otto Wacker was accused of selling fakes that he claimed were painted by Van Gogh. De Wild explained to the court that he had found traces of lead and resin in the paint, concluding that the paintings sold by the dealer as Van Goghs had used pigments that were never employed by the artist in his authenticated works.[48] Forgers as well as connoisseurs and conservationists became aware of chemical analysis and changed the ingredients of their fakes in response to this challenge. Thanks to his training as a restorer, the famous Dutch forger Han van Meegeren, for example, knew how to make a painting look old, imitating the fine cracks in the surface that reveal an antique by cooking his productions in an oven. He mixed his paints with bakelite, a kind of plastic invented in 1907, to make his paintings impervious to scientific tests.[49]

The year 1930 marks a turning point in the history of conservation, the date of an international conference on the subject held in Rome and of the establishment of the Department of Conservation and Technical Research at the Fogg Museum in Harvard. The National Gallery in London established their scientific department in 1934. The Doerner Institute in Munich was established in 1937 and the Istituto Centrale per il Restauro in Rome, in 1939, with the support of the Fascist minister of education, Giuseppe Bottai.

Scientific evidence was also taken seriously in debates over attribution. Joyce Plesters, who was appointed to a post in the scientific department of the National Gallery in London in 1949, has been described by Jaynie Anderson as 'the first chemist connoisseur'. Plesters combined her science with her love of Venetian painting and began collecting samples of paint from famous pictures as an aid to their attribution. For example, her microscopic analysis of Bellini's *Feast of the Gods* disposed of the argument that Titian had finished it by adding the attributes of the gods by showing that these attributes belonged to the earliest layers of the painting. The successor of Plesters at the National Gallery, Jill Dunkerton, together with her team used cross-sections of paint to study late works by Titian, concluding (among other things) that 'In conjunction with traditional connoisseurship . . . the scientific examination of paintings can help to resolve certain issues of workshop participation.'[50]

X-Rays

X-rays were discovered in 1895. They rapidly came into use in medicine and a little later in connoisseurship, since they revealed what was under the surface of the painting: a sketch, alterations (known in Italian as *pentimenti*, 'repentances') and on occasion another painting. In Munich, the Alte Pinakothek was using X-rays by 1916 to detect second thoughts by artists. In Vienna, from 1928 onwards, Johannes Wilde (together with restorer Sebastian Isepp) employed X-rays to study works by Giorgione and Titian at the Kunsthistorisches Museum. In the United States in the 1920s, Alan Burroughs (illus. 30) used X-ray photographs to assist in attributions as well as in conservation.[51] He also established an archive of X-ray photos at the Fogg Museum at Harvard. In 1932 a witness in the Wacker trial used X-rays to demonstrate that the paintings sold as 'Van Goghs' did not employ the same techniques as seen in genuine paintings by the artist.

Infrared photography, together with its successor infrared reflectography (used by Jill Dunkerton in her study of Titian), has revealed underdrawings that help with the attribution of paintings, while ultra-violet photography makes some later retouching visible. The binocular and optical microscopes allow the different stages of a painting to be seen clearly, from the ground and the preparatory drawing to the different layers of paint, glazes and varnish.[52] The result of these investigations has sometimes surprised the investigators. Infrared reflectography was employed in the 1970s to establish attributions to individual masters, but what the underdrawings of Early Netherlandish paintings revealed was actually the importance of assistants, leading one scholar to write about 'the end of a connoisseurship era'.[53]

These findings from 'technical art history', a new subdiscipline, are generally accepted by connoisseurs and art historians. Berenson

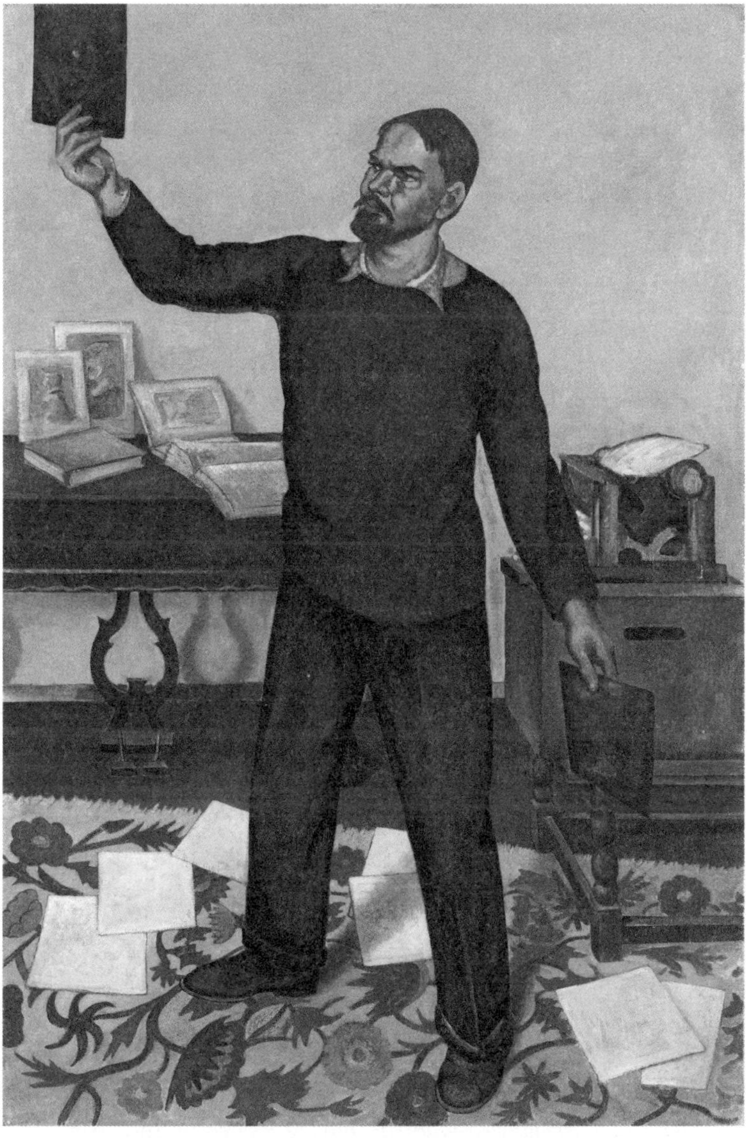

30 Molly Luce, *Alan Burroughs with X-Ray*, 1925, oil on canvas.

was relatively unusual in opposing their use. However, as the art historian Erwin Panofsky noted, the employment of X-rays is 'methodically not different from the use of spectacles or a magnifying glass'. Another point was neatly made by Justice Vivien Rose in the *Thwaytes v Sotheby's* trial (discussed in the following chapter):

'Although most scholars would conclude that technical analysis can establish that a painting is *not* from a particular period or not by a particular artist, its value in establishing a positive dating or attribution is less widely recognized.'[54]

New Technologies

A problem with chemical analysis is that it is destructive, relying on the removal of tiny samples of paint for analysis in the laboratory. It is being replaced by a new, non-destructive technology, known as Fourier-transform infrared spectroscopy.

Other technologies have come into use in the last few years. It is now possible, for example, to measure changes in the colour of paintings as a result of the lighting, humidity and temperature of the gallery in which they are displayed. Dendrochronology allows a painting on panel to be dated on the basis of a study of the annual growth rings (thick or thin according to the rainfall) on the tree from which it was made. For example, the attribution of a painting of *St John the Baptist Preaching* to Rembrandt, or at least to his workshop, was confirmed by the discovery that three more major works with this attribution had been painted on panels cut from the same tree.[55]

The Italian engineer Maurizio Seracini, who describes himself using the well-known medical metaphor 'diagnostician' and as an 'expert for scientific authentication of works of art', founded Editech, a company for the scientific analysis of paintings that employs multi-spectral imaging and even radar to study art, in 1977. In particular, Seracini's work focused on the *Battle of Anghiari* by Leonardo, a lost painting that Seracini claimed to have discovered hidden behind Vasari's *Battle of Marciano* in the Palazzo Vecchio in Florence.[56] Orion Analytical, another company for the scientific analysis of works of art, was founded in 2000 by James Martin, a scientist who previously worked in conservation. His company was bought by Sotheby's in 2016.[57]

Still more recently, artificial intelligence has entered the world of art, since computers are even better than human brains at pattern recognition. Programs have been written for AI to compare the brushstrokes of a given painting to those of a possible artist in a databank, thus assisting attribution. Thanks to one of these programs, Art Recognition declared in 2025 that a painting of a lute player believed to be a copy of a Caravaggio had an 85.7 per cent chance of being an original.[58] The use of AI in this way is still in its infancy, but it is likely that the infant will grow up fast, as in the case of machine translation a few years ago.

Nevertheless, while admitting that AI may be able to carry out stylistic analysis more rapidly and perhaps more thoroughly than traditional connoisseurs with their magnifying glasses, we should remember that human intervention is required both to establish the databank in the first place and then to select what to test. Updating Panofsky, we may say that AI, which is likely to be used more and more often for attribution in the future, remains methodically no different from the use of spectacles or a magnifying glass.

Forging and Detecting

The entangled histories of art, globalization and science have been particularly visible in the case of forgeries and their detection. Both practices have a long history, but as the price of both Old and Modern Masters has increased, it has become increasingly common – and increasingly profitable – to forge their works.

The connoisseurial eye still plays an important role in the detection of fakes. Max Friedländer once described the forger as 'a child of his time' who 'succumbs to the prejudices of taste that belong to his own period'.[59] Some practised eyes have been able to detect stylistic anachronisms. It was Kenneth Clark, for example, who recognized that the *Madonna of the Veil*, discovered in the 1930s and attributed to Botticelli, was a forgery, pointing out that the Madonna had 'something of the silent cinema star' about her, taking the example of Jean Harlow. As he wrote later, 'most forgeries have agreeable faces according to the ideal of prettiness of the time.'[60] Later scientific analysis confirmed Clark's conclusion, and the work has now been dated to the 1920s.[61]

On the other hand, some skilled forgers have been able to deceive even leading connoisseurs, as in the notorious case of Abraham Bredius and Han van Meegeren, discussed below, or (if his testimony can be trusted) the English forger Eric Hebborn, who claimed to have deceived Ellis Waterhouse, Byam Shaw, John Pope-Hennessy, Philip Pouncey, David Carritt and John Gere with drawings attributed to Cossa, Rubens, Tiepolo, Gainsborough, Piranesi, Corot and others.[62]

It is hardly surprising to find that some professional restorers have been able to detect fakes, since the restoration of paintings requires even closer looking and also slower looking than that of the gaze of even the most patient connoisseur. Some restorers, or ex-restorers, are also to be found on the side of the forger rather than the detective. They include Van Meegeren and also Hebborn, who began his career by working for one of the Tate Gallery's restorers. A spectacular case of a restorer turned forger is that of the Belgian Joseph ('Jef') van der Veken, who worked at the Royal Museum of Fine Arts in Brussels and specialized in Early Netherlandish paintings, notably Jan van Eyck, Rogier van der Weyden and Hans Memling. Veken began by making copies and pastiches, in other words original paintings that imitate earlier ones. He discovered that his works were sometimes taken to be originals, even by experts, though Friedländer was suspicious of some of them. One of his copies was exhibited in Burlington House as a Flemish 'primitive', and when the artist confessed to having painted it, he was, like Van Meegeren later, met with disbelief. Veken turned to restoration, especially 'hyper-restoration', the creation of a new work on the basis (literal as well as metaphorical) of an old one. The transition from one activity to the other was not too difficult in an age before the repair and repainting of damaged paintings ('restoration') was replaced by care for them ('conservation').[63] Veken specialized in masters such as Jan van Eyck and Roger van der Weyden, completely repainting parts of their work but imitating the cracks in the paint that naturally occur over the centuries. It remains uncertain whether the famous painting of *The Mystic Lamb* by Jan van Eyck in Ghent Cathedral is or is not a copy by Veken, a problem made even more complicated by the fact that conservators may have mistakenly removed Jan van Eyck's revisions of his brother's work.[64]

'Hyper-restorations' might be described less euphemistically as 'semi-forgeries'. The German restorer and connoisseur Hubert von Sonnenburg, whose career was divided between the Metropolitan Museum in New York and the Doerner Institute in Munich, made a careful study of one semi-forgery of this kind. He described it as 'a late fifteenth-century panel painting [*The Man of Sorrows*, now in the Metropolitan Museum] that had been restored in a highly deceptive manner'.[65] Sonnenburg was also quick to recognize that some paintings attributed to Lucas Cranach were actually recent fakes. They turned out to have been painted by the German forger Christian Goller, who, on being found out, praised the quality of Sonnenburg's eye.[66]

One might have thought that forgeries of contemporary art would be easier to identify than forgeries of Old Masters, since it is possible to ask the original painter whether or not a given work is by their hand. Picasso wrote on a photo of one painting 'No es mio', and Matisse on another, 'Ce tableau est un faux'.[67] Ironically, these texts by famous artists will have increased the value of the fakes. More recently, in 1993, a picture attributed to Fernando Botero offered for sale by Christie's was withdrawn when the artist denied that he had painted it.[68] All the same, forgeries of this kind have multiplied, driven not only by profit but by the resentment of unsuccessful artists and their desire for revenge on the reviewers who dismissed their work, the dealers who failed to sell it and the public who failed to buy it. In 1948, for example, an anonymous expert complained that another false Utrillo could be found every week in the famous Paris auction house Drouot.[69] The spread of fake Kahlos has already been mentioned. Other popular choices for forgers are Amedeo Modigliani and Vincent van Gogh.

A notorious producer of Modiglianis was the Hungarian Elmyr de Hory (one of the fake names employed by Elemér Albert Hoffmann). Hory has been described as 'the most prolific and successful art forger that the world has ever known' (unless, of course, his rivals remain undiscovered).[70] Hory also produced works supposedly by Picasso, Matisse, Derain, Vlaminck and Dufy, which he and his partners (who cheated him in their turn) sold for large sums in Paris, New York and Rio de Janeiro before a curator at the Fogg Museum began to have doubts about the authenticity of the Modiglianis that the museum had bought. One reason for Hory's success, besides an uncanny skill in imitating the style of other artists and a rapidity of production that made the imitations look spontaneous, was his concentration on painters who were active when he was himself a young artist in Paris, where he was trained by Léger and met Picasso, Vlaminck and Derain. In the case of drawings, he was careful to create the fakes on paper produced at the time when the artists were active, and in that of Dufy's paintings, to use the zinc white favoured by the artist. Hory sometimes faked certificates of authenticity but apparently received a genuine one from the famous Italian connoisseur Lionel Venturi for a 'Sisley' by his hand.[71]

Like genuine art, forgery has become increasingly globalized. Since the 1980s, Dafen, an urban village in Shenzhen in China, has become a centre of production for art in the Western style, with some 8,000 artists at work. Their work may be described by the apparently self-contradictory phrase 'mass-production by hand'. These artists specialize in the work of modern masters such as Van Gogh and Monet. They imitate small reproductions of paintings they have never seen, and soon learn to work from memory so as to produce paintings more rapidly. Hence their work does not easily fit standard categories such as 'original', 'pastiche', 'copy' or 'forgery'. The paintings are not exact copies, although they are too close to the original to be described as pastiches. Whether they can be described as forgeries depends on whether or not they are sold as originals by their chosen master. As in the case of Bastianini, discussed earlier, the artists receive little money for their work. The profit goes to the entrepreneurs who employ them.[72]

The flood of crude imitations is often easy to recognize. In contrast, the less obvious ones still require to be identified by connoisseurs, who are not always successful in their task. The gifted Dutch connoisseur Abraham Bredius is now most often remembered as the victim of a forger. Late in his career, shortly before the Second World War, he was delighted to find what he thought to be an unknown early work, *The Supper at Emmaus*, by one of his favourite artists: Vermeer. One can feel the excitement in the letter that Bredius wrote to the *Burlington Magazine* in which he announced the discovery of 'A New Vermeer', describing it as '*the* masterpiece' of the painter.[73] Unfortunately for Bredius, *The Supper at Emmaus* was not a Vermeer at all. It had recently been painted by Han van Meegeren, an unsuccessful artist who had become a successful forger.

In addition to his skills at evading scientific detection, Van Meegeren was bold enough to produce a painting that differed from the 'classic' Vermeers because the subject was religious. Bredius had already discovered an early work of the master, the *Allegory of Faith* (still thought to be a genuine Vermeer) and he doubtless wanted to believe that he had found another. The forgery was tailor-made for Bredius, just as Casanova's *Jupiter and Ganymede* was tailor-made for Winckelmann (above, Chapter Four). In both cases, connoisseurs who had already demonstrated sharp eyes for fakes fell into the traps set for them.[74]

The story of the unmasking of Van Meegeren, which has been retold many times, has the allure of a good thriller. During the Second World War, the artist, who had Nazi sympathies, was involved in the sale of another of his forgeries, *Christ and the Woman Taken in Adultery*, to the collector Hermann Goering. For this reason, at the end of the war, Van Meegeren was arrested and charged with collaboration with the enemy. In gaol, faced with the possibility of execution for selling a national treasure, he declared, 'I painted it.'[75] His confession was met with disbelief. To prove it, he was required to paint another Vermeer.

This story reads like a re-telling of Michelangelo's revelation to Cardinal Riario that he was the creator of the *Sleeping Cupid*, or the confession of the eighteenth-century artist Giuseppe Guerra that he had forged some ancient Roman paintings (he too was asked to prove his claim).[76] Van Meegeren actually produced what was required, a painting of *Christ in the Temple*, which is not one of his best fakes but was good enough to convince the court. Yet another version of the story, which would qualify as a myth were it not for the documents, appears in an account of the life of the Mexican potter Brigido Lara, who was arrested in 1974 on a charge of smuggling antiquities across the border into the USA. His reply, like Van Meegeren's, was that he had made the objects himself. As in the Dutch case, Lara was asked to prove his claim by making new forgeries and passed the test successfully. It turned out that examples of his work were displayed as Pre-Columbian originals in a number of major museums.[77]

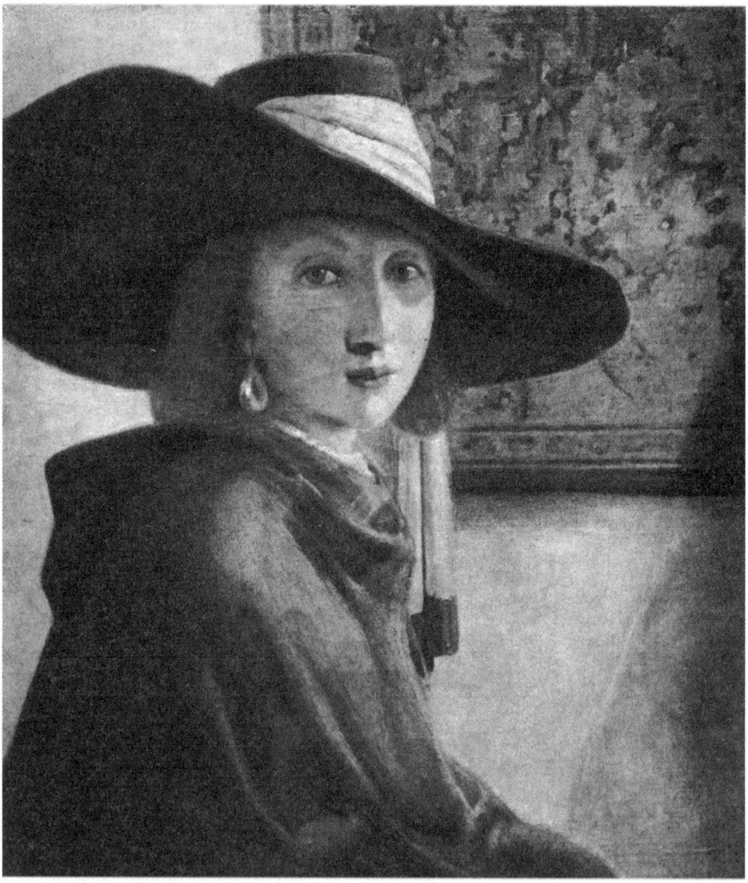

31 Vermeer (manner of), *Young Woman with a Blue Hat*, n.d., oil on canvas.

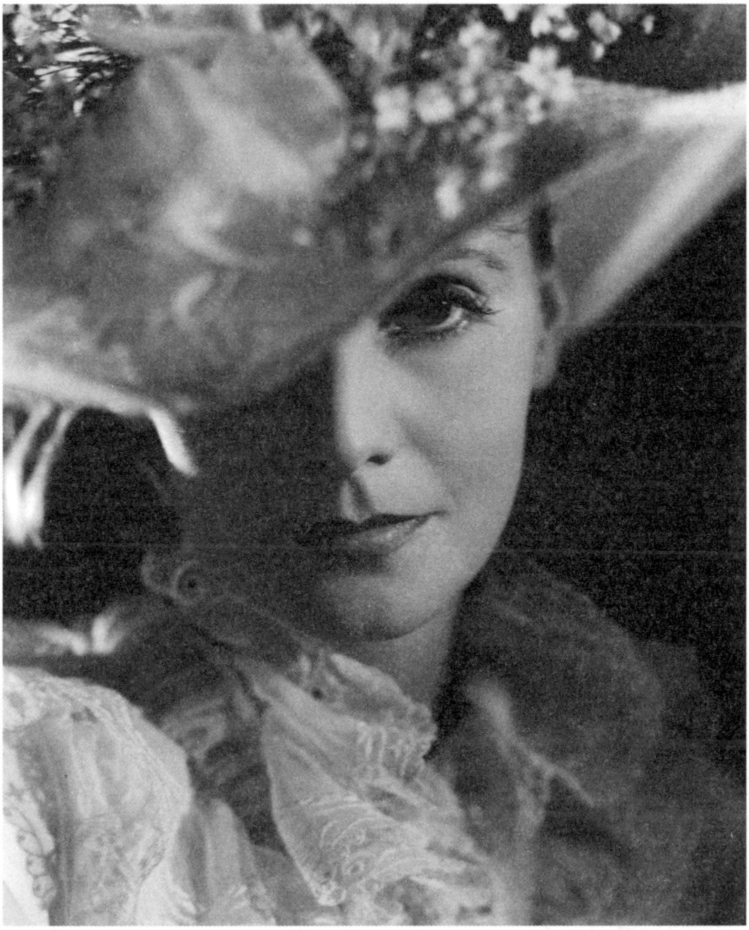

32 Greta Garbo in a publicity still for *Anna Karenina*, 1935.

Returning to the problem of anachronism, it has often been observed in the last few years that Van Meegeren's fakes no longer look right. Morelli would surely have drawn attention to the hooded eyes of Christ and other figures as giving the game away. One of the fakes, featuring a girl wearing a sombrero, has been nicknamed 'the Greta Garbo Vermeer' (illus. 31, 32). The name may remind us of Clark's reference to the American film star Jean Harlow and also of Friedländer's remark about the forger as a 'child of his time'. Ironically enough, the 'Greta Garbo' was authenticated by Friedländer himself.[78]

It is no accident that a recent course on connoisseurship at the National Gallery in London was entitled 'The Forensic Eye'.[79] Comparisons between Morelli and Sherlock Holmes have been made a number of times, as we have seen, but they are particularly appropriate in a period when the police have become officially involved with art, not only with its theft but with its forgery as well. In France, for instance, Guy Isnard was one of the first police officers to specialize in the discovery of art forgeries. He went on to write a series of books on the subject, calling himself 'the Sherlock Holmes of Painting'.[80] In the United States, James Martin, the founder of Orion Analytical, once worked for the FBI.

Art Historians versus Connoisseurs

Art history may be described as yet another *savoir* that complements the *connaissance* of the connoisseur, since it is based on documents as well as autopsy. As we have seen, early and mid-nineteenth-century scholars such as Rumohr and Waagen, Crowe and Cavalcaselle practised both approaches without any sense of conflict between the two. However, in an age of increasing specialization and the consequent territorialization of knowledge, difference has often been perceived as competition.

A century after Anton Springer had described connoisseurship as no more than an ancillary discipline to the history of art, an obituary of the distinguished English connoisseur Philip Pouncey quoted 'a young art historian' as saying, 'Oh yes, Pouncey. He just knows who things are by.'[81] This dismissive attitude is self-undermining. As Pouncey himself put it, 'It can hardly make sense to study an artist's style, development or iconography before you have learnt to distinguish the object of your studies.'[82] For a spectacular case in his favour, consider the posthumous fortune of Leonardo as a painter.

Judgements of Leonardo's work were based on different information in different centuries. Some paintings were lost, such as *Leda and the Swan*. Others survived but were attributed to another artist, as in the case of the *Madonna of the Carnation* now in Munich. It used to be attributed to Leonardo's master Verrocchio but is now generally thought to be by Leonardo himself. Yet others had been attributed to the master but were later claimed to be the work of someone else, collaborators, pupils or followers such as Ambrogio de'Predis, Giovanni Antonio Boltraffio or Bernardino Luini. Waagen, for instance, re-attributed a painting of *Christ Among the Doctors* from Leonardo to Luini. Charles Eastlake, viewing a painting of a boy as St Sebastian, was 'inclined to think it by Beltraffio [*sic*]', and re-attributed the *Virgin of Columbine* to Luini.[83] In one case, that of the *Medusa*, the former 'Leonardo' came to be attributed to a painter from another part of Europe and another century: seventeenth-century Flanders.

On the positive side, it was Wilhelm Bode who recognized the portrait of Ginevra de' Benci as a Leonardo. A Baltic German aristocrat, Eduard Karl von Liphart, and his son Ernst both identified a work by Leonardo: the *Annunciation* (now in the Uffizi) in the case of the father and the *Benois Madonna* (now in the Hermitage) in the case of his son. In short, the reconstruction of the list of Leonardo's paintings owes much to a succession of connoisseurs.

For their part, some connoisseurs have claimed the primacy of their form of knowledge over history based on documents. As we saw in the previous chapter, Berenson relied on the eye (more exactly, his eye) and had little interest in documentary evidence. The Italian scholar Pietro Toesca used to say, and his more famous pupil Roberto Longhi to repeat, 'First the connoisseurs, then the historians' (*Prima conoscitori, poi storici*). Since documents such as letters, contracts and provenance as well as works themselves offer evidence of 'who things are by', it might be more exact to say, 'first attribution, then interpretation'.

Conflicts remain. We still see, on one side, attribution treated as an inferior activity; on the other, the dismissal of an art history based on texts. It is no wonder that the French scholar Frédéric Elsig recently complained of what he calls 'the gulf between the academic sphere, the museum world and the art market'. It is a gulf that he, among others, has done much to bridge in the last few years by working in all three domains.[84]

The Emergence of Female Connoisseurs

From the point of view of a social historian of connoisseurship, an important development over the centuries has been the emergence of female connoisseurs, first as amateurs and then as professionals, whether as advisers, dealers, curators, conservators, critics or art historians.

The term 'conjugal patronage' was recently coined to describe the commissioning of art by a couple rather than by the husband alone.[85] In a similar fashion, we might speak of the 'conjugal connoisseurship' of the Arundels, Eastlakes, Berensons, Tietzes, Gronaus and Pounceys. Female connoisseurs in their own right appear in public around the beginning of the twentieth century (the nineteenth-century scholar Anna Jameson was concerned with iconography and art criticism rather than attribution).[86] As we have seen, the followers of Morelli included Constance Ffoulkes and Maud Cruttwell in the field of Renaissance art, as well as the classicist Eugénie Sellers Strong.[87] Female collectors included Lady Dorothy Nevill (née Walpole: one might say that collecting was in her blood). Her interests ranged from porcelain to ironwork, while she discovered that 'one of the best ways of learning how to distinguish the good from the bad was to make a practice of frequenting Christie's.'[88]

The 'school of Berenson' included not only his wife but the Florentine Luisa Vertova and the Englishwoman Evelyn Sandberg. Vertova worked at Christie's as a specialist of Old Masters and published many books on Italian Renaissance painting. Sandberg, who specialized in late medieval Italian art, was admired by leading connoisseurs such as Zeri and Pope-Hennessy. The latter called her 'a mentor and a valued friend' and confessed that 'the debt I owe her is immeasurable.'[89]

If there were not many more female connoisseurs at this time, the reason was probably that so few opportunities were available for them to study and still fewer for them to work. The Englishwoman Christiana Herringham, for instance, described by her friend Ffoulkes as *distinta conoscitrice* (a distinguished connoisseur), was active as an artist.[90] Sandberg made a living in Florence as a guide to tourists and as a teacher of art history. Carmen Gronau and Myril Pouncey also practised connoisseurship, as Lady Eastlake and Mary Berenson had done, in partnership with their husbands, and Carmen succeeded her husband Dietrich as an adviser on Old Masters at Sotheby's.

The academic world slowly opened its doors to women. In Austria, Erica Tietze-Conrat was able to study art history in Vienna from 1902 onwards and to gain her PhD before marrying Hans Tietze and working with him on Venetian drawings. The German Frida Schottmüller presented her dissertation on Donatello at the University of Zurich at a time when this was not yet possible for a woman in Germany. She found a place at the Kaiser Friedrich Museum in Berlin in 1905 as assistant to Wilhelm Bode and was later appointed a curator.[91] The classicist Eugénie Strong was appointed assistant director of the British School in Rome in 1909. Another classicist, Margarete Bieber, was appointed a professor at the University of Giessen in 1919, the second woman in Germany to hold a chair in any discipline. Carmen Gronau studied art history in Freiburg, Frankfurt and Göttingen, writing a dissertation on the baroque artist Ludovico Cigoli.

A few women have become successful dealers, spotters of new talent in the manner of Durand-Ruel and Vollard, Cassirer and Kahnweiler. One was Berthe Weill, who owned a gallery in Paris from 1901 to 1941. Like Vollard, she was one of the first dealers to appreciate Matisse and Picasso, while she gave Modigliani his first solo exhibition. Another dealer-connoisseur was Betty Parsons, a former artist who opened her own gallery in New York in 1946, supporting Abstract Expressionism and exhibiting works by Mark Rothko and Jackson Pollock before moving on to discover Robert Rauschenberg and Eduardo Paolozzi.[92] Eleanor Ward, founder of Stable Gallery in New York, showed works by Andy Warhol and Cy Twombly. The Brazilian Luisa Strina opened a gallery in São Paulo in 1974 and acted as an intermediary between cultures, promoting the work of Brazilian artists such as Lygia Pape abroad and introducing Brazilians to the art of Andy Warhol and Roy Lichtenstein.

In 1992 she became the first owner of a Latin American gallery to be invited to the Basel Art Fair.

Female connoisseurs who are active as curators or professors are no longer unusual, even if they remain less numerous than their male colleagues. At the Louvre, Sylvie Béguin stood out as a connoisseur. So does Mina Gregori, a former student of Longhi's who shared his interest in Caravaggio and Caravaggio's followers and who succeeded him in the chair of art history in Florence.

Women are also important in the growing profession of art advisers. The American Amy Cappellazzo, for instance, a former curator in Miami, became an adviser at Christie's. In 2014 she co-founded Art Agency, which was bought by Sotheby's two years later. The Latin American examples of female consultants mentioned earlier are not alone.

Although connoisseurship has been changing its shape, some traditional connoisseurs survived until the end of the twentieth century or even later. Two famous examples of the species are Roberto Longhi and Federico Zeri.

One of the young men who visited Berenson to express their admiration was Longhi, though he later distanced himself from his former idol, describing Berenson's lists of attributions as the artistic equivalent of railway timetables and his essay on Caravaggio as 'clumsy and spiteful'.[93] Longhi became the greatest of Italian connoisseurs since Cavalcaselle, whom he much admired, and Morelli, whom he dismissed as a simple 'attributionist' (*rinconoscitore*), rather than a true *conoscitore* with a sense of quality.[94] Like Berenson, he made a living from advising collectors, including the collector-dealer Alessandro Contini-Bonacossi, with whom he visited galleries all over Europe in 1920–21.[95] Longhi entered the academic world relatively late, becoming a professor at the University of Bologna in 1934 and transferring to the University of Florence in 1949. He was a spellbinding speaker – a former student, the poet and film director Pier Paolo Pasolini, used the term *carismatico*, while another listener, the art historian Enrico Castelnuovo, confessed to having been overwhelmed by the lectures.[96] It is no surprise to discover that Longhi was often asked to speak on the radio.

As a connoisseur, Longhi's achievements include the discovery of Poussin's *Midas* and the re-attribution to Giovanni Bellini of *The Drunkenness of Noah* (which Berenson had assigned to a lesser painter, Giovanni Cariani).[97] His famous attributions to Caravaggio include the recognition of a *Narcissus*, a *Bacchus* and a *Flagellation of Christ*. In the case of the *Flagellation*, Longhi's way of looking was vividly described by an eyewitness, the French connoisseur Michel Laclotte, as 'a kind of mute dance around the painting', viewing it from different angles until some incisions became visible. Since Caravaggio painted directly onto the canvas without an under-drawing, the incisions were made to guide his hand.[98] On another occasion, Longhi suggested a link between the art of Caravaggio and that of a minor Lombard painter, Simone Peterzano. A contract discovered later, by the young Nikolaus Pevsner, revealed that Peterzano had been Caravaggio's first teacher.[99] Longhi was able to identify lost works by Caravaggio thanks to contemporary copies – he had an unusual ability to discriminate between copies and originals, thanks to an eye that was hypersensitive to the lack of spontaneity in an imitation.

An even more spectacular achievement, involving an extraordinary memory as well as a sharp eye, was Longhi's recognition that some scattered paintings by Domenico Veneziano were in fact fragments of the same work.[100] Like Berenson earlier and Zeri later, he was able to fit fragments together in his mind like pieces of a jigsaw puzzle. Longhi later repeated this feat of recognition in the case of a work by Giotto.[101]

These examples concern only a few of Longhi's insights, but they may be sufficient to explain his reputation as a master connoisseur with an uncanny ability to date paintings and what Pope-Hennessy called 'a flawless memory and an eye of great speed and often of great accuracy'.[102] Longhi has been criticized for relying on intuition and not bothering to explain how he reached his conclusions.[103] This judgement applies to many connoisseurs, and I shall return to it in the conclusion to this book. In Longhi's case, a distinction has been made between the young connoisseur, whose judgements were based on his eye, and the later scholar, who took other kinds of evidence into account when he dated or attributed works of art, while continuing to consider this evidence as less important.[104] It is clear, for instance, that he studied seventeenth-century biographies of artists with great care.

Longhi is also much admired as an art critic, evaluating works ranging from Cimabue to the connoisseur's friend Giorgio Morandi. The best known examples of Longhi's impact on taste are surely his early championship of Piero della Francesca (on whom he published a study in 1914 and a major work in 1927), together with his 'resurrection' of Caravaggio, on whom he wrote his dissertation in 1911, when the artist was still out of favour.[105] Unlike other famous connoisseurs of Old Masters such as Berenson and Bode, he also expressed enthusiasm for modern art and published studies of the Futurist Umberto Boccioni.

Longhi stands out most clearly from his fellow connoisseurs, as has often been noted, in the evocative power of his descriptions of paintings, major contributions to the tradition of *ekphrasis*.[106] Indeed, a major literary critic, Gianfranco Contini, claimed that Longhi's book on Piero della Francesca is a classic of Italian literature, although the author later criticized his early style as 'too romantic'.[107] Here and elsewhere, Longhi's aim was what he called a 'verbal transposition' (*trasferimento verbale*) of what he saw, representing as well as describing each work. He combined precise descriptions of its form with evocative adjectives and metaphors, making use of dialect on occasion to give his descriptions local colour and of archaisms to give them period flavour. For fun (a *scherzo*, as he put it), Longhi once produced a brilliant pastiche of early nineteenth-century Italian in the form of a letter from 'an unknown correspondent' to the art historian Luigi Lanzi.[108] His prose style, sometimes described as 'modern baroque', shifts between a number of tones or registers: poetic, dramatic, conversational, ironic and sarcastic. As for his rich vocabulary, a glossary has proved to be necessary even for Italian readers.[109] Like Morelli, Longhi sometimes presented his ideas in the form of a dialogue, interviewing himself or imagining a conversation between the two artists in his *Masolino and Masaccio* (1940) and another between Caravaggio and Tiepolo, which he read aloud on Radio Venice in 1951.

It is no wonder that Longhi attracted a new generation of connoisseurs to study with him, including Giuliano Briganti, Giovanni Previtali, Enrico Castelnuovo, Mina Gregori and Federico Zeri.

Zeri in particular was another remarkable connoisseur, an expert on minor Italian masters. For a long time, for instance, he was 'the only art historian' to take the seventeenth-century Venetian painter Pietro della Vecchia 'really seriously'.[110] Like Longhi, who praised Zeri's connoisseurship, he had 'a prodigious visual memory' (*una prodigiosa memoria visiva*) as well as 'a dazzling capacity to make attributions' (*folgorante capacità attributiva*).[111] His memory enabled him, among other achievements, to recognize that a work discovered in England was a lost fragment of a crucifix by Giotto. Unlike Longhi, Zeri was interested in the social history of art, but he also asserted the primacy of the eye, as his master Longhi and Longhi's master Toesca had done before him.[112]

Like Berenson and Longhi, Zeri made a fortune as an art adviser, to John Paul Getty among others. In all three cases, their main income came from their eyes, enabling them to resist specialization. Zeri also became a television personality (as Berenson would doubtless have been if he had been born a generation later). A scholar with a good nose for forgeries who was also an *enfant terrible*, Zeri became notorious for declaring, after a moment's inspection, that an apparently ancient Greek statue of a young man (for which the J. Paul Getty Museum had paid $10 million) was a fake, explaining in Morellian style that the fingernails were wrong as well as noting that the marble had been deliberately discoloured in order to appear old.[113]

A Very English Connoisseur: Philip Pouncey among Friends

Unlike Zeri (and Kenneth Clark, whose BBC series *Civilization* shown from 1966 onwards in the UK and abroad made him a household name), the English connoisseurs discussed here would have shunned television. They were all experts on Italian Renaissance drawings, a genre in which attribution by the eye is particularly important, since the works are not signed. The group – one is tempted to call them a 'school' – worked together as a team, a collaboration that was doubtless facilitated by their common education at public school and Oxbridge.

The senior member of the group, Arthur Popham, joined the Department of Prints and Drawings at the British Museum in 1912. The evacuation of the museum's collection, together with its staff, to Aberystwyth in Wales during the Second World War allowed Popham to study drawings in private hands from Windsor Castle and Chatsworth and publish studies of the work of Correggio, Parmigianino and Leonardo.[114] The younger members of the group were Philip Pouncey, who joined the department in 1945 and published a catalogue together with Popham in 1950, and John Gere, who joined in 1946, published studies of the drawings of Taddeo Zuccari and was described by Kenneth Clark as having 'a better eye and deeper knowledge than anyone else alive today'.[115]

As a schoolboy at Marlborough College, Pouncey acquired and studied the famous book on Renaissance art by Crowe and Cavalcaselle. At Cambridge, where he read English, he also volunteered to work at the Fitzwilliam Museum. In 1932, on his first visit to Italy, Pouncey paid a call on Bernard Berenson, who later told a French scholar that Pouncey was 'the best connoisseur he had ever met', quite a compliment to a youth of 22 from his senior by 45 years (it would be fascinating to know the works with which Berenson had tested Pouncey's eye).[116]

It might have been predicted that Pouncey would begin his career as an assistant keeper at the National Gallery, cataloguing the early Italian paintings. However, his true vocation was the study of drawings, as he discovered during the Second World War, when he was evacuated to Aberystwyth, along with the gallery's paintings, and so met Popham and two gifted exiled Hungarian connoisseurs of drawings, Frederick Antal and Johannes Wilde.[117] As a result, when the war was over, he moved from the National Gallery to the Department of Prints and Drawings in the British Museum, specializing (if that can be said of such a large field) in Italian Renaissance art. Pouncey was methodical, cautious and modest. He loved catalogues, as connoisseurs often do, and even made one, according to his wife Myril, of his excellent collection of French wine. One of his colleagues noted 'how closely Philip and Myril worked together, and how dependent he was on her constant help and her own expertise in the subject'.[118]

Given the rarity of signatures, cataloguing drawings raises even more problems of attribution than cataloguing paintings. Pouncey was ideally qualified to respond to this challenge, comparing drawings to one another or to finished paintings in order to reveal the personality of the artist. For example, a sketch of a *Woman Washing Her Child's Feet* (now in Oporto) had been given to a minor artist until Pouncey recognized it as a Leonardo, noting the left-handed hatching and the similarity to a Leonardo drawing at Windsor.[119] He identified an *Agony in the Garden* as the work of Giulio Romano (an identification that was later confirmed by the discovery of an inscription on the back of the drawing). Pouncey had a Morellian eye for detail, attributing a sketch of a couple to Lorenzo Lotto on the basis of the shape of their hands. Again, 'Typical of Lotto is the tendency of the drapery to crumple itself into a series of more or less parallel billowy folds.'[120]

A vivid example of Pouncey's flair, as well as his knowledge of the work of minor artists in Renaissance Italy, is his remark on a drawing of a naked man crouching, that 'If Bastianino had made drawings, this is exactly the sort of drawing that one would have expected from him.' The attribution was confirmed when a similar figure was noticed by his wife Myril in a painting of the *Last Judgement* already ascribed to Bastianino (not to be confused with Bastianini), a minor follower of Michelangelo.[121]

Like Longhi, Pouncey was a master of *ekphrasis*, though much more laconic. He described drawings precisely, vividly and sometimes with humour, noting the 'rhythmic lucidity' of Andrea del Sarto, for instance, 'the placid, somewhat cow-like faces of the Virgin and the annunciate angel' in a work by Mariotto di Nardo, and, for once letting himself go in the case of Correggio: 'the figures, whose plasticity is conveyed by contours of varying intensity, ranging between sharply accented definition and blurred touches achieving a *sfumato* suggestive of quivering movement, are enveloped, one may say caressed, by a faint haze obtained by a mesh of shading of the utmost subtlety.'[122] Pouncey published relatively little, apart from catalogues, but did not waste words and each of his articles made an original contribution to its subject.

Earlier in this chapter, I referred to a series of challenges faced by twentieth-century connoisseurs. More recently, the accumulation of challenges, often the consequence of globalization, has provoked what is sometimes described as a 'crisis' of connoisseurship as well as continuing the long debate about the reliability of the eye. This crisis is the theme of the following chapter.

7
Crisis

As we saw earlier, connoisseurs, peering through their magnifying glasses, have been the targets of satirists and cartoonists ever since the eighteenth century. They have often been described as charlatans, while Bernard Berenson complained about being compared to fortune-tellers and astrologers.[1] In the notorious *Hahn v Duveen* trial in New York in 1929, over which of two portraits of the same woman – both known as *La Belle Ferronnière* – was the original by Leonardo da Vinci, Judge Black dismissed the testimony of experts who included Berenson.[2] Prejudice against connoisseurship is still expressed in public places. In 2016, in the Knoedler trial, again in New York, in which that famous gallery was accused of selling fake Pollocks and Rothkos, one of the attorneys told the jury to 'put aside the fancy art words like "connoisseurship" and "catalogue raisonné" that the supposed experts use'.[3] In 2021 connoisseurship was even described as 'a C-word long fallen out of usage'.[4]

Even experts on art have expressed embarrassment about the term. As early as 1948, the editor of the *Burlington Magazine for Connoisseurs* deleted the phrase 'for Connoisseurs' from its title because 'The word connoisseur now conjures up a picture of an elderly gentleman in white bow tie and trim imperial,' complete with cigar and magnifying glass.[5] In 1960 Edgar Wind, who viewed art as essentially the embodiment of ideas, devoted one of his Reith Lectures on *Art and Anarchy* to the 'Critique of Connoisseurship'.

In the twenty-first century, criticisms from inside have increased. In 2002 the director of the Metropolitan Museum of Art remarked that 'If you go to the College Art Association, connoisseurship is practically a dirty word.'[6] In 2014, at a conference on 'Connoisseurship Now' at the Paul Mellon Center for British Art, Bendor Grosvenor complained that 'the basic element of being a connoisseur isn't appreciated or encouraged enough anymore,' while Hugo Chapman, Keeper of the Department of Prints and Drawings at the British Museum, went still further, capturing the attention of the media with his remark that he would 'rather gouge my eyes out with a rusty penknife than describe myself as a connoisseur'.[7]

What is the problem? Part of it, at least, may be described as a rejection of both the importance and the reliability of attributions, at a time, ironically enough, when more millions of pounds (euros, dollars, yen . . .) depend on whether a given painting is or is not an original Rembrandt or Van Gogh. However, as we have seen, the rejection of attribution, like that of the word 'connoisseur', is not new. Kenneth Clark, writing to Berenson in the 1920s, dismissed what he called 'petty fogying [*sic*] attributions' and described himself as someone 'who, though fond of the attribution game, would like to try another approach to the study of art'.[8] As we saw in Chapter Five, the cultural historians Jacob Burckhardt and Aby Warburg had made similar points still earlier.

The late twentieth century was not the first time that the study of art was described in terms of crisis. As early as 1925, Longhi had suggested that the 'race of connoisseurs' had almost 'died out', while Hans Tietze published a book about the crisis of art studies (*Kunstwissenschaft*). The German art historian Lothar Brieger referred to the same 'crisis' in 1932.[9] Half a century later, a sense of crisis resurfaced. In 1976 Federico Zeri remarked on 'the decline of connoisseurship'. Zeri's friend and colleague Giuliano Briganti discussed the question in 1984, quoting the art critic Cesare Brandi, who had written in 1980 that connoisseurs were an endangered species. The American art historian Gary Schwartz claimed in 1993 that the 'age of connoisseurship' was over.[10] Another American art historian, James Beck, took up this theme in 2006, using the term 'crisis' to refer to what he called the 'decline in authority, prestige and quality' of connoisseurs since 1998, following the deaths of Zeri and Pope-Hennessy (he failed to mention Denis Mahon and Konrad Oberhuber, both of whom were still alive when Beck's book was published, or Mina Gregori, who is still alive as I write in 2024).[11]

However, Gregori herself believes in what she calls 'the decadence and unpopularity of connoisseurship today', comparing it with its 'apex' in the age of Friedländer and Longhi. Asked in an interview whether connoisseurship is in crisis, she immediately answered 'yes', on the grounds that there were 'too many people' in the field, so that the percentage of good eyes and memories had declined. 'Without a good visual memory,' she declared, 'it is better not to practise this profession.'[12]

A British connoisseur has gone so far as to assert that 'we are less good at seeing than our Victorian predecessors.'[13] In similar fashion, the French connoisseur Philippe Costamagna claims that 'the great eyes ... are becoming more and more rare.' His colleague Frédéric Elsig makes an allied point, suggesting that 'the discipline is going through a crisis of growth and identity.'[14] An article published in 2013 asked whether 'the end of the art connoisseur' was in sight, replaced by 'equal participation in art evaluation'.[15] The rise of high-definition online reproductions of paintings has made the playing field of attribution more level than it was, although it is still no substitute for the experienced eye.

Some of the comments on the crisis are dramatic – perhaps too dramatic. Briganti concluded his discussion of connoisseurs by suggesting that the species was not becoming extinct. The British connoisseur Bendor Grosvenor has gone further, suggesting that 'the pendulum is swinging back in favour of connoisseurship,' noting its new place in exhibitions at the National Gallery in London, including one about Charles Eastlake in 2011.[16] It is worth noting that some connoisseurs of the traditional kind (including Grosvenor) still exist and that they have made some remarkable discoveries, even in the domain of Old Masters, despite the shrinking numbers of such masters in the art market.

Discoveries of lost works by Caravaggio have hit the headlines more than once in the last few decades. In 1990 Sergio Benedetti, a Florentine conservator at the National Gallery in Dublin, recognized a painting in the Jesuit house in that city as Caravaggio's *Taking of Christ*, a discovery confirmed by a study of its provenance. In 2019 Eric Turquin, who had worked in Sotheby's before founding his own firm of advisers, discovered a painting of *Judith and Holofernes* under a mattress in an attic in Toulouse. After he had declared it to be a work by Caravaggio, the painting was valued at $170 million, though some experts remained sceptical of his attribution.[17] In 2021 the Italian art historian Massimo Pulini recognized a painting of Christ at an auction in Madrid as a work by Caravaggio ('I instantly knew this was a Caravaggio').[18]

The demand for attributions has recently been increasing, along with the dizzying increase in the prices of the works of both Old and Modern Masters. For example, when the National Gallery in Washington acquired Leonardo's portrait of Ginevra de' Benci in 1967, they paid $5 million for their prize. However, when the *Salvator Mundi* was up for sale half a century later, the price was $450 million, in other words ninety times as much. In consequence, auction rooms and dealers are under increasing pressure from both buyers and sellers to establish whether a given painting is an original, a copy or a fake.

Indeed, according to one journalist writing in 2001, a 'crisis of fakes' has arrived (though what criminologists call the 'dark figure' of undiscovered crimes makes it impossible to be sure whether forgery is increasing).[19] Thanks to the demand for their skills, professionals, whether described as 'connoisseurs', 'advisers', 'experts' or 'consultants', are not about to disappear. Some now work for auction rooms, while others have founded their own enterprises, charging for attributions and sometimes selling works of art as well. They include the following:

1987 Eric Turquin Expertise
1994 Cabinet d'expertise (Millet)
2001 Fine Art Group (Hoffman)

2011 Pall Mall Art Advisors
2012 Gnyp Art Advisory
2014 Art Agency (Cappelazzo/Allan Schwartzman)
2015 Arndt Art Agency
2015 Art Authentication Service (Polsky)
2019 Gagosian Art Advisory

Another recent development has been the rise of 'authentication boards', in other words committees that decide which works attributed to a given artist are genuine and, like traditional connoisseurs, issue certificates of authenticity, as in the case of the board linked to the Warhol Foundation for the Visual Arts. However, this board and similar ones for Jean-Michel Basquiat, Alexander Calder, Roy Lichtenstein and others have now shut down. The problem is that declaring a work to be inauthentic makes a board vulnerable to lawsuits by aggrieved owners.[20] The famous anonymous artist who works under the name of 'Banksy' handed the task of authenticating his works to a body called 'Pest Control'. In 2024, however, it emerged that two collectors are suing Pest Control for breach of contract for failure to say whether a certain work, a print of *Monkey Queen* attributed to Banksy, is authentic or not (it is possible that in the course of the trial, the artist's identity will finally be revealed).[21] For similar reasons, there has been a decline in one traditional practice of connoisseurs, the publication of a catalogue of the works of a particular artist. Scholars now fear being sued by both buyers and sellers, since exclusion from such a catalogue lowers the value of particular paintings.

'Crisis' is a concept that is often used vaguely, but it remains possible to employ it in a relatively precise manner. I would define a crisis as a moment of turbulence that accompanies a transition between two systems. In this case, the term functions as a kind of umbrella raised over at least five transitions that are taking place at more or less the same time: the crisis of attribution, the crisis of curatorship, the crisis of art history, the crisis of the art market and the crisis of art itself.

The Crisis of Attribution

As we have seen, the practice of attribution was an essential part of connoisseurship in early modern Europe, in the context of the work of artists who came to be known as the Old Masters. It was this kind of art that dominated the market, and it was to judge this art that the stars of the profession developed their methods, from the early seventeenth century to the twentieth. However, as Philip Hook has suggested, 'the "connoisseurial" demands that Modernism makes . . . are different from those of previous generations,' so that 'a new sort of eye is needed to make correct judgements, one less tied to traditional standards of quality.'[22]

Traditional practices of attribution are also threatened by the blurring of the distinction between originals and copies and the distinction between great masters and their assistants. Art historians have undermined belief in connoisseurship by showing that its leading concepts – 'original', 'copy', 'forgery' and 'authenticity' – have all changed their meaning over the centuries. In the seventeenth century, when they were appreciated, copies of one master might be made by another, some copies were said to be better than the originals, and some connoisseurs were 'interested in the attribution of such works'.[23] Artists such as Rubens made copies of their own paintings, with or without variations. Awareness of this fluid situation led the French connoisseur Sylvie Béguin to coin the phrase 'original copy' (*réplique originale*) and the art historians Kathleen Preciado and Maria Loh to write about 'multiple originals' and 'repetition as originality'.[24] In other words, the distinction between 'original' and 'copy' needs to be historicized, like the concepts of forgery and authenticity.

Yet another candidate for historicization is the distinction between master and disciple. It has long been known that certain Old Masters, notably Raphael, Titian, Rembrandt and Rubens, presided over large workshops of apprentices and assistants. On one occasion, Rubens distinguished between works entirely painted by him, those painted with the help of assistants and those painted by assistants but touched up by the master.[25] There has long been a tension between this practice and that of attributing paintings to an individual artist.[26]

That the conflict between traditional attribution to individuals and awareness of collaboration has been becoming sharper is suggested by the recent history of studies of Rembrandt, whose more than fifty pupils and assistants included future leading artists such as Ferdinand Bol, Gerard Dou and Govert Flinck. No wonder then that attributions to Rembrandt have long been controversial. Maximalists attributed 714 paintings to the master, while minimalists reduced the number to 265.[27]

To settle the controversy, a team of scholars in the Netherlands began work in 1969 on the Rembrandt Research Project (known as the RRP), involving a team of scholars located at the University of Amsterdam with the task of dividing possible works by the master into three categories: A, authentic; B, uncertain; and C, inauthentic, whether they were imitations, copies or works by the 'school' of Rembrandt. In carrying out this task, however, the team encountered serious problems. They disagreed not only about the attribution of individual paintings but about the relative weight given to the eye, to documents or to science. Dendrochronology and X-rays were employed but the team concluded that 'technical examination rarely provided absolute certainty regarding attributions.'[28]

Controversy focused on the nature of collaboration between the master and his disciples. How much should the master have contributed for a painting to be labelled a 'Rembrandt'? Disagreement turned into a 'crisis', marked by the resignation of some leading members of the team, the emergence of a new leader, Ernst van de Wetering, and the abandonment of sharp distinctions between the categories A, B and C.[29]

In short, the history of the project is a history of what sociologists describe as 'perverse consequences', in this case of an enterprise in which the participants gradually undermined the assumptions on which that enterprise had originally been based. The point has been generalized by the British-American scholar Ivan Gaskell, who 'engaged with connoisseurship, especially very early in my career', but is now 'one of its most trenchant critics', noting that 'the dominant obsession with trying to decide on the single maker of any given thing, regardless of the circumstances of making, is extremely limiting.'[30]

The Crisis of Art History

The crisis of attribution forms part of a larger crisis, the crisis of art history. In 1988, when the American art historian Svetlana Alpers published a book with the provocative title *Rembrandt's Enterprise*, it was met by a wave of shock and anger, vividly expressed in a review by the critic Hilton Kramer, who accused the author of assimilating Rembrandt to Andy Warhol and treated her book as 'wholly destructive', an illustration of what had gone wrong with art history.[31]

The problem is that like Vasari, most art historians have focused attention on the biographies of great artists. As we have seen, the growing interest in the individual in early modern Europe became still more important in the nineteenth century. Despite the Swiss scholar Heinrich Wölfflin's call for a history of art 'without names', a focus on individual genius has long dominated the field. It is only in the last few decades that this emphasis has been challenged in art history as well as in other disciplines, leading to the perception of the study of Old or Modern Masters as similarly 'elitist', but also opening the way for appreciation of non-Western, 'folk' and decorative arts.[32] The context for these developments includes the reaction of some scholars of Anglophone literature against the 'canon' of classical texts, denounced on occasion as a collection of the works of dead white men.

More generally, some art historians have come to historicize or even to reject the idea of 'art history' itself. The German scholar Hans Belting, for instance, claimed that the term is only appropriate to works produced in the West between the fifteenth and the late twentieth century. He argued that art history had come to an end and should be replaced by 'Image Studies' (*Bildwissenschaft*), in the manner of Aby Warburg in the 1920s.[33] By the 1990s the term 'Visual Culture Studies' was coming into use in the USA to describe a rival to art history in which the canon of great works was either rejected or ignored and artefacts were studied irrespective of artistic quality.[34]

The trend towards globalization discussed in the previous chapter has also played its part, leading to a critique of traditional art history as Eurocentric. To correct this bias, there has been a call for 'decentering' the concept of Modernism to include works of art produced in India, China, Japan, Africa, Latin America and elsewhere. A growing number of scholars now speak about 'modernisms' in the plural and discuss artists from outside Europe and the USA who, as we saw in Chapter Six, combined what they learned from European and North American modernists with their own traditions.[35] The art historian Partha Mitter, for instance, has written about the 'Picasso Manqué Syndrome', in other words the double standard of critics who dismissed the work of artists such as Gaganendranath Tagore as derivative because he was inspired by Cubism, while treating Picasso as original although he was inspired by traditional African art.[36] A place in art histories should also be made for artists who combine elements from two non-Western traditions. For example, Tagore learned from the Japanese tradition of brush painting, thanks to meeting the art critic Okakura Kazuko, who spent two years in India and knew the Tagore family.[37]

From the 1980s, books and courses have regularly offered a 'world history of art'.[38] However, this approach faces a challenge in its turn, that of incorporating images that were made in cultures which lacked a concept of 'art'. Inevitably the question was posed, 'Is a global art history possible?' One answer, a controversial one, is Carlo Ginzburg's suggestion that such a history might be based on connoisseurship in an 'expanded' sense of the term.[39]

The Crisis of Curatorship

Curators, who have often been trained as art historians and may continue to practise the craft, have also faced a crisis in the last generation. The roles of the scholar and the curator have become increasingly incompatible. Stephen Deuchar, the director of Tate

Britain from 1998 to 2010, identified three challenges that emerged, at least in the British case, in the 1980s. The first was a 'squeeze' on public funding for the arts. The second was an extension to museums of commercial criteria according to which the success of an exhibition was measured by the numbers of visitors who attended it, leading to pressure on curators to choose popular themes. The third challenge was that the role expected from a curator (sometimes by directors of museums, sometimes by ministers) was shifting from scholar to manager. We might add a fourth challenge to curators of works of art, the rise of the New Art History, especially its critique of traditional Western ideas of 'art'.[40] More recently, curators of museums and galleries have had to respond to increasing criticism of their 'colonialism' and to increasing pressure to return artefacts in their keeping – the Elgin Marbles, the Benin Bronzes and many more – to the places where they were made.[41]

The Crisis of the Art Market

As for the art market, it is certainly flourishing but at the same time it is changing shape. As we saw in the previous chapter, it is becoming increasingly global. Globalization is linked to the shift in demand away from the Old Masters and towards modern and contemporary art. According to the consulting firm Arts Economics, Old Masters still accounted for 16 per cent of the value of sales of paintings at auction in 2003, but this proportion had declined to 4 per cent in 2023.[42] This decline has obviously reduced the commercial need for what is sometimes called 'classical' connoisseurship. However, selling modern and contemporary art raises its own problems. Modern art is easier to fake than Old Masters, as the career of Elmyr de Hory (discussed in Chapter Six) suggests. So is contemporary art, where the market, as noted earlier, is unusually unstable, since artistic reputations have not had time to settle.

In the detection of fakes, scientific methods now play a more important role than ever before. A recent development is the use of artificial intelligence in attribution, by comparing the pattern of brushstrokes in a given painting with a databank of works generally attributed to a given artist. AI carries out stylistic analysis more rapidly and more completely than traditional connoisseurs with their magnifying glasses, prints and photos. Hephaestus Analytical, a company based in London and founded in 2018, makes use of AI alongside the traditional methods of connoisseurship, provenance and scientific analysis. Art Recognition, a company based in Zurich and founded in 2019, places more emphasis on AI in what is coming to be called 'authentication', a term with overtones of certainty, rather than the older word 'attribution', which stresses the fallible human element. There is an obvious parallel between the use of AI in connoisseurship and its use in espionage, another area of current controversy.[43]

Problems remain, illustrated by some recent controversies. For example, two tests making use of the analysis of brushstrokes by AI produced opposite results in the case of the de Brécy Tondo Madonna. It was attributed to Raphael in an investigation carried out by Bradford and Nottingham universities but rejected by Art Recognition. The founder of the company, Carina Popovici, has argued that the rival diagnosis was carried out by a system programmed to spot similarities rather than differences and that the discrepancy between the results of the two investigations 'doesn't undermine the tool's potential'. We shall see. Today, AI is even being used for talent spotting in the field of contemporary art, at least in the sense of predicting the artists whose work will be most in demand in the near future.[44]

Science, from chemical analysis to X-rays, used to be a resource for connoisseurs but in the age of artificial intelligence it might turn into a threat. Are today's connoisseurs the last of the dinosaurs? The argument is still in progress. On one side, asked for his reaction to these developments, Bendor Grosvenor asserted in 2021 that 'computers still don't understand how artists worked. And probably never will.' Three years later, he appeared to be more positive, commenting that 'the main drawback at the moment is the quality of the inputs given to the attribution programmes currently being used.'[45] Meanwhile, in 2022, an article in *The Economist* suggested that future connoisseurs may, like translators, become cyborgs, in other words 'human beings with mechanical enhancements'.[46] Whether or not this prediction comes true, the story of the impact of AI on connoisseurship has only just begun.

The Crisis of Art

As was suggested earlier, the art of judgement that is known as connoisseurship developed in the age of the Old Masters and is showing more and more signs of wear. In the case of abstract art, which lacks Morelli's famous clues to authorship, judgement is especially difficult. The problem is even more acute in the case of *objets trouvés*, going back to Marcel Duchamp's notorious urinal, *Fountain*, rejected for exhibition in 1917, where the artist's contribution was limited to the 'signature', 'R. Mutt' and to his decision to exhibit the object. Paradoxically, the attribution of *Fountain* to Duchamp has now been contested, on grounds that include the handwriting. It is claimed that the idea came from the German artist Elsa von Freytag-Loringhoven.[47]

As for installations, video art, street art, land art, performance art, digital art, AI art and other contemporary forms, they offer no place for the traditional connoisseur. Take the case of Andy Warhol's famous silk-screen prints, which began with a photograph, transferred to a small acetate, after which the artist would telephone the printers to tell them what colours to use. In what sense is such a print 'by' Warhol? It is intriguing to discover that the art adviser Richard Polsky claims to distinguish genuine Warhols from fakes by a 'sixth sense', like traditional connoisseurs in the case of Old Masters.[48]

As we have seen, it was in the 1980s that the art historian Hans Belting suggested that the idea of 'art' was inappropriate for describing both medieval images, made before that idea existed, and contemporary images, made after it had been rejected. In similar fashion, the American philosopher Arthur Danto proclaimed the 'end of art', on the grounds that since 1964, when Warhol exhibited *Brillo Boxes*, 'anything goes . . . There is no special way works of art have to be.'[49]

A New Connoisseurship?

Do we now live in an age of 'post-connoisseurship'?[50] Or might the practices of classical connoisseurship be adapted to meet the new challenges? If so, how?

There has been talk of a 'new connoisseurship', a 'reinvention' of the discipline or at least a new emphasis on certain elements in traditional connoisseurship at the expense of other ones.[51] This new model or paradigm is gradually displacing attention from the individual 'genius' to studies that revive the notion of 'schools' by speaking of 'networks' of artists or pay increasing attention to collective production in the workshop or studio.[52] This move away from the big names, however desirable from a historian's point of view, will of course be resisted by dealers.

The new connoisseurship is in tune with, if not driven by, a 'social turn', in other words, an increasing recognition of the importance of collaboration in art.[53] In 2021, for instance, Britain's Turner Prize was won by a group, the Array Collective, illustrating the official acceptance of art 'after individualism'. It is worth noting at this point that at the end of the eighteenth century, the art historian Luigi Lanzi, discussing attribution, suggested that the 'amateur' (*dilettante*) should be able to attribute paintings, 'if not to an individual author, at least to a certain period of taste', like the antiquaries who dated artefacts to a given century.[54] Again, in the nineteenth century, Giovanni Morelli argued that schools of painting were a result of local geography and complained that 'the majority of the so-called connoisseurs' know nothing about schools and so attribute all works of the school to a given individual.[55]

In the case of Renaissance Italy, modern studies of collaboration in the workshop go back to the 1930s, when the Viennese art historian Hans Tietze suggested that a signature on a painting did not necessarily signify that it was an autograph work by the artist. Indeed, Tietze presented the paradox that Titian signed precisely the paintings that were not by his hand, as if to guarantee that they were up to the standard of 'brand Titian'.[56] Since then, the ambiguities of the use of the phrase 'by his hand' in early modern documents have been studied in detail. Once again, what might appear to be timeless has been historicized.[57]

A few years ago, Frédéric Elsig distinguished between the collaborator, the follower and the circle of a given painter (*collaborateur*, *suiveur*, *entourage*).[58] A place also needs to be found for a mixture of hands of the kind described to Carleton by Rubens, where the master gives the finishing touches to the work of the assistant. The sale catalogues of Sotheby's and Christie's have been following a new model from 1985 onwards, distinguishing six categories: by the master, attributed to the master, studio of the master, circle of the master, style of the master (painted at the time) and manner of the master (painted later). In similar fashion, the labels on paintings in museums might be adjusted – and on occasion have been adjusted – in order not to give the impression of false certainty in cases where this is unwarranted. For example, the label 'Rembrandt' might sometimes be replaced by 'probably Rembrandt', or 'Rembrandt with the possible assistance of Gerard Dou'.

In this situation it seems appropriate to return to a problem that has resurfaced a number of times in the course of our voyage, without receiving a definite answer (if such a thing is possible). Can we trust connoisseurs?

Conclusion: Can We Trust Connoisseurship?

This book has tried to show how the practice of connoisseurship has changed over the centuries, while individual connoisseurs have also differed in both skills and interests. Some of them have been specialists while others, notably Bode and Zeri, have ranged widely. Individuals have also differed in their methods or at least in the emphasis that they placed on different approaches. Some, notably Morelli, stressed attention to the details of a painting, while others preferred general impressions of the whole. Some have taken the evidence of documents or chemical analysis very seriously, while others have rejected it or at least, like Berenson, Toesca, Longhi and Zeri, reiterated the primacy of the connoisseur's eye.[1]

The emphasis on the eye distinguishes the connoisseur from other knowledgeable people, but at the same time it raises serious problems. As we saw in Chapter One, it is possible to demystify the idea of intuition, but the question of its reliability remains.

The debate over the connoisseurial eye has been going on for centuries, as two books published over three hundred years ago testify. As we have seen, in his *Réflexions critiques* (1719), Jean-Baptiste Du Bos treated connoisseurship as an art of guessing, calling it 'the most unreliable of all the arts apart from medicine' (*le plus fautif de tous les arts après la Médecine*). As if replying to Du Bos, Jonathan Richardson described connoisseurship as a science and gave the second part of his *Two Discourses*, also published in 1719, the title 'That disagreement among connoisseurs is not an objection to the science'.[2]

The parallel between connoisseurs and scientists is worth pursuing for a moment. Attributions are like hypotheses in natural science. Scientists produce rival hypotheses, often on the basis of intuition, and then proceed to test them.[3] They sometimes disagree with their colleagues or change their mind, but these changes or disagreements do not cast doubt on the validity of scientific enterprise. How different is the case of connoisseurship?

The failure of connoisseurs to agree is notorious. A famous nineteenth-century case concerned a Madonna attributed to Hans Holbein, one version of which was displayed in Dresden and the other in Darmstadt. In a public debate in 1871, Morelli took one side and Bode the other.[4] In New York in 1929, in the notorious Hahn case, concerning which of two paintings was an original by Leonardo and which a copy, well-known connoisseurs testified on both sides. Their disagreement led Judge Black to tell the jury to disregard their testimonies, dismissing experts as 'those who claim to have a sixth sense which enables some of them after they have seen a picture even for five minutes to definitely determine whether it is genuine or not'.[5] As for changes of mind, they are sometimes spectacular, as in the case of Berenson, for instance, but also of Longhi, who repudiated in 1961 conclusions about the painter Aniello Falcone that he had reached in 1915. He now regarded his earlier judgement as 'incomprehensible'.[6]

In the case of two leading Old Masters in particular, Rembrandt and Caravaggio, disagreements have taken the form of conflicts between the maximalists (or 'expansionists) and the minimalists (or 'restrictionists'). It would be illuminating if we could eavesdrop on the conversations of leading connoisseurs to hear how they justified their disagreements. These exchanges are occasionally documented in letters that reveal connoisseurship in action. In 1956, for instance, Longhi attributed a *Holy Family* to Francesco Bissolo while Berenson gave it to Giovanni Cariani, claiming that 'the Joseph is typically Carianesque,' while Longhi saw him as 'subtler and more strictly giorgionesque than the usual Cariani'. In this regard, the long correspondence between Longhi and Zeri is also revealing.[7]

Disagreement might be expected. More serious is the disparagement of leading connoisseurs by their colleagues. Wilhelm Bode described Giovanni Morelli as a 'quack doctor'.[8] In his turn, Bode was described by Max Friedländer as a 'sort of charlatan'. Berenson complained about being viewed as someone who 'invented a trick by which one could infallibly tell the authorship of an Italian picture'.[9] The art historian Anthony Blunt was described by one famous connoisseur, John Pope-Hennessy (nicknamed 'The Pope' by his colleagues), as having 'a defective eye'. Another famous connoisseur, Denis Mahon, agreed that Blunt 'did not have an eye'.[10] In his turn, the eye of Mahon, when he was in his nineties, was criticized by former admirers of his connoisseurship.[11] Bode had been the object of similar criticisms towards the end of his career.

Even the stars can be shown to have made serious mistakes of attribution or accepted forgeries as originals. As we have seen, Abraham Bredius accepted Han van Meegeren's *Supper at Emmaus* as a genuine Vermeer. As he once confessed, 'Our métier is so difficult that the best connoisseur may blunder.'[12] Few connoisseurs, if any, are in a position to cast stones at Bredius. The best and the bravest have sometimes erred. Mariette confessed on one occasion that 'I have been wrong about names which I should have known as well as my own,' and on another, writing about a painting attributed to Raphael that he believes to be by Fra Bartolommeo, that he cannot be sure, 'since I find nothing more equivocal than these kinds of christenings' (*car je ne trouve rien de si équivoques que ces sortes de baptêmes*).[13] Morelli once identified a 'Moroni' in Dresden but later recognized its 'Flemish origin' and apologized for the mistake.[14] Even Berenson admitted, in one of his more modest moments, that 'I do not flatter myself that my attributions are final, but I dare hope that, at the worst, they are on the way to truth and not to error.'[15] Unfortunately, the habit of rapid judgements often leads to overconfidence, as the cases of Bode, Bredius and Berenson demonstrate.

No wonder then that the French sociologist Bernard Lahire, reflecting on the transformation of a painting of the *Flight into Egypt* from 'a simple copy' considered in 1986 to be worth about €12,000 into 'a masterpiece by Nicolas Poussin sold for €17,000,000 in 2007', concluded that this event illustrates the power of 'social magic' in the contemporary Western world, a power that deserves to be studied by anthropologists.[16] The connoisseur is a kind of magician in the sense that a few words from him or her can produce important changes in the real world.

Connoisseurship on Trial

Court cases about the authenticity of certain paintings have been mentioned a number of times in this book. A particularly interesting example is *Thwaytes v Sotheby's* (2015). The claimant was informed by the auction room that his painting of *Cardsharps* was a copy after Caravaggio. He subsequently learned that the connoisseur who bought the painting, Denis Mahon, believed it to be an original work that was worth much more than the £42,000 he had paid for it. The claimant therefore accused Sotheby's of neglecting their duty of diligent research into the painting before it was offered for sale.

A number of well-known connoisseurs testified in this case, including Mina Gregori, who agreed with Mahon, and Richard Spear, who disagreed with him. Spear later published a book about the trial, noting that all the witnesses were submitted to rigorous cross-examination by the lawyers for the two sides, discussing, for instance, which features counted as 'characteristics' of Caravaggio.[17] Counsel for Sotheby's stressed the primacy of connoisseurship in the process of attribution, while counsel for the claimant argued that it was inadequate. Hence one might say that the practice of connoisseurship was itself on trial and that the case provided a privileged moment for connoisseurs to explain their methods in public.

As has often been the case, they differed. Gregori, for instance, simply declared that 'my judgement was based on my "eye".' Spear, on the other hand, followed Morelli's famous method and contrasted the representation of the ears in the version of the *Cardsharps* in the Kimbell Art Museum in Fort Worth (generally accepted as an original work by Caravaggio) with 'the inorganic, dry, awkwardly formed ears by the copyist'.[18] An unusual feature of the trial was that the judge, Justice Vivien Rose, regarded it as part of her 'inescapable' task to 'come to terms with Caravaggio connoisseurship'. In this respect she offers a remarkable contrast to Judge Black in the case of *Hahn v Duveen*, discussed earlier. Justice Rose made her own assessment of quality, going to see the work in question and concluding that it could not have been painted by the master.[19] For her, the trial offered a visual education.

In the case of *Thwaytes v Sotheby's*, connoisseurship (to be distinguished from individual connoisseurs) emerged from the ordeal unscathed. In any case, the many successes of the stars, from Baldinucci to Mariette, from Cavalcaselle to Morelli and from Longhi to Pouncey, have often been noted in these pages. Another striking example of a string of successful attributions is offered by the British dealer David Carritt, a former pupil of the Hungarian connoisseur Frederick Antal. Before his early death in 1982, Carritt had discovered a Caravaggio (*Musicians*), a Fragonard (*Psyche*, which had been described in the auction catalogue as the work of a lesser master, Carle van Loo), a Tiepolo (on the dining-room ceiling of the Egyptian embassy) and some Guardis (in a shed in Dublin). It is unsurprising to learn that, as a young man, Carritt's eye for paintings had impressed Bernard Berenson.[20]

In short, in connoisseurship, as in certain other domains such as the battlefield, where rapid decisions are required in conditions of uncertainty, some individuals are able to assess the situation in a flash. Napoleon had this gift, for instance, and so did Federico Zeri. So do a number of individuals today, in professions that range from medicine to firefighting. It is of course necessary to re-examine attributions that were originally arrived at in this way, using the close looking of the psychologist Daniel Kahneman's 'System Two' to verify the conclusions arrived at by the rapid 'System One'.[21] In similar fashion the British connoisseur John Gere concluded that 'Connoisseurship . . . is not exactly a science in the sense of being a rational system of inference from verifiable data, nor is it exactly an art. It stands somewhere between the two.'[22]

Verification has often been successful, sometimes dramatically so, thanks to the discovery of formerly hidden signatures that confirmed Bode's recognition of a work by Dürer, for instance, and of another by Gerard ter Borch, or Pouncey's recognition of a drawing by Giulio Romano before the discovery of an inscription confirming the connoisseur's judgement. Conversely, occasions recur when documents have come to light that contradict the judgements of even the best eyes. For example, Longhi attributed a painting of the *Martyrdom of St Ursula* to a follower of Caravaggio, while Mina Gregori claimed it was by the master himself. The question was settled by the discovery in 1980 of a letter to the patron, the nobleman Marcantonio Doria, in which his agent informed him that Caravaggio had finished painting the picture.[23]

It is obviously time to move on from the conflict between supporters of documents and supporters of the connoisseurial eye, to forget 'either . . . or' and adopt 'both . . . and'. The last word in this debate should probably go to Bode's former assistant Max Friedländer, a fine connoisseur himself who also had a ringside seat for observing both Bode's successes and his failures. Friedländer both employed and defended intuition as a method of attribution but added that 'one should also sceptically and coolly put this opinion to the test.' He also remarked that the 'occupational disease' of the connoisseur is to become a charlatan. In other words, connoisseurs are to be 'trusted and mistrusted'.[24] No one is infallible, not even 'The Pope'.

REFERENCES

Abbreviations

DA *Dictionary of Art*, ed. Jane Turner, 34 vols (New York, 1996)
DBI *Dizionario biografico degli italiani*, ed. Alberto Maria Ghisalberti, 100 vols (Rome 1960–)
ODNB *Oxford Dictionary of National Biography*, ed. H.G.C. Mathew and Brian Harrison, 60 vols (Oxford, 2004)

Preface

1 Roberto Longhi, 'Per una storia dei conoscitori' [1954], reprinted in Longhi, *Critica d'arte e buongoverno* (Florence, 1985), pp. 149–52; Enrico Castelnuovo in *Giovanni Morelli e la cultura dei conoscitori*, ed. Giovanni Agosti et al. (Bergamo, 1993), vol. 1, p. 10.
2 Pierre Bourdieu, *Outline of a Theory of Practice* [1972], trans. Richard Nice (Cambridge, 1977); Roger Chartier, *Cultural History: Between Practices and Representations* (Cambridge, 1988); Arndt Brendecke, ed., *Praktiken der Frühen Neuzeit* (Cologne, 2015).
3 See Michael Baxandall's famous concept of the 'period eye': *Painting and Experience in Fifteenth-Century Italy* (Oxford, 1972), p. 32.
4 Bruno Latour, 'Visualization and Cognition: Thinking with Eyes and Hands', *Knowledge and Society: Studies in the Sociology of Culture Past and Present* (1986), VI, pp. 1–40; Lissa Roberts, Simon Schaffer and Peter Dear, *The Mindful Hand: Inquiry and Invention from the Late Renaissance to Early Industrialization* (Amsterdam, 2007).
5 Pierre Bourdieu, *Pascalian Meditations* [1997], trans. Richard Nice (Cambridge 2000), pp. 128–63. See Graham Harding, '"The Stock of a Connoisseur": The Development and Commercialization of Wine Connoisseurship in the Long Nineteenth Century', in *Connoisseurship*, ed. Christina M. Anderson and Peter Stewart (Oxford, 2023), pp. 165–89.
6 Michael Polanyi, *Personal Knowledge* (London, 1958), p. 49.
7 Daniel Kahneman, *Thinking Fast and Slow* (New York, 2011).
8 Max Friedländer, *On Art and Connoisseurship* (London, 1942), p. 173.

1 What Is Connoisseurship?

1 Jaynie Anderson, 'Otto Mündler and His Travel Diary', *Walpole Society*, LI (1985), pp. 7–59 (p. 12).
2 Emanuele Lugli, 'Connoisseurship as a System', *Word and Image*, XXIV/2 (2008), pp. 162–75. On the 'three domains', Joris Heyder, 'Doing Connoisseurship', *Journal of Art Historiography*, XXIV (2021), pp. 1–9 (p. 2).
3 Robert Merton, 'The Matthew Effect in Science', *Science*, CLIX/3810 (1968), pp. 56–63.
4 Ivan Gaskell, 'A Rembrandt Puzzle and the Limits of Connoisseurship', paper given at the symposium 'Hans Heinrich Thyssen as an Art Collector', Museo Nacional Thyssen Bornemisza, Madrid, 2021; Ernest Samuels, *Bernard Berenson: The Making of a Connoisseur* (Cambridge, MA, 1979), p. 155.
5 Christopher de Hamel, *Meetings with Remarkable Manuscripts* (London, 2016).
6 Wen C. Fong, 'The Problem of Forgeries in Chinese Painting', *Artibus Asiae*, XXV (1962), pp. 95–119 (p. 107).
7 Kokan Nagayama, *The Connoisseur's Book of Japanese Swords* (Tokyo and London, 1997); Akiko Yano, ed., *Salon Culture in Japan: Making Art, 1750–1900* (London, 2024), especially pp. 8–47.
8 Wilhelm von Bode and Ernst Kühnel, *Antique Rugs from the Near East* [1902], trans. Charles Ellis (London, 1970).
9 A wide range of domains are discussed in Christine M. Anderson and Peter Stewart, eds, *Connoisseurship* (Oxford, 2023).
10 Bernard Lahire, *This Is Not Just a Painting: An Inquiry into Art, Domination, Magic and the Sacred* [2015], trans. Helen Morrison (Cambridge, 2019), pp. 381–98.
11 Alberto Frigo, 'Can One Speak of Painting if One Cannot Hold a Brush? Giulio Mancini, Medicine and the Birth of the Connoisseur', *Journal of the History of Ideas*, LXXIII/3 (2012), pp. 417–36.
12 Lahire, *This Is Not Just a Painting*, p. 391.
13 Donata Levi, *Cavalcaselle: il pioniere della conservatione dell'arte italiana* (Turin, 1988).
14 Luke Uglow, 'Giovanni Morelli and His Friend Giorgione: Connoisseurship, Science and Irony', *Journal of Art Historiography*, XI (2014), pp. 1–30; Jaynie Anderson, *The Life of Giovanni Morelli in Risorgimento Italy* (Milan, 2019).
15 Mina Gregori quoted in *Il mestiere del conoscitore: Roberto Longhi*, ed. Anna Maria Ambrosini et al. (Bologna, 2017), p. 22.
16 Philippe Costamagna, *Histoires d'oeils* (Paris, 2019), p. 92.
17 Eric Hebborn, *Confessions of a Master Forger* (London, 1997), p. 342.
18 Andrew Gumbel, 'Art Forger's Death in Rome a Mystery', *The Independent*, 13 January 1996.
19 Roger de Piles, *Conversations sur la connoissance de la peinture* (Paris, 1677), p. 300.

20 Max Friedländer, *On Art and Connoisseurship* (London, 1942), pp. 172–3.
21 Malcolm Gladwell, *Blink: The Power of Thinking without Thinking* (London, 2005), pp. 23, 3–17; Federico Zeri, *J'avoue m'être trompé* (Paris, 1995), pp. 24–7.
22 Christopher Brown, Jan Kelch and Pieter van Thiel, eds, *Rembrandt: The Master and His Workshop* (New Haven, CT, 1991), pp. 117, 123.
23 Bernard Berenson, *Three Essays on Method* (Oxford, 1926).
24 Sydney Cockerell, Director of the Fitzwilliam, letter of 30 January 1925, https://yashiro.itatti.harvard.edu/cockerell-letters, accessed 1 June 2025.
25 Mina Gregori quoted in Andrea Vogt, 'Caravaggio's Original Mary Magdalene in Ecstasy "Discovered"', *Daily Telegraph*, 24 October 2014.
26 Peter Dent, ed., *Sculpture and Touch* (Farnham, 2014); Adrian Randolph, *Touching Objects* (New Haven, CT, 2014).
27 Lesley Lewis, *Connoisseurs and Secret Agents in Eighteenth-Century Rome* (London, 1961), p. 39; John Pope-Hennessy, *Learning to Look* (London, 1991), pp. 113, 115; Edmund de Waal, *The Hare with Amber Eyes* (London, 2010), p. 16.
28 Joseph Addison, *Dialogues upon the Usefulness of Ancient Medals* [1720], ed. Adolph Guthkelch, 2 vols (London, 1914), vol. II, the third dialogue.
29 Quoted in Thomas Hoving, *False Impressions* (London, 1996), p. 19 (without reference to a source); Swarzenski's colleague Perry Rathbone, quoted in Belinda Rathbone, *The Boston Raphael* (Jaffrey, NH, 2014), p. 122.
30 Marco Boschini, *Carta de navegar pittoresco* [1660], ed. Anna Pallucchini (Venice, 1966).
31 Quoted in Rudolf Wittkower, 'Inigo Jones – "Puritanissmo Fiero"', *Burlington Magazine*, XC/539 (1948), pp. 50–51.
32 Edmond Bonnaffé, *Les collectionneurs de l'ancienne France* (Paris, 1873), p. 86 (my translation). See Érika Wicky, 'L'oeil, le goût et le flair: les compétences sensorielles du collectionneur fin de siècle', *Société et Représentations*, XLIV (2017), pp. 151–62 (p. 156).
33 Carlo Ginzburg, 'Clues: Roots of an Evidential Paradigm' [1978], English translation in Ginzburg, *Clues, Myths, and the Historical Method* (Baltimore, MD, 1989), pp. 96–125, 200–214.
34 Gladwell, *Blink*, p. 23.
35 Jonathan Richardson, *An Essay on the Whole Art of Criticism as it Relates to Painting and an Argument in Behalf of the Science of a Connoisseur* (London, 1719), p. 54; Jaś Elsner, 'Significant Details: Systems, Certainties and the Art-Historian as Detective', *Antiquity*, LXIV (1990), pp. 950–52; Daniel Arasse, *Le détail: pour une histoire rapprochée de la peinture* (Paris, 1992).
36 Quoted in Valerie Kobi, *Dans l'oeil du connoisseur: Pierre-Jean Mariette (1694–1774) et la construction des savoirs en histoire de l'art* (Rennes, 2018), p. 99 (my translation).

37 Rachel Cohen, *Bernard Berenson: A Life in the Picture Trade* (New Haven, CT, 2021), pp. 84, 86.
38 Françoise Viatte, 'Paul Joannides: A Connoisseur at Work', *Artibus et Historiae*, XXXVII (2016), pp. 13–23 (p. 14; my translation).
39 Quoted in Frances Spalding, *Roger Fry: Art and Life* (London, 1980), p. 133.
40 Quoted in Max Seidel, 'Adolph Goldschmidt', in *I conoscitori tedeschi*, ed. Francesco Caglioti, Andrea De'Marchi and Alessandro Nova (Milan, 2018), p. 350.
41 Friedländer, *Art and Connoisseurship*, p. 177.
42 Berenson quoted in Cohen, *Bernard Berenson*, pp. 224–5, and Ernest Samuels, *Bernard Berenson: The Making of a Legend* (Cambridge, MA, 1987), p. 137.
43 Zeri, *J'avoue*, p. 71.
44 Leo Steinberg, quoted in John A. Gere, 'Philip Pouncey, 1910–1990', *Proceedings of the British Academy*, LXXVI (1991), pp. 529–44 (pp. 537–8).
45 Quoted from Pietro Guarienti's preface to Pellegrino Orlandi, *Abecedario pittorico* (Venice, 1753).
46 Pope-Hennessy, *Learning to Look*, pp. 309–10, 303.
47 Carlo Ginzburg, 'Piccole differenze: ekphrasis e connoisseurship', *Paragone*, LXXI (2020), pp. 98–116.
48 Jean-Baptiste Du Bos, *Réflexions Critiques* (Paris, 1719); Marc-Antoine Laugier, *Manière de bien juger les ouvrages de peinture* (Paris, 1771), p. 10.
49 Berenson, *Three Essays*.
50 Gail Feigenbaum and Inge Reist, eds, *Provenance: An Alternate History of Art* (Los Angeles, CA, 2012).
51 Margarete Bieber, *Ancient Copies* (New York, 1977); Brunilde Ridgway, *Roman Copies of Greek Sculpture* (Ann Arbor, MI, 1984).
52 Adolph Borbein, 'Connoisseurship', in *Oxford Handbook of Greek and Roman Architecture*, ed. Clemente Marconi (Oxford, 2014), pp. 518–40 (p. 528).
53 Lucian, *Philopseudes*; Callistratus, *Descriptions* (London, 1979); Pliny, *Natural History* (London, 1938–62). See Andrew S. Becker, *The Shield of Achilles and the Poetics of Ekphrasis* (Lanham, MD, 1995).
54 Franciscus Junius the Younger, *On the Painting of the Ancients* [1638], new edn (Oxford 1991), p. 68.
55 Philostratus, *Imagines* (London, 1931), pp. 11, 221.
56 Fong, 'The Problem of Forgeries', p. 96.
57 Chu Sing-Chai, *On the Connoisseurship of Chinese Calligraphy and Painting* (Hong Kong, 1961); Craig Clunas, *Superfluous Things: Material Culture and Social Status in Early Modern China* (Cambridge, 1991), p. 86.
58 Fong, 'The Problem of Forgeries', p. 96n.
59 Michel Beurdeley, *The Chinese Collector through the Centuries* (Rutland, VT, 1966), pp. 66–74; Craig Clunas, *Art in China* (Oxford, 1997), p. 139.

60 Clunas, *Art in China*, p. 151.
61 Clunas, *Superfluous Things*, pp. 57–8.
62 'Notes on Pure Esoterica', quoted in Timothy Brook, *The Confusions of Pleasure: Commerce and Culture in Ming China* (Berkeley, CA, 1998), p. 228.
63 Craig Clunas, *Chinese Painting and Its Audiences* (Princeton, NJ, 2017), pp. 42–60.
64 Quoted in Brook, *Confusions*, pp. 224–5.
65 Quoted in Clunas, *Superfluous Things*, p. 111. The poem was by Shao Changheng.
66 Fong, 'Problem of Forgeries', pp. 96–100; Judith Smith and Wen Fong, eds, *Issues of Authenticity in Chinese Painting* (New York, 1999).
67 Anna Tummers, 'By His Hand: The Paradox of Seventeenth-Century Connoisseurship', in *Art Market and Connoisseurship*, ed. Koenraad Jonckheere and Anna Tummers (Amsterdam, 2021), pp. 31–66.
68 Maria Loh, 'New and Improved: Repetition as Originality in Italian Baroque Practice and Theory', *Art Bulletin*, LXXXVI/3 (2004), pp. 477–504 (p. 477).
69 Marc Bloch, *Apologie pour l'histoire* [1944] (Paris, 1974), pp. 37–41.
70 Jeffrey Muller, *Rubens: The Artist as Collector* (Princeton, NJ, 1989), pp. 94–146; Evelyn quoted in *Old Masters Worldwide*, ed. Susanna Avery-Quash and Barbara Pezzini (London, 2019), p. 5.
71 Francis Haskell, *The Ephemeral Museum: Old Master Paintings and the Rise of the Art Exhibition* (New Haven, CT, 2000), p. 4.
72 Creighton Gilbert, ed., *Italian Art 1400–1500* (Englewood Cliffs, NJ, 1980), pp. 31–2.
73 Jaynie Anderson, 'The Political Power of Connoisseurship in Nineteenth-Century Europe', *Beiheft Jahrbuch der Berliner Museen*, XXXVIII, pp. 107–19 (p. 109); Nigel Llewellyn, 'Une science du regard: les connaisseurs', in *Histoire de l'histoire de l'art*, ed. Edouard Pommier, 2 vols (Paris, 2000), vol. II, p. 309; Christopher Hodkinson, *A Question of Attribution: Art Connoisseurship in the Nineteenth Century* (Wrightington, 2014).
74 Irene Haberlandt, *Jonathan Richardson: Die Begründung der Kunstkennerschaft* (Münster, 1991); Donatella Levi Sparti, 'Novità su Giulio Mancini: arte e presunta "connoisseurship"', *Mitteilungen des Kunsthistorischen Institutes in Florenz*, LII (2008), pp. 53–72; Pascal Griener, 'Le connoisseurship, science et art de réussir', in *La République de l'oeil: l'expérience de l'art au siècle des lumières* (Paris, 2010), pp. 91–115.

2 The Birth of the Connoisseur

1 Roberto Weiss, 'The Collection of Antiques', in *The Renaissance Discovery of Classical Antiquity* [1969], new edn (Oxford 1988), pp. 180–202; Xavier Salomon, 'Cardinal Pietro Barbo's Collection and Its Inventory Reconsidered', *Journal of the History of Collections*,

xv (2003), pp. 1–18; Kathleen Christian, *Empire without End* (New Haven, CT, 2010), p. 94.

2 Clifford M. Brown, 'Isabella d'Este e il mondo Greco-romano', in *Isabella d'Este: la primadonna del Rinascimento*, ed. Daniele Bini (Modena, 2001) pp. 109–28.

3 Laurie Fusco and Gino Corti, *Lorenzo de'Medici: Collector and Antiquarian* (Cambridge, 2004), pp. 29–30, 208, 211.

4 Phyllis Gordan, ed., *Two Renaissance Book Hunters: The Letters of Poggius Bracciolini to Nicolaus de Niccolis* (New York, 1974), letter 84.

5 Vespasiano da Bisticci, 'Niccolò Niccoli', in *The Vespasiano Memoirs*, trans. William George and Emily Waters (New York, 1926), p. 399; Brown, 'Isabella'.

6 Margarete Bieber, *Ancient Copies* (New York, 1977); Brunilde Ridgway, *Roman Copies of Greek Sculpture* (Ann Arbor, MI, 1984).

7 Lynn Catterson, 'Michelangelo's "Laocoön"?', *Artibus et Historiae*, XXVI/52 (2005), pp. 29–56.

8 Giorgio Vasari, *Vite de' pittori* [1550], ed. Rosanna Bettarini and Paola Barocchi, 6 vols (Florence, 1966–87); Ascanio Condivi, *Vita di Michelangelo Buonarotti* (Rome, 1553).

9 Enea Vico, *Discorsi sopra le medaglie de gli antichi* (Venice, 1555). See Giulio Bodon, *Enea Vico: fra memoria e miraggio della classicità* (Rome, 1997).

10 Georgia Clarke, 'Ambrogio Traversari: Artistic Adviser in Early Fifteenth-Century Florence?', *Renaissance Studies*, XI/3 (1997), pp. 161–78 (p. 167); Joseph Alsop, *The Rare Art Traditions* (London, 1982), p. 348.

11 Fusco and Corti, *Lorenzo*, p. 211.

12 Isabella d'Este, *Selected Letters*, ed. and trans. Deanna Shemek (Toronto, 2017).

13 David Chambers, ed., *Patrons and Artists in the Italian Renaissance* (London, 1972), no. 95. See Michael Baxandall, *Painting and Experience in Fifteenth-Century Italy* (Oxford, 1972), pp. 109ff.

14 Ernst Gombrich, 'The Leaven of Criticism in Renaissance Art', in *Art, Science and History in the Renaissance*, ed. Charles S. Singleton (Oxford, 1967), pp. 3–42.

15 Michiel quoted in Rosella Lauber, 'Per la descrizione delle opere d'arte in Marcantonio Michiel', in *Testi, immagini e filologia nel* XVI *secolo*, ed. Eliana Carrara and Silvia Ginzburg (Pisa, 2007), pp. 1–36 (p. 30).

16 Theodor Frimmel, ed., *Der Anonimo Morelliano* (Vienna, 1888), p. 80.

17 Philip Sohm, *Pittoresco: Marco Boschini, His Critics and Their Critiques of Painterly Brushwork in Seventeenth- and Eighteenth-Century Italy* (Cambridge, 1991), p. 10; Mario Pozzi and Enrico Mattioda, *Giorgio Vasari Storico e Critico* (Florence, 2006), pp. 148–55.

18 Baldassare Castiglione, *Il Cortegiano*, Book 1 (1528), chapter 7.

19 Jacob Burckhardt, *Civilization of the Renaissance* [1860], trans. S.G.C. Middlemore (London, 1944), pp. 81–103, 199–202.

20 T. C. Price Zimmermann, *Paolo Giovio* (Princeton, NJ, 1995), p. 214.

21 Lorenzo Ghiberti, *Commerntarii*, ed. Lorenzo Bartoli (Florence, 1998).

22 Edwin Panofsky, 'The First Page of Vasari's Libro' [1930], in *Meaning in the Visual Arts* (Garden City, NY, 1955), pp. 169–225; Stefano Pierguidi, 'Che si conoscono al suo già detto segno: Vasari's Connoisseurship in the Field of Engravings', *Journal of Art Historiography*, XVI (2017), pp. 1–8.

23 Carol Gibson-Wood, *Studies in the Theory of Connoisseurship from Vasari to Morelli* (London, 1982).

24 Giorgio Vasari, 'Life of Garofalo', quoted in Ingrid Rowland and Noah Charney, *The Collector of Lives: Giorgio Vasari and the Invention of Art* (New York, 2017), p. 307. Given the number of editions and translations of Vasari, page numbers are not given when citing.

25 Quoted in Jennifer Fletcher, 'Marcantonio Michiel's Collection', *Journal of the Warburg and Courtauld Institutes*, XXXVI/1 (1973), pp. 382–5 (p. 382).

26 Frimmel, *Anonimo Morelliano*, p. 84.

27 Jeffrey Müller, 'Measures of Authenticity: The Detection of Copies in the Early Literature on Connoisseurship', *Studies in the History of Art*, XX (1989), pp. 141–51 (pp. 144–5).

28 Frimmel, *Anonimo Morelliano*, p. 78.

29 Felipe de Guevara, *Comentarios de la pintura* (Madrid, 1788).

30 Otto Kurz, 'Early Art Forgeries from the Renaissance to the Eighteenth Century', *Journal of the Royal Society of Arts*, CXXI/5198 (1973), pp. 74–90 (p. 75).

31 Albrecht Dürer to Willibald Pirckheimer, 7 February 1506, in Jeffrey Ashcroft, *Albrecht Dürer: Documentary Biography*, 2 vols (New York, 2017), vol. 1, p. 139; Salvatore Settis, *Giorgione's Tempest* [1978], trans. Ellen Bianchini (Cambridge, 1990), p. 129.

3 Codifying Connoisseurship

1 On codification, Matteo Valleriani, 'The Epistemology of Practical Knowledge', in *The Structures of Practical Knowledge*, ed. Valleriani (Cham, 2017), pp. 1–19 (pp. 3–5).

2 Karel van Mander, *Het Schilderboek* (Haarlem, 1604). See Hessel Miedema, *Kunst, Kunstenaar en Kunstwerk bij Karel van Mander* (Alphen, 1981).

3 Denis Mahon, *Studies in Seicento Art and Theory* (London, 1947), p. 273; Flore César, 'Amateur, connaisseur, curieux', in *LexArt: les mots de la peinture*, ed. Michele-Caroline Heck (Paris, 2018), pp. 40–48.

4 Jeffrey Muller, *Rubens: The Artist as Collector* (Princeton, NJ, 1989). The correspondence with Carleton is most accessible in the English translation of Jacob Burckhardt's *Recollections of Rubens* (London, 1950), pp. 204–13.

5 Cennino Cennini, *The Craftsman's Handbook*, trans. Daniel Thompson (New York, 1960).

6 Rudolph Bell, *How to Do It: Guides to Good Living for Renaissance Italians* (Chicago, IL, 1999); Patricia Smith, *From Lived Experience to the Written Word* (Chicago, IL, 2022), pp. 117–37.
7 Giambattista Armerini, *De'veri precetti della pittura* [1587], ed. Marina Gorreri (Turin, 1998), p. 12.
8 Martin Warnke, 'Nah und Fern zum Bild', in *Forma et subtilitas*, ed. Wilhelm Schlink and Martin Sperlich (Berlin, 1986), pp. 190–97; Philip Sohm, *Pittoresco: Marco Boschini, His Critics and Their Critiques of Painterly Brushwork in Seventeenth- and Eighteenth-Century Italy* (Cambridge, 1991).
9 Giambattista Marino, *La galeria* [1619], ed. M. Pieri, 2 vols (Padua, 1979).
10 Nikolaus Pevsner, *Academies of Art Past and Present* (London, 1940), pp. 69, 90, 115, 119, 128.
11 Francis Haskell, 'The Market for Italian Art in the Seventeenth Century', *Past and Present*, XV (1959), pp. 48–56; Haskell, 'Art Exhibitions in Seventeenth Century Rome', *Studi Secenteschi*, I (1960), pp. 107–21; John Michael Montias, 'Art Dealers in the Seventeenth-Century Netherlands', *Simiolus*, XVIII/4 (1988), pp. 244–56; Christina Anderson, *The Flemish Merchant of Venice: Daniel Nijs and the Sale of the Gonzaga Art Collection* (New Haven, CT, 2015).
12 William Weber, *The Rise of Musical Classics in Eighteenth-Century England* (Oxford, 1992).
13 Clifford Brown, *Isabella d'Este and Lorenzo da Pavia* (Geneva, 1982), pp. 169–71.
14 Theodor Frimmel, ed., *Der Anonimo Morelliano* (Vienna, 1888), pp. 98, 104.
15 Bob van den Boogert, *Maria van Hongarije: konigin tussen keisers en kunstenaars* (Zwolle, 1993); Rosemary Mulcahy, *Philip II of Spain, Patron of the Arts* (Dublin, 2004), pp. 29–31.
16 Robert Evans, *Rudolf II and His World* (Oxford, 1973), pp. 162–95; Andrea Bubenik, *Reframing Albrecht Dürer: The Appropriation of Art, 1528–1700* (Farnham, 2013), pp. 57–62; Ulinka Rublack, *Dürer's Lost Masterpiece* (Oxford, 2023).
17 Hans Belting, *Likeness and Presence: A History of the Image before the Age of Art* [1990], trans. Edmund Jephcott (Chicago, IL, 1996); Antonia Putzger, *Kult und Kunst – Kopie und Original* (Berlin, 2021), introduction.
18 Patricia Allerton, 'The Second-Hand Trade in the Arts in Early Modern Italy', in *The Art Market in Italy*, ed. Marcello Fantoni, Louisa Matthew and Sara Matthews-Greco (Modena, 2003), pp. 301–2.
19 Bernard Aikema, *Pietro della Vecchia and the Heritage of the Renaissance in Venice* (Florence, 1990).
20 Maria Loh, 'New and Improved: Repetition as Originality in Italian Baroque Practice and Theory', *Art Bulletin*, LXXXVI (2004), pp. 477–504 (p. 498).
21 Friso Lammertse and Jaap van der Veen, *Uylenburgh and Son: Art and Commerce from Rembrandt to de Lairesse* (Zwolle, 2006).

22 Jeffrey Muller, 'Measures of Authenticity: The Detection of Copies in the Early Literature on Connoisseurship', *Studies in the History of Art*, xx (1989), pp. 141–51 (pp. 141–9).
23 Aikema, *Pietro della Vecchia*, p. 37; Loh, 'New and Improved', p. 490.
24 Claude Lorrain, *Liber veritatis*, ed. Michael Kitson (London, 1978).
25 Vincentius Placcius, *De scriptis et scriptoribus anonymis atque pseudonymis syntagma* (Hamburg, 1674).
26 Simone Savini Branca, *Il collezionismo veneziano del '600* (Padua, 1965), pp. 122, 125, 126, 141.
27 Marcus Burke and Peter Cherry, *Collections of Paintings in Madrid, 1601–1755* (Los Angeles, CA, 1995), no. 43.
28 Ibid., no. 115.
29 Ibid., p. 190 and no. 109.
30 J. Michael Montias, *Artists and Artisans in Delft* (Princeton, NJ, 1982); Michael North, *Art and Commerce* (1992), trans. North (New Haven, CT, 1997), pp. 118–28 (p. 121).
31 Elizabeth Honig, *Painting and the Market in Early Modern Antwerp* (New Haven, CT, 1998), pp. 200–202.
32 Muller, *Rubens*, pp. 94–146.
33 Paolo Coen, 'L'attribuzione e la stima di quadri nel contesto accademico capitolino: il ruolo di Giovanni Maria Morandi (1622–1717)', in *In Arcadia: saggi di storia delle arti per Elisa Debenedetti*, ed. M. Bevilacqua, M. C. Cola and M. Tabarrini (Rome, 2024), pp. 187–93.
34 Enriqueta Harris, 'Velázquez as Connoisseur', *Burlington Magazine*, CXXIV/952 (1982), pp. 436–40.
35 Paul Fréart de Chantelou, *Diary of the Cavaliere Bernini's Visit to France*, trans. Margery Corbett (Princeton, NJ, 1985), pp. 77, 79.
36 Ibid., pp. 288–9; Franco Mormando, 'Bernini's Painting Collection', *Journal of the History of Collections*, XXXIV/1 (2022), pp. 33–50 (p. 40).
37 Vicente Carducho, *Las Excelencias de la Pintura* [1633], cited in José Juan Pérez Preciado, 'Art Aficionados at Court', in *On Art and Painting: Vicente Carducho and Baroque Spain*, ed. Jean Andrews et al. (Chicago, IL, 2016), pp. 57–67.
38 Rudolf Wittkower, 'Inigo Jones, "Puritanissimo Fiero"', *Burlington Magazine*, XC/539 (1948), pp. 50–51.
39 Quoted in Francis Haskell, *The King's Pictures* (New Haven, CT, 2013), p. 11.
40 Quoted in Bernadette Py, 'Introduction', in *Everard Jabach Collectioneur* (Paris, 2001), pp. 11–22 (p. 11).
41 Quoted in Anna Tummers, 'By His Hand: The Paradox of Seventeenth-Century Connoisseurship', in *Art Market and Connoisseurship*, ed. Koenraad Jonckheere and Anna Tummers (Amsterdam, 2021), pp. 31–66 (pp. 31–2).
42 Chantelou, *Diary*, p. 251.
43 Rubens to Carleton, 12 May 1618, in Burckhardt, *Recollections*, p. 208. See Tummers, 'By His Hand'.
44 Giulio Mancini, *Considerationi sulla pittura*, ed. Adriana Marucchi, 2 vols (Rome, 1956–7), vol. 1, pp. 1, 120, 134.

45 Alberto Frigo, 'Can One Speak of Painting if One Cannot Hold a Brush? Giulio Mancini, Medicine and the Birth of the Connoisseur', *Journal of the History of Ideas*, LXXIII/3 (2012), pp. 417–36; Stefano Pierguidi, 'Giulio Mancini e la nascita della connoisseurship', *Zeitschrift für Kunstgeschichte*, LXXIX/1 (2016), pp. 63–71.

46 Barbara Agosti, ed., *Le postille di Padre Sebastiano Resta* (Vatican City, 2015).

47 Genevieve Warwick, *The Arts of Collecting* (Cambridge, 2000), p. 95. On the *dilettante*, see also pp. 98, 125, 171–2, 239.

48 Arthur Popham, 'Sebastiano Resta and His Collections', *Old Master Drawings*, XI (1936–7), pp. 1–19; Warwick, *The Arts of Collecting*, pp. 80–81; Angelo Mazza, 'Lelio Orsi e l'expertise collegiale di padre Sebastiano Resta' in *Federico Zeri: dietro l'immagine*, ed. Anna Ottani Cavina (Bologna, 2010), pp. 65–9.

49 Warwick, *Arts of Collecting*, p. 86.

50 Isabel Franconi, *Die Notizie de' professori del disegno von Filippo Baldinucci* (Berlin, 2021).

51 Edward Goldberg, *After Vasari* (Princeton, NJ, 1988), p. 59.

52 Filippo Baldinucci, *Opere*, 14 vols (Milan, 1808–12), vol. VI, pp. 461–85.

53 Mancini, *Considerationi*, p. 5; Frigo, 'Can One Speak of Painting'; Baldinucci, *Opere*, vol. VI, pp. 462–7.

54 Baldinucci, *Opere*, vol. VI, pp. 467–71.

55 Ibid., pp. 471–9.

56 Baldinucci, *Vocabolario Toscano dell'Arte del Disegno* (Florence, 1681); Philip Sohm, 'Filippo Baldinucci: Cataloguing Style and Language', in *Style in the Art Theory of Early Modern Italy* (Cambridge, 2001), pp. 165–84; see Oskar Bätschmann, 'Félibien's *Dictionnaire* von 1676 und Baldinuccis *Vocabolario* von 1681', in *Begrifflichkeit, Konzepte, Definitionen in der Kunstliteratur der Frühen Neuzeit*, ed. Elisabeth Oy-Marra, Marieke von Bernstorff and Henry Keasor (Wiesbaden, 2014), pp. 21–45.

57 Philip Sohm, *Pittoresco* (Cambridge, 1991), pp. 28–30.

58 Ibid., p. 19.

59 Mancini, *Considerationi*; Carlo Ginzburg, 'Clues and Scientific Method' [1978], trans. John and Ann Tedeschi, in *Myths, Emblems, Clues* (London, 1990), pp. 96–125. See Frances Gage, *Painting as Medicine in Early Modern Rome: Giulio Mancini and the Efficacy of Art* (Philadelphia, PA, 2016).

60 Giovanni Bonifacio, *L'arte de'cenni* [1616], ed. Silvia Gazzola (Treviso, 2018).

61 Camillo Baldi, *Trattato come de una lettera massiva si conoscano la natura e qualità dello scrittore* (Carpi, 1622). He was compared to Mancini and Morelli by Carlo Ginzburg in his famous essay on clues.

62 Duveen quoted in John Brewer, *The American Leonardo: A Twentieth-Century Tale of Obsession, Art and Money* (New York, 2007), p. 157.

63 Isaac Casaubon, *De rebus sacris* (Geneva, 1663); Anthony Grafton, 'Protestant versus Prophet: Isaac Casaubon on Hermes Trismegistus', *Journal of the Warburg and Courtauld Institutes*, XLVI (1983), pp. 78–93 (pp. 87–8). On parallels between the detection of forgeries in literature, art and antiquities, Tamara Griggs, 'Ancient Art and the Antiquarian', *Huntington Library Quarterly*, LXXIV/3 (2011), pp. 471–503 (pp. 475–6).

64 Richard Bentley, *A Dissertation upon the Epistles of Phalaris* [1697], ed. Wilhelm Wagner (Berlin, 1874), p. 51; Kristine Haugen, *Richard Bentley: Poetry and Enlightenment* (Cambridge, MA, 2011), pp. 110–23.

65 Daniel Papebroch, *Propylaeum antiquarium*, prefixed to *Acta Sanctorum*, tomus II (Antwerp, 1675); Maciej Dorna, 'Von der Hagiographie zur Diplomatik: Daniel Papebrochs Lehre zur Erkennung von frühmittelalterlichen Urkundenfälschungen', *Archiv für Diplomatik*, LX (2014), pp. 165–89. Gabriele Bickendorf noted analogies and links between philology and connoisseurship in 'Luigi Lanzis *Storia Pittorica della Italia* und das Entstehen der historich-kritischen Kunstgeschreibung', *Jahrbuch des Zentralinstituts für Kunstgeschichte München*, II (1986), pp. 231–72 (pp. 232–4).

66 Jean Mabillon, *De Re Diplomatica* (Paris, 1681), p. 2. See Maciej Dorna, *Mabillon und Andere: Die Anfänge der Diplomatik* [2014], German trans. Martin Faber (Wiesbaden, 2019).

67 Brian Cowan, 'An Open Elite: The Peculiarities of Connoisseurship in Early Modern England', *Modern Intellectual History*, I/2 (2004), pp. 151–183 (pp. 163–4).

68 Carlo Ginzburg, personal communication, 2024.

69 Abraham Bosse, *Sentiments sur la distinction des diverses manières de peinture, dessin et gravure et des originaux d'avec leurs copies* [1649] (reprint, Geneva, 1973); Marianne Le Blanc, 'Les *Sentiments* d'Abraham Bosse', in *Littérature et Peinture au temps de Le Sueur*, ed. Jean Serroy (Grenoble, 2003), pp. 35–42; Chambray and Sorbière quoted in Donald Posner, 'Concerning the "Mechanical" Parts of Painting and the Artistic Culture of Seventeenth-Century France', *Art Bulletin*, LXXV/4 (1993), pp. 583–98 (pp. 583–4, 587).

70 Antoine Schnapper, *Curieux du Grand Siècle* (Paris, 1994), pp. 202–5; Patrick Michel, *Mazarin: prince des collectionneurs* (Paris, 1999).

71 Comte de Brienne, *Mémoires*, ed. Paul Bonnefon, 3 vols (Paris, 1916), vol. I, pp. 3, 90.

72 Ibid., pp. 290–91, 303.

73 Schnapper, *Curieux*, pp. 243–6.

74 André Félibien, *Entretiens sur les vies et les ouvrages des plus excellens peintres* [1725 edn] (Farnborough, 1967).

75 Ibid., pp. 184–7, 276–8, 280–81.

76 Roger de Piles, *Conversations sur la connoissance de la peinture* (Paris, 1677), pp. 10–11, 19.

77 Roger de Piles, *Balance des peintres* (Paris, 1708).

78 'Por unas muy ruines pinturas con tanto gusto que antes sufrirán que digais mal de sus personas propias, que de sus pinturas': Felipe

de Guevara, *Comentarios de la pintura*, quoted in Francisco Javier Sánchez Cantón, *Fuentes literárias por la historia del arte* (Madrid, 1923), p. 156.

79 Vicente Carducho, *Diálogos de la pintura* [1633], new edn (Madrid, 1865); Jeremy Roe, 'Carducho and *pintura de borrones*', in *On Art and Painting: Vicente Carducho and Baroque Spain*, ed. Jean Andrews et al. (Cardiff, 2016), pp. 283–307.

80 See Jonathan Brown, 'Theory and Art in the Academy of Francisco Pacheco', in *Images and Ideas in Seventeenth-Century Spanish Painting* (Princeton, NJ, 1978), pp. 21–83.

81 Jonathan Brown and Richard L. Kagan, 'The Duke of Alcalà: His Collection and Its Evolution', *Art Bulletin*, LXIX/2 (1987), pp. 231–55 (p. 231). See Marcus Burke, 'A Golden Age of Collecting', in *Collections of Paintings in Madrid, 1601–1755*, ed. Burke and Peter Cherry (Los Angeles, CA, 1995), pp. 109–87; and Sara Schroth and Ronni Baer, eds, *El Greco to Velázquez: Art during the Reign of Philip III* (London, 2008).

82 Miguel Morán and Fernando Checa, *El coleccionismo en España* (Madrid, 1985), pp. 231–306; Jonathan Brown, *Kings and Connoisseurs: Collecting Art in Seventeenth Century Europe* (New Haven, CT, 1995), pp. 95–112; José Juan Pérez Preciado, 'Art Aficionados at Court', in *On Art and Painting*, ed. Andrews et. al., pp. 121–47 (p. 121).

83 Brown, *Kings*, p. 37.

84 Hopton quoted in Jonathan Brown, *Velázquez: Painter and Courtier* (New Haven, CT, 1986), p. 196; Palomino in Harris, 'Velázquez', p. 439.

85 Francis Haskell, *Patrons and Painters* (London, 1963), pp. 190–91; Morán and Checa, *Coleccionismo*, pp. 297–8.

86 Walter E. Houghton Jr, 'The English Virtuoso in the Seventeenth Century: Part I', *Journal of the History of Ideas*, III (1942), pp. 190–209; Claire Pace, 'Virtuoso to Connoisseur', *Seventeenth Century*, II/2 (1987), pp. 167–88.

87 David Howarth, *Lord Arundel and His Circle* (New Haven, CT, 1985); Francis Haskell, *The King's Pictures: The Formation and Dispersal of the Collections of Charles I and His Courtiers* (New Haven, CT, 2013), p. 207.

88 Mary Hervey, *The Life, Correspondence and Collections of Thomas Howard, Earl of Arundel* (Cambridge, 1921), pp. 267–80, 382–95 (p. 383); Charles Saumarez Smith, 'Rev. William Petty', https://charlessaumarezsmith.com, 13 April 2015.

89 Howarth, *Arundel*, p. 69.

90 David Howarth, 'The Patronage and Collecting of Aletheia, Countess of Arundel, 1606–54', *Journal of the History of Collections*, X/2 (1998), pp. 125–37; Elizabeth Chew, 'The Countess of Arundel and Tart Hall', in *The Evolution of English Collecting: Receptions of Italian Art in the Tudor and Stuart Periods*, ed. Edward Chaney (New Haven, CT, 2003), pp. 285–314.

91 Hervey, *Arundel*, pp. 404–5; see Bernadette Py, *Everard Jabach Collectioneur* (Paris, 2001), p. 11.

92 Lord Arundel to Petty, quoted in Hervey, *Arundel*, p. 395.
93 Quoted in Wittkower, 'Inigo Jones', pp. 50–51.
94 Ronald Lightbown, 'Van Dyck and the Purchase of Paintings for the English Court', *Burlington Magazine*, CXI (1969), pp. 418–21 (p. 420).
95 Haskell, *Collections of Charles I*, p. 203.
96 Oliver Millar, *The Age of Charles I: Painting in England, 1620–1649*, exh. cat., Tate Gallery (London, 1972); Brown, *Kings*.
97 Quoted in Wittkower, 'Inigo Jones', pp. 50–51; see John Newman, 'Jones, Inigo', ODNB, vol. XXX, pp. 527–38 (p. 536).
98 Paul Shakeshaft, 'The Letters of James, Third Marquis of Hamilton and Basil, Viscount Feilding', *Burlington Magazine*, CXXVIII/995 (1986), pp. 114–34 (p. 123). I have modernized the spelling of the letters.
99 Ibid., pp. 124–5.
100 Logan Pearsall Smith, *The Life and Letters of Sir Henry Wotton*, 2 vols (Oxford, 1907), vol. I, p. 49.
101 Rubens to Carleton in Burckhardt, *Recollections*, p. 208.
102 William Aglionby, *Painting Illustrated in Three Dialogues* (London, 1685), p. 4.
103 Ibid., pp. 21, 66, 88.
104 Michael Jaffé, 'Rubens as a Collector', *Journal of the Royal Society of Arts*, CXVII/5157 (1969), pp. 641–60; Muller, *Rubens*; Kristin Lohse Belkin and Fiona Healy, *A House of Art: Rubens as a Collector* (Antwerp, 2004).
105 Brown, *Kings*, pp. 151–3; Honig, *Painting and the Market*, pp. 196–210.
106 Anne-Marie Logan, *The 'Cabinet' of the Brothers Gerard and Jan Reynst* (Amsterdam, 1979), pp. 33, 40, 98.
107 Montias, 'Art Dealers', pp. 244–56; North, *Art and Commerce*.
108 North, *Art and Commerce*, pp. 92–5; Lammertse and Van der Veen, *Uylenburgh and Son*; on Constantijn; Otto Kurz, 'Early Art Forgeries from the Renaissance to the Eighteenth Century', *Journal of the Royal Society of Arts*, CXXI/5198 (1973), pp. 74–90 (p. 84).
109 J. Michael Montias, *Art at Auction in 17th Century Amsterdam* (Amsterdam, 2002), p. 28.
110 Walter Melion, *Shaping the Netherlandish Canon: Karel van Mander's 'Schilder-Boeck'* (Chicago, IL, 1991).
111 Ibid., p. 5.
112 Miedema, *Kunst*, pp. 120–22, 169–70; Paul Taylor, 'The Concept of *Houding* in Dutch Art Theory', *Journal of the Warburg and Courtauld Institutes*, LV/1 (1992), pp. 210–32.
113 Michèle-Caroline Heck, *Théorie et pratique de la peinture: Sandrart et la Teutsche Academie* (Paris, 2006), pp. 130, 354.
114 Frigo, 'Can One Speak of Painting'.

4 The Age of the Amateurs

1 Neil McKendrick, John Brewer and J. H. Plumb, *The Birth of a Consumer Society* (London, 1983). See Roman Sandgruber, *Die Anfänge der Konsumgesellschaft* (Vienna, 1982), and Daniel Roche, *A History of Everyday Things* [1997], trans. Brian Pearce (Cambridge, 2000).

2 Horace Walpole, *Anecdotes of Painting* [1762], quoted in Paul Baines, *The House of Forgery in Eighteenth-Century Britain* (Farnham, 1999), p. 165.

3 William Whitley, *Thomas Gainsborough* (London, 1915), p. 279; Kristin Campbell, '"Such Is Picture Dealing": Noel Joseph Desenfans and the Perils of Purchasing in 18th-Century London', in *Inganno: The Art of Deception*, ed. Sharon Gregory and Sally Ann Hickson (Farnham, 2012), pp. 187–98 (pp. 193–4).

4 Irene Haberland, *Jonathan Richardson: Die Begründung der Kunstkennerschaft* (Münster, 1993); Donatella Livia Sparti, 'Novità su Giulio Mancini', *Mitteilungen des Kunsthistorischen Institutes in Florenz*, LII/1 (2008), pp. 53–72; Pascal Griener, 'Le connoisseurship, science et art de réussir', in *La République de l'oeil: l'expérience de l'art au siècle des lumières* (Paris, 2010), pp. 91–115.

5 Lisa Sogh, 'The Varied Role of the Amateur', *Nuncius*, XXXI (2016), pp. 489–98, the introduction to a special issue on this theme. See Flore César, 'Amateur, connaisseur, curieux', in *LexArt: les mots de la peinture*, ed. Michèle-Caroline Heck (Montpellier, 2018), pp. 41–7.

6 Ernst Cassirer, *Philosophy of the Enlightenment* [1932], trans. Fritz Koellin and James Pettegrove (Princeton, NJ, 1951), pp. 275–360.

7 Margaret Stuffmann, 'Les tableaux de la collection de Pierre Crozat', *Gazette des Beaux Arts*, CX (1968), pp. 11–144; Cordélia Hattori, 'The Drawings Collection of Pierre Crozat (1665–1740)', in *Collecting Prints and Drawings in Europe, c. 1500–1750*, ed. Christopher Baker, Caroline Elam and Genevieve Warwick (London, 2003), pp. 173–81.

8 Francis Haskell, *The Painful Birth of the Art Book* (London, 1987), pp. 42–55; Benedict Leca, 'An Art Book and Its Viewers: The "Recueil Crozat" and the Uses of Reproductive Engraving', *Eighteenth-Century Studies*, XXXVIII/4 (2005), pp. 623–49.

9 Quoted in JoLynn Edwards, *Alexandre-Joseph Paillet, expert et marchand de tableaux à la fin du 18e siècle* (Paris, 1996), p. 103.

10 Louis Olivier, 'The Other Bachaumont', *Studies on Voltaire*, CLXI (1976), pp. 219–44 (p. 243).

11 Nicolas Kronk and Kris Peeters, eds, *Le Comte de Caylus* (Amsterdam, 2004); Joachim Rees, *Die Kultur des Amateurs: Studien zu Caylus* (Weimar, 2006); Tamara Griggs, 'Ancient Art and the Antiquarian: The Forgery of Giuseppe Guerra, 1755–1765', *Huntingdon Library Quarterly*, LXXIV/3 (2011), pp. 471–503.

12 Haskell, *Painful Birth*; Eva Manikowska, 'The *Galeriewerk* and the Self-Fashioning of Artists at the Dresden Court', in *Art and Its Geographies*, ed. Ingrid Vermeulen (Amsterdam, 2024), pp. 147–62.

13 Ibid., p. 20.
14 Patrick Michel, *Le commerce du tableau à Paris dans la seconde moitié du XVIIIe siècle* (Villeneuve d'Ascq, 2007). See Paolo Coen, 'The Art Market in Rome in the 18th Century', in *The Art Market in Rome in the Eighteenth Century*, ed. Coen (Leiden, 2019), pp. 1–27.
15 Kristel Smentek, *Mariette and the Science of the Connoisseur in Eighteenth-Century Europe* (Farnham, 2014); Valerie Kobi, *Dans l'oeil du connoisseur: Pierre-Jean Mariette (1694–1774) et la construction des savoirs en histoire de l'art* (Rennes, 2018).
16 Kobi, *Oeil*, p. 79.
17 Quoted in Smentek, *Mariette*, p. 98.
18 Ibid., pp. 144–54.
19 Ibid., p. 94; Leca, 'Art Book', p. 52n.
20 Kate Steinitz, *Pierre-Jean Mariette and the Comte de Caylus and their Concept of Leonardo da Vinci* (Los Angeles, CA, 1974), p. 13.
21 Quoted in Smentek, *Mariette*, pp. 116–17.
22 Mariette, *Lettere a Giovanni Gaetano Bottari* (Rome, 2022), pp. 426–7.
23 Kobi, *Oeil*, p. 61.
24 Haskell, *Painful Birth*, pp. 46–7.
25 Mariette, *Traité des pierres gravées* (Paris, 1750), pp. 48–9; Mariette, *Lettere*, p. 548.
26 Smentek, *Mariette*; Leca, 'Art Book', n.50.
27 Mariette, 'La vie et les ouvrages de Mellan', in Anatole de Montaiglon, *Catalogue de l'oeuvre de Claude Mellan* (Abbeville, 1856), pp. 15–76 (pp. 15, 20, 23, 27–8).
28 Michel, *Commerce du tableau*.
29 Andrew McClellan, 'Watteau's Dealer: Gersaint and the Marketing of Art in Eighteenth-Century Paris', *Art Bulletin*, LXXVIII/3 (1996), pp. 439–53; Guillaume Glorieux, *À l'enseigne de Gersaint* (Seyssel, 2002). On sale catalogues, Krzysztof Pomian, *Collectors and Curiosities* [1987], trans. Elizabeth Wiles-Portier (Cambridge, 1990), pp. 139–68.
30 François Marandet, 'Pierre Rémy (1715–97)', *Apollo*, CLVIII (2003), pp. 32–42 (p. 39); Patrick Michel, 'Pierre Rémy', in *Mélanges Pierre Rosenberg* (Paris, 2001), pp. 328–36; Michel, *Commerce du tableau*, pp. 229–40.
31 Edwards, *Paillet*, p. 164.
32 Francis Haskell, *Rediscoveries in Art: Some Aspects of Taste, Fashion and Collecting in England and France* (Oxford, 1976), pp. 25–37 (pp. 25, 32).
33 Antoine-Joseph Pernety, 'Touche', in *Dictionnaire portatif de peinture* (Paris, 1757). See Christian Michel, 'Manière, goût, faire, style: les mutations du vocabulaire de la critique d'art en France au 18e siècle', in *Rhétorique et discours critiques* (Paris, 1989), pp. 153–9; Pascal Griener and Cecilia Hurley, 'Une norme en transformation: la systématique du vocabulaire artistique au XVIIIe siècle', in *L'art et les normes sociales au XVIIIe siècle*, ed. Thomas Gaehtgens et al. (Paris, 2001), pp. 3–14.
34 Michel, *Commerce du tableau*, p. 243. See Linda Whiteley, 'The Language of Sale Catalogues, 1750–1820', in *Collections et marché*

d'art en France, 1789–1848, ed. Monica Preti-Hamard and Philippe Sénéchal (Rennes, 2005), pp. 35–45.

35 A vivid example in Gita May, *Diderot et Baudelaire, critiques d'art* (Geneva, 1957), p. 112. See Else Marie Bukdahl, *Diderot, critique d'art* (Copenhagen, 1980–82), vol. 1, pp. 300ff.

36 Anita Brookner, *The Genius of the Future: Essays in French Art Criticism* (Ithaca, NY, 1971), p. 15; May, *Diderot*, p. 9.

37 Quoted in May, *Diderot*, p. 159.

38 Brian Cowan, 'An Open Elite: The Peculiarities of Connoisseurship in Early Modern England', *Modern Intellectual History*, 1/2 (2004), pp. 151–83 (p. 151) (in Bernard Mandeville's *Fable of the Bees*); Iain Pears, *The Discovery of Painting: The Growth of Interest in the Arts in England, 1680–1768* (New Haven, CT, 1988).

39 Quoted in Cowan, 'Open Elite', p. 163.

40 David Ormrod, 'Dealers, Collectors and Connoisseurship in Seventeenth and Eighteenth Century London', in *Kunstsammeln und bürgerlicher Geschmack im 18. Jahrhundert*, ed. Michael North (Cologne and Weimar, 2002), pp. 15–23.

41 Jonathan Richardson, *Two Discourses* (London, 1719), part 2, pp. 7, 64.

42 John Pope-Hennessy, 'Connoisseurship', in *Study and Criticism of Italian Sculpture* (Princeton, NJ, 1980), vol. 1, pp. 11–38 (p. 11).

43 Richardson, *Two Discourses*, part 2, pp. 27–30, 130.

44 Ibid., p. 54.

45 Carol Gibson-Wood, *Jonathan Richardson: Art Theorist of the English Enlightenment* (New Haven, CT, 2000), pp. 179, 187.

46 Ibid., p. 192.

47 Richardson, *Two Discourses*, part 1, pp. 104–5, 117, 125, 140.

48 Cinzia Maria Sicca, ed., *John Talman: An Early 18th-Century Connoisseur* (New Haven, CT, 2008).

49 Charles Collins Baker and Muriel Baker, *The Life and Circumstances of James Brydges Duke of Chandos* (Oxford, 1949), pp. 69–92 (p. 82).

50 Susan Jenkins, *Portrait of a Patron: The Patronage and Collecting of James Brydges, 1st Duke of Chandos, 1674–1744* (Aldershot, 2007), pp. 127–8, 131; Aaron Graham, 'Connoisseurship, Consumption, Company and James Brydges, First Duke of Chandos, 1705–13', *Huntington Library Quarterly*, LXXX/4 (2017), pp. 539–77.

51 J. H. Plumb, *Robert Walpole*, 2 vols (London, 1958–60), vol. 1, pp. 2, 85–7.

52 Louise Lippincott, *Selling Art in Georgian London: The Rise of Arthur Pond* (New Haven, CT, 1983), pp. 22–4, 103–4, 108.

53 John Brewer, *The Pleasures of the Imagination: English Culture in the Eighteenth Century* (Chicago, IL, 1997), p. 266; Michael Clarke and Nicholas Penny, eds, *The Arrogant Connoisseur* (Manchester, 1982).

54 Frank Messman, 'Richard Payne Knight and the Elgin Marbles Controversy', *British Journal of Aesthetics*, XIII/1 (1973), pp. 69–75.

55 Claudia Cremer, *Hagedorns Geschmack: Studien zu Kunstkennerschaft in Deutschland im 18. Jht* (Bonn, 1989); Griener, *La République de l'oeil*, pp. 107–15.

56 Alex Potts, *Flesh and the Ideal: Winckelmann and the Origins of Art History* (New Haven, CT, 1994); Elisabeth Décultot, *Johann Joachim Winckelmann: enquête sur la genèse de l'histoire de l'art* (Paris, 2000); Édouard Pommier, *Winckelmann, inventeur de l'histoire de l'art* (Paris, 2003); Katherine Harloe, *Winckelmann and the Invention of Antiquity* (Oxford, 2013).
57 Adolf Heinrich Borbein, 'Winckelmann und die klassische Archäologie', in *Johann Joachim Winckelmann, 1717–1768*, ed. Thomas Gaehtgens (Hamburg, 1986), pp. 289–99.
58 Krzysztof Pomian, 'Mariette et Winckelmann', *Revue germanique internationale*, XIII (2000–2001), pp. 11–38; Pommier, *Winckelmann*, pp. 119, 157; Harloe, *Winckelmann*, pp. 62, 67–8, 72–4.
59 Quoted and translated in Griggs, 'Ancient Art', p. 492.
60 Winckelmann, *Briefe*, ed. Walther Rehm, 4 vols (Berlin, 1957), vol. I, pp. 4, 266.
61 Thomas Pelzel, 'Winckelmann, Mengs and Casanova', *Art Bulletin*, LIV/3 (1972), pp. 300–315.
62 Patrick Michel, *Peinture et plaisir: les goûts picturaux des collectionneurs parisiens au XVIIIe siècle* (Rennes, 2010), p. 19.
63 Rees, *Kultur des Amateurs*; Charlotte Guichard, *Les amateurs d'art à Paris au XVIIIe siècle* (Seyssel, 2008).
64 Marc-Antoine Laugier, *Manière de juger les oeuvres de peinture* [1771] (Geneva, 1972).
65 Renée Loche, 'Quand François Tronchin visitait les cabinets de peinture d'Aix-en-Provence', in *Mélanges Marcel Roethlisberger* (Milan, 2007), pp. 201–10.
66 On Adriana, see Gerrit Verhoeven, 'Mastering the Connoisseurs' Eye: Paintings, Criticism and the Canon in Dutch Travel Culture, 1600–1750', *Eighteenth Century Studies*, XLVI/1 (2012), pp. 29–56 (p. 36). More French examples in Michel, *Peinture et plaisir*, pp. 102–3.
67 Verhoeven, 'Mastering the Connoisseurs' Eye', pp. 47–8.
68 Roger de Piles, *Balance des peintres* (Paris, 1708), pp. 26–7.
69 Michel, *Peinture et plaisir*, pp. 124, 130, 372.
70 Thomas Crow, *Painters and Public Life in Eighteenth-Century Paris* (New Haven, CT, 1985).
71 Oliver Goldsmith, *The Citizen of the World* [1760], quoted in Pears, *Discovery of Painting*, p. 197.
72 Pears, *Discovery of Painting*, pp. 173–5, 198; Brewer, *Pleasures*, pp. 218–21.
73 Brewer, *Pleasures*, pp. 240–48.
74 Pears, *Discovery of Painting*, p. 93; Brewer, *Pleasures*, p. 223.
75 Jürgen Habermas, *The Structural Transformation of the Public Sphere* [1962], trans. Thomas Burger (Cambridge, MA, 1989); James Van Horn Melton, *The Rise of the Public in Enlightenment Europe* (Cambridge, 2001).
76 Quoted in Crow, *Painters and Public Life*, p. 10.
77 Laugier, *Manière de bien juger*, preface.
78 Richardson, *Two Discourses*, part 1, p. 40; part 2, p. 143.

79 Quoted in Philip Hook, *Breakfast at Sotheby's: An A–Z of the Art World* (London, 2014), p. 302.
80 Pears, *Discovery*, pp. 97, 195.
81 Harry Mount, 'The Monkey with the Magnifying Glass: Constructions of the Connoisseur in Eighteenth-Century Britain', *Oxford Art Journal*, XXIX/2 (2006), pp. 167–83.
82 Ibid., p. 180.

5 The Age of the Professionals

1 Donata Levi, 'La professionalizzazione della figura dell'esperto in Inghilterra e in Francia', in *Collections et marché de l'art en France, 1789–1848*, ed. Monica Preti-Hamard and Philippe Sénéchal (Rennes, 2005), pp. 57–72.
2 Antoinette Friedenthal, 'John Smith's Rembrandt Research Project', in *Connoisseurship and the Knowledge of Art*, ed. Perry Chapman, Thijs Weststeijn and Dulcia Meyers (Leiden, 2019), pp. 212–47 (p. 223).
3 Harold Perkin, *The Rise of Professional Society* (London, 1989).
4 Udo Kultermann, *History of Art History* [1966], Eng. trans. (anon.) (New York, 1993), p. 87.
5 Karl Friedrich Rumohr, *Über die Antike Gruppe Castor und Pollux oder von dem Begriffe der Idealität im Kunstwerken* (Hamburg, 1812).
6 Rumohr, 'Behandlung italienischer Kunstgeschichte', *Kunstblatt*, XXXIX (1820), quoted in Gabriel Bickendorf, *Der Beginn der Kunstgeschichtsschhreibung unter dem Paradigma Geschichte* (Worms, 1985), p. 131; Rumohr, *Italienische Forschungen* [1827–31], ed. Julius Schlosser (Frankfurt, 1920), p. 225; Rumohr, *Über Raphael und sein Verhältniss zu den Zeitgenossen* (Berlin, 1831). See Bickendorf, 'Die Tradition der Kennerschaft von Lanzi über Rumohr und Waagen zu Morelli', in *Giovanni Morelli e la cultura dei conoscitori*, ed. Giovanni Agosti, Maria Elisabetta Manca and Matteo Panzeri (Bergamo, 1993), vol. I, pp. 25–48.
7 Leopold von Ranke, 'Critique of Modern Historians', appended to his *History of the Latin and Germanic Nations* [1824], trans. Philip Ashworth (London, 1887).
8 David Alan Brown, *Leonardo da Vinci: Origins of a Genius* (New Haven, CT, 1998), p. 168.
9 Chiara Battezzati, 'Carl Friedrich von Rumohr', in *I conoscitori tedeschi tra otto e novecento*, ed. Francesco Caglioti, Andrea de Marchi and Alessandro Nova (Milan, 2018), pp. 5–26. See Pia Müller-Tamm, *Rumohrs 'Haushalt der Kunst'* (Hildesheim, 1991); Enrica Yvonne Dilk, *Ein 'praktischer Aesthetiker': Studien zum Leben und Werk Carl Friedrich Rumohrs* (Hildesheim, 2000); Enrica Yvonne Dilk, *Das 'verzweifelte allerhand Talent': Neue Studien zu Carl Friedrich Rumohr* (Hildesheim, 2010).
10 Johann David Passavant, *Raphael of Urbino and His Father Giovanni Santi* [1839], Eng. trans. (anon.) (London, 1872).

11 Adolph Cornill, *Johann David Passavant: Ein Lebensbild* (Frankfurt, 1864–5); Alfonso Litta and Miriam Laffranchi, 'Johan David Passavant', in *Conoscitori tedeschi*, ed. Caglioti, de Marchi and Nova, pp. 27–38; Corina Meyer, '"To see once again the glorious picture by Moretto before it is forever lost for Rome": How an Artist's Position in the Canon of Taste Was Enhanced in the Nineteenth Century', in *Art Markets, Agents and Collectors*, ed. Susan Bracken and Adriana Turpin (London, 2021), pp. 185–200.

12 Gustav Waagen, *Über Hubert und Jan van Eyck* (Breslau, 1822). See Bickendorf, *Beginn*, pp. 129–35, 143–8; Waagen, 'Gustav Friedrich Waagen und der Historismus in der Kunstgeschichte', *Jahrbuch der Berliner Museen*, XXXVII (1995), pp. 23–32.

13 Giles Waterfield and Florian Illies, 'Waagen in England', *Jahrbuch der Berliner Museen*, XXXVII (1995), pp. 47–59.

14 Elizabeth Pergam, *The Manchester Art Treasures Exhibition of 1857* (Farnham, 2011).

15 Gustav Waagen, *Galleries and Cabinets of Art in Great Britain* (London, 1857), pp. 394–5, 269, 358–9.

16 Brown, *Leonardo*, p. 169.

17 Waagen, *Galleries*. See David Ekserdjian, 'Gustav Friedrich Waagen', in *Conoscitori tedeschi*, ed. Caglioti, de Marchi and Nova, pp. 52–60 (p. 55).

18 Luigi Lanzi, *Reale Galleria di Firenze accresciuta e reordinata* [1782] (Florence, 1982), pp. 67ff; Christian von Mechel, *Verzeichniss der Gemälde der kaiserlich königlichen Bilder Gallerie in Wien* (Vienna, 1783).

19 Gabriele Bickendorf, 'Luigi Lanzis *Storia Pittorica della Italia* und das Entstehen der historich-kritischen Kunstgeschreibung', *Jahrbuch des Zentralinstituts für Kunstgeschichte München*, II (1986), pp. 231–72.

20 Friedenthal, 'John Smith's Rembrandt Research Project', p. 218.

21 Michael Hunter, *John Aubrey and the Realm of Learning* (London, 1975), pp. 156–63.

22 Friedrich Meinecke, *Historism: The Rise of a New Historical Outlook* [1959], trans. J. E. Anderson (London, 1972), p. 12; Otto Gerhard Oexle, 'Aufklärung und Historismus: Zur Geschichtswissenschaft in Göttingen um 1800', in *Johann Dominicus Fiorillo*, ed. Antje Middeldorf Kosegarten (Göttingen, 1997), pp. 28–56; Gabriele Bickendorf, 'Des Mauristes à l'école berlinoise', in *Histoire de l'histoire de l'art*, ed. Édouard Pommier, 3 vols (Paris, 1997), vol. II, pp. 141–76; Jörg Rüsen, 'La floraison des sciences historiques en Allemagne: historiser l'art et esthétiser l'histoire', *Histoire de l'histoire de l'art*, ed. Édouard Pommier, pp. 177–94. See Stephen Toulmin and June Goodfield, *The Discovery of Time* (London, 1965); Michel Foucault, *The Order of Things* [1966], trans. Alan Sheridan (London, 1970), chapter 7.

23 Philippe Lejeune, *Le pacte autobiographique* (Paris, 1971). See Peter Burke, 'Historicizing the Self, 1770–1830', in *Controlling Time and Shaping the Self: Developments in Autobiographical Writing since the*

Sixteenth Century, ed. Ariel Baggerman, Rudolf Dekker and Michael Mascuch (Leiden, 2011), pp. 13–32.

24 Denis Mahon, *Studies in Seicento Art and Theory* (London, 1947), p. 1.

25 Christian Thomsen, *Guide to Northern Archaeology* [1836], trans. Francis Ellesmere (London, 1848). See Bo Gräslund, *The Birth of Prehistoric Chronology* (Cambridge, 1987), pp. 17–30; Bruce Trigger, *A History of Archaeological Thought* (Cambridge, 2006), pp. 121–9.

26 Jaś Elsner, 'Significant Details: Systems, Certainties and the Art-Historian as Detective', *Antiquity*, LXIV (1990), pp. 950–52; Richard Neer, 'Beazley and the Language of Connoisseurship', *Hephaistos*, XV (1997), pp. 7–30; Richard Neer, 'Connoisseurship and the Stakes of Style', *Critical Inquiry*, XXXII/1 (Autumn 2005), pp. 1–26.

27 John Smith, *A Catalogue Raisonné*, vol. VII (Berlin, 1836), quoted in Friedenthal, 'John Smith's Rembrandt Research Project'.

28 Bylvan Gaskell, 'Tradesmen as Scholars', in *Art History and Its Institutions*, ed. Elizabeth Mansfield (London, 2002), pp. 146–62.

29 Quoted in Jeremy Melius, 'Connoisseurship, Painting and Personhood', *Art History*, XXXIV/2 (2011), pp. 288–309 (p. 298).

30 Bichendorf, *Beginn*, pp. 121–9. On 'the primacy', Jeroen Boomgaard and Robert Scheller, 'A Delicate Balance: A Brief Survey of Rembrandt Criticism', in *Rembrandt: The Master and His Workshop*, ed. Christopher Brown, Jan Kelch and Pieter van Thiel (New Haven, CT, 1991), pp. 106–23 (p. 113); Julie Sheldon, 'Lady Eastlake and the Characteristics of the Old Masters', *Interdisciplinary Studies in the Long Nineteenth Century*, XXVIII (2019), pp. 1–12 (p. 10).

31 Waagen's letter is quoted in Wietse De Boer, 'Expressions of the Self in Burckhardt's Renaissance', in *A Renaissance Reclaimed: Jacob Burckhardt's Civilization of the Renaissance in Italy Reconsidered*, ed. Stefan Bauer and Simon Ditchfield (Oxford, 2022), pp. 120–41 (p. 121).

32 Charles Clément, *Michel-Ange, Léonard de Vinci, Raphael* (Paris, 1861); Ernst Cassirer, *The Philosophy of the Enlightenment* [1932], trans. Fritz Koellin and James Pettegrove (Princeton, NJ, 1951), pp. 312–21.

33 Andrea Wulf, *Magnificent Rebels: The First Romantics and the Invention of the Self* (London, 2022), pp. 28, 48, 132, 142, 168, 180, 227, 242, 250, 271, 333–5, 351.

34 Virginia Cox, 'The Performance of Identity in Renaissance Italy', in *A Renaissance Reclaimed*, pp. 99–119 (p. 100).

35 William Buchanan, *Memoirs of Painting, with a Chronological History of the Importation of Pictures of Great Masters into England since the French Revolution* (London, 1824).

36 Pamela Fletcher and Anne Helmreich, eds, *The Rise of the Modern Art Market in London, 1850–1939* (Manchester, 2011); Thomas M. Bayer and John R. Page, *The Development of the Art Market in England: Money as Muse, 1730–1900* (London, 2011); Susanna Avery-Quash and Christian Huemer, eds, *London and the Emergence of a European Art Market, 1780–1920* (London, 2019).

37 Oliver Garnett, 'Agnew, Thomas and Sons', *DA*, vol. I, pp. 453–4; Dennis Farr, 'Agnew Family', *ODNB*, vol. I, pp. 461–2; Barbara

Pezzini, 'Agnews: From Modern Art to Old Masters', in *Old Masters Worldwide*, ed. Susanna Avery-Quash and Barbara Pezzini (London, 2019), pp. 117–30.

38 Henry Marillier, *Christie's, 1766–1925* (London, 1926).

39 Donald Garstang, *Art, Commerce, Scholarship: A Window onto the Art World: Colnaghi, 1760 to 1984* (London, 1984); Jeremy Howard, *Colnaghi* (London, 2010).

40 Francis Haskell, *Rediscoveries in Art: Some Aspects of Taste, Fashion and Collecting in England and France* (Oxford, 1976), p. 98; Simon Turner, 'Samuel Woodburn', *Print Quarterly*, XX/2 (2003), pp. 131–44 (p. 131).

41 Gaskell, 'Tradesmen as Scholars', pp. 153, 156.

42 Antoinette Friedenthal, 'John Smith and the "Stigma of PICTURE DEALER"', *Journal of Art Historiography*, IX/9 (2013), pp. 1–20 (p. 10).

43 Jaynie Anderson, ed., *Collecting, Connoisseurship and the Art Market in Risorgimento Italy: Giovanni Morelli's Letters to G. Melli and P. Zavaritt* (Venice, 1999), pp. 5–61 (p. 40). See Peter Burke, '"Buying Half of Italy": The Drain Abroad of Works of Art, 1650–1850', in *'Esportare opere, plasmare uno stile': il fenomeno delle esportazioni di opere d'arte dall'Italia nel lungo period*, ed. Paolo Coen (Leiden, forthcoming).

44 Patrizia Cappellini, 'Trading Old Masters in Florence, 1890–1914', *Journal of the History of Collections*, XXXI/2 (2019), pp. 363–71; Rosanna Pavoni, ed., *Reviving the Renaissance: The Use and Abuse of the Past in Nineteenth-Century Italian Art and Decoration* (Cambridge, 1997); Anita Moskowitz, *Forging Authenticity: Bastianini and the Neo-Renaissance in Nineteenth-Century Florence* (Florence, 2013).

45 Lynn Catterson, 'Duped or Duplicitous? Bode, Bardini and the Many Madonnas of South Kensington', *Journal of the History of Collections*, XXXIII/1 (2021), pp. 71–92 (p. 71); Joanna Smalcerz, 'A Lesson in Loopholes: Stefano Bardini and the Export of the Botticelli Frescoes from Villa Lemmi', in *Dealing Art on Both Sides of the Atlantic, 1860–1940*, ed. Lynn Catterson (Leiden, 2017), pp. 291–309.

46 Cynthia Saltzman, *Old Masters, New World: America's Raid on Europe's Great Pictures* (New York, 2008).

47 Natalia Semenova, *The Collector: The Story of Sergei Shchukin and His Lost Masterpieces* (New Haven, CT, 2018), pp. 87, 103.

48 Andrew McClellan, *Inventing the Louvre: Art, Politics and the Origins of the Modern Museum in Eighteenth-Century Paris* (Berkeley, CA, 1999); James Sheehan, *Museums in the German Art World from the End of the Old Regime to the Rise of Modernism* (Oxford, 2000).

49 Otto Mündler, *Essai d'une analyse critique de la notice des tableaux italiens du Musée du Louvre* (Paris, 1850). See Jaynie Anderson, 'Otto Mündler and His Travel Diary', *Walpole Society*, LI (1985), pp. 7–59 (p. 11).

50 The *Report* is reprinted in Christopher Hodkinson, *A Question of Attribution: Art Connoisseurship in the Nineteenth Century* (Wrightington, 2014), pp. 295–307.

51 *Report*, pp. 295, 299.
52 Charles Eastlake, 'How to Observe', in *Contributions to the History of the Fine Arts*, Second Series (London, 1870), pp. 199–300. See Lucy Hartley, 'How to Observe: Charles Eastlake and a New Professionalism for the Arts', *Journal of Art Historiography*, XVIII (2018) pp. 261–81.
53 Anderson, 'Otto Mündler'.
54 David Robertson, *Charles Eastlake and the Victorian Art World* (Princeton, NJ, 1978).
55 Susanna Avery Quash and Julie Sheldon, *Art for the Nation: The Eastlakes and the Victorian Art World* (London, 2011), p. 152.
56 Ibid., p. 154.
57 Wilhelm Bode, *Italienische Bildhauer der Renaissance* (Berlin, 1887), preface.
58 James David Draper, 'Wilhelm von Bode, attributeur', *Revue de l'art*, XLII (1978/4), pp. 32–6.
59 Catherine Scallen, 'Wilhelm Bode's and Giovanni Morelli's Debates about Connoisseurship', in *Rembrandt, Reputation and the Practice of Connoisseurship* (Amsterdam, 2004), pp. 87–102 (p. 51).
60 Manfred Ohlsen, *Wilhelm von Bode: Zwischen Kaisermacht und Kunsttempel* (Berlin, 1995).
61 Esmée Quodbach, 'Wilhelm Bode and Johannes Vermeer: Creating a Taste and a Market', in *Wilhelm Bode and the Art Market*, ed. Joanna Smalcerz (Leiden, 2023), pp. 67–96.
62 Rolf Kultzen, 'Otto Mündler als Freunde und Förderer des junge Bode', *Beiheft Jahrbuch der Berliner Museen*, XXXVIII (1996), pp. 49–55 (p. 53).
63 Joseph Crowe and Giovanni Battista Cavalcaselle, *Raphael* (London, 1885), p. 322n.
64 Wilhelm von Bode, *Mein Leben*, ed. Thomas Gaehtgens, 2 vols (Berlin, 1997), vol. I, p. 36. See Wilheml von Bode, 'Karl Eduard von Liphart', XIV (1891), pp. 448–50.
65 Kultzen, 'Otto Mündler', p. 54; Max Friedländer in *Wilhelm Bode zum Gedächtnis* (Berlin, 1929); John Pope-Hennessy, *Learning to Look* (London, 1991), p. 44.
66 Bode, *Leben*, p. 279.
67 Simon Elson, *Der Kunstkenner: Max J. Friedländer* (Cologne, 2016); Max Friedländer, *Von Kunst und Kennerschaft* (Oxford, 1946), p. 26.
68 Francesco Caglioti, 'Wilhelm Bode', in *Conoscitori tedeschi*, ed. Caglioti, de Marchi and Nova, pp. 73–86.
69 Jan Kelch, ed., *Bilder in Blickpunkt: Der Mann mit dem Goldhelm* (Berlin, 1986).
70 Catterson, 'Duped or Duplicitous?', p. 84.
71 Jonathan Lopez, *The Man Who Made Vermeers* (Boston, MA, 2008), pp. 23, 64–71.
72 Bode, *Leben*, pp. 356–63; Ohlsen, *Bode*, pp. 238–50; Ulrike Wolff-Thomsen, *Die Wachsbüste einer Flora und das System Wilhelm Bode* (Kiel, 2006).

73 Quoted in Ohlsen, *Bode*, p. 261.
74 David Alan Brown, 'Bode and Berenson', *Jahrbuch der Berliner Museen*, XXXVIII (1996), pp. 101–6 (p. 104).
75 Bode, *Leben*, p. 192; Scallen, 'Wilhelm Bode's and Giovanni Morelli's Debates', pp. 73–84.
76 Quoted in Gary Schwartz, 'Rembrandt Research after the Age of Connoisseurship', *Annals of Scholarship*, X (1993), pp. 313–35 (pp. 318–19).
77 Scallen, *Rembrandt, Reputation*, p. 271. See Michael Ripps, 'A Faustian Bargain? Charles Sedelmeyer, Wilhelm Bode and the Expansion of Rembrandt's Painted Corpus', in *The Challenge of the Object*, ed. Ulrich Grossmann and Petra Krutisch (Nuremberg, 2013), pp. 745–7; Joanna Smalcerz, 'The Entanglement of Art Historical Scholarship, Connoisseurship and the Art Trade in the Late Nineteenth Century', in *Bode*, ed. Smalcerz, pp. 1–15; Catherine Scallen, 'Authority and Expertise in the Old Master Market: Bode and Duveen', in *Old Masters Worldwide*, ed. Avery-Quash and Pezzini, pp. 147–60.
78 Alessandro Conti, *History of the Restoration and Conservation of Works of Art* [1988], trans. Helen Glanville (Amsterdam, 2007), pp. 146–57; Gilberte Émile-Mâle, *Pour une histoire de la restauration des peintures en France* (Paris, 2008), pp. 259–60; Ann Massing, 'The Transfer Technique in France', *Burlington Magazine*, CLVIII/1357 (2016), pp. 283–9.
79 Conti, *Restoration*, pp. 190–216; Elizabeth Darrow, 'Pietro Edwards: The Restorer as "Philosophe"', *Burlington Magazine*, CLIX/1369 (2017), pp. 308–17.
80 Giovanni Secco Suardo, *Manuale ragionato per la parte meccanica dell'arte del ristauratore dei dipinti* (Milan, 1866). See Evelina Borea, ed., *Giovanni Secco Suardo* (Rome, 1998).
81 Morelli to Layard, 3 January 1864, quoted in Anderson, 'Otto Mündler', p. 54. See Jaynie Anderson, *The Restoration of Painting in Mid-Nineteenth-Century Milan* (Florence, 2014).
82 Anderson, 'Otto Mündler', p. 18.
83 Conti, *Restoration*, pp. 327–49, 370–75; Giorgio Bonsanti, 'From Guizzardi to Cavenaghi: Nineteenth-Century Italian Conservators', *Burlington Magazine*, CXVIII/1365 (2016), pp. 968–78; Donata Levi, *Cavalcaselle: il pioniere della conservatione dell'arte italiana* (Turin, 1988); Isabelle Brajer, ed., *Conservation in the Nineteenth Century* (London, 2013).
84 Quoted in John Fleming, 'Art Dealing and the Risorgimento II', *Burlington Magazine*, CXXI/917 (1979), pp. 492–508 (p. 499).
85 Hartley, 'How to Observe', p. 272.
86 Otto Kurz, *Fakes* (London, 1948), p. 148; Kenneth Clark, 'Forgeries', *History Today* (1979), pp. 724–33 (p. 730); Moskowitz, *Forging Authenticity*, p. xiii.
87 Jeremy Warren, 'Forgery in Risorgimento Florence', *Burlington Magazine*, CXLII/1232 (2005), pp. 729–41.

88 Anita Moskowitz, 'The Case of Giovanni Bastianini: A Fair and Balanced View', *Artibus et Historiae*, XXV/50 (2004), pp. 157–85; Anita Moskovitz, 'The Case of Giovanni Bastianini: A Hung Jury?', *Artibus et Historiae*, XXVII/54 (2006), pp. 201–17; Carol Helstosky, 'Giovanni Bastianini, Art Forgery and the Market in Nineteenth-Century Italy', *Journal of Modern History*, LXXXI/4 (2009), pp. 793–823.
89 Barbara Strachey and Jayne Samuels, eds, *Mary Berenson: A Self-Portrait from Her Letters and Diaries* (London, 1983), pp. 81, 84, 115.
90 Icilio Federico Joni, *Le memorie di un pittore di quadri antichi* (Sancasciano, n.d.), pp. 107, 137, 154, 231, 278.
91 Ibid., pp. 120, 140.
92 Heinrich Dilly, *Kunstgeschichte als Institution* (Frankfurt, 1979).
93 Joseph Crowe and Giovanni Battista Cavalcaselle, *A New History of Painting in Italy* [1866], trans. Edward Hutton, 3 vols (London, 1909), vol. I, pp. 3, 13.
94 Ibid., p. 501.
95 Anon, 'Cavalcaselle, Giovanni Battista', *Dizionario biografico degli italiani*, 100 vols (Milan, 1960), vol. XX, pp. 640–44; Levi, *Cavalcaselle*; David Ekserdjian, 'Crowe and Cavalcaselle Then and Now', in *Exiles, Emigrés and Intermediaries: Anglo-Italian Cultural Transactions*, ed. Barbara Schaff (Amsterdam, 2010), pp. 357–74.
96 Quoted in Levi, *Cavalcaselle*, p. 216.
97 Flaminia Gennari Santori, 'La National Gallery e la pittura de Carlo Crivelli', in *Giovanni Battista Cavalcaselle conoscitore e conservatore*, ed. Anna Chiara Tommasi (Venice, 1998), pp. 291–312.
98 Tommasi, *Cavalcaselle*, p. 95; Anderson, *Collecting*, pp. 32–3.
99 Quoted in Santori, 'National Gallery', p. 310, n82.
100 'Ivan Lermolieff' [Giovanni Morelli], *Italian Painters* [1890], trans. Jocelyn Ffoulkes (London, 1892).
101 Ibid., pp. 1–2, 17.
102 Morelli to Sir James Hudson (1871), quoted in John Fleming, 'Art Dealing and the Risorgimento I', *Burlington Magazine*, CXV/838 (1973), pp. 4–17 (p. 12).
103 Morelli, *Italian Painters*, pp. 31, 266.
104 Ibid., pp. 158ff; Luke Uglow, 'Giovanni Morelli and His Friend Giorgione: Connoisseurship, Science and Irony', *Journal of Art Historiography*, XI (2014), pp. 1–30.
105 Morelli, *Italian Painters*, pp. 5–6.
106 Quoted in Harry Mount, 'The Monkey with the Magnifying Glass: Constructions of the Connoisseur in Eighteenth-Century Britain', *Oxford Art Journal*, XXIX/2 (2006), pp. 167–83 (p. 176).
107 Morelli, *Italian Painters*, p. 84; Carlo Ginzburg, *Indagini su Piero* [1981], new edn (Milan, 2022), pp. 322, 328.
108 Quoted in John Brewer, 'Art and the Evidence of Attribution', *Insights*, IX/3 (2016), pp. 2–9 (p. 5).
109 Morelli, *Italian Painters*; Jack Spector, 'The Method of Morelli and Its Relation to Freudian Psychoanalysis', *Diogenes*, XVII/66 (1969),

pp. 63–83; Richard Wollheim, 'Giovanni Morelli and the Origins of Scientific Connoisseurship', in *On Art and the Mind* (London, 1973), pp. 177–201; Carlo Ginzburg, 'Clues: Roots of an Evidential Paradigm' [1978], trans. John and Ann Tedeschi, in *Clues, Myths, and the Historical Method* (Baltimore, MD, 1989), pp. 96–125, 200–214.

110 Josefine Leistra, in *Connoisseurship: Bredius, Jan Steen and the Mauritshuis*, ed. Guido Jansen (The Hague, 2014), p. 19.

111 Scallen, *Rembrandt, Reputation*, p. 130.

112 Austen Layard, *Autobiography*, 2 vols (London, 1903), vol. I, p. 37; Jaynie Anderson, 'Layard and Morelli', in *Austen Henry Layard*, ed. Frederick Fales and Bernard Hickey (Rome, 1987), pp. 109–37.

113 Gianluca Kannès, 'Frizzoni, Gustavo', *DBI*, vol. I, pp. 581–3.

114 Clark to Bing, quoted in Elizabeth Sears, 'Kenneth Clark and Gertrud Bing', *Burlington Magazine*, CLIII/1301 (2011), p. 531.

115 Francesco Ventrella, 'Writing under Pressure: Maud Cruttwell and the Old Master Monograph', *Interdisciplinary Studies in the Long Nineteenth Century*, XXVIII (2019), pp. 1–27.

116 Constance Ffoulkes and Rodolfo Maiocchi, *Vincenzo Foppa of Brescia* (London, 1909), pp. xiii, 52, 120, 123; Francesco Ventrella, 'Constance Jocelyn Ffoulkes and the Modernization of Scientific Connoisseurship', *Visual Resources*, XXXIII/1–2 (2017), pp. 117–39.

117 Julius von Schlosser, 'The Vienna School of the History of Art' [1934], English translation in *Journal of Art Historiography*, I (2009), pp. 1–50.

118 Wilhelm Vöge, *Bildhauer des Mittelalters* (Berlin, 1958), with an introduction by Erwin Panofsky; Franz Wickhoff, *Roman Art* [1895], ed. and trans. Mrs S. Arthur Strong (London, 1900).

119 Gladys Thomson, *Mrs Arthur Strong* (London, 1949); Mary Beard, *The Invention of Jane Harrison* (Cambridge, MA, 2000), pp. 14–29; Mary Beard, 'Mrs Arthur Strong, Morelli and the Troopers of Cortés', in *Ancient Art and Its Historiography*, ed. Alice Donohue and Mark Fullerton (Cambridge, 2003), pp. 148–70; J.C.M. Toynbee, 'Strong, Eugénie', *ODNB*, vol. III, pp. 97–8.

120 Elsner, 'Significant Details', pp. 950–52.

121 John Beazley, 'Citharoedus', *Journal of Hellenic Studies*, XLII (1922), pp. 70–98; Bernard Ashmole, 'Sir John Beazley', *Proceedings of the British Academy*, XLVI (1971), pp. 443–61; Donna Kurtz, 'Beazley and the Connoisseurship of Greek Vases', in *Greek Vases in the J. Paul Getty Museum* (Malibu, CA, 1985), pp. 237–50; Michael Vickers, 'Artful Crafts', *Journal of Hellenic Studies*, CV (1985), pp. 108–28; Richard Neer, 'Beazley and the Language of Connoisseurship', *Hephaistos*, XV (1997), pp. 7–30; Eric Driscoll, 'Beazley's Connoisseurship: Aesthetics, Natural History and Artistic Development', *Corps Antiques* (Paris, 2019), pp. 101–20; Peter Stewart, 'Beazley, Daubert and the Burden of Proof', in *Connoisseurship*, ed. Christina Anderson and Peter Stewart (Oxford, 2023), pp. 17–40.

122 Quoted by Enrico Castelnuovo in *Giovanni Morelli*, ed. Agosti, Manca and Panzeri, p. 11; Ernst Gombrich, *Aby Warburg: An Intellectual Biography* (London, 1970), p. 143.

123 Anton Springer, 'Kunstkenner und Kunsthistoriker' [1881], in *Kunstkenner und Kunsthistoriker* (Leipzig, 1886), pp. 377–404, quoted in English in Antoinette Friedenthal, 'John Smith', *Journal of Art Historiography*, IX (2013), pp. 1–20 (p. 17).
124 Morelli, *Italian Painters.*
125 Wilhelm Bode, 'Morelli', *Fortnightly Review* (1891). See Catherine Scallen, 'Wilhelm Bode's and Giovanni Morelli's Debates'.
126 Quash and Sheldon, *Art for the Nation*, p. 154.
127 Edgar Wind, *Art and Anarchy* (London, 1963), pp. 30–46.
128 Julius von Schlosser, *Schriftquellen zur Geschichte der Karolingischen Kunst* (Vienna, 1892).
129 Max Dvořák, *Art History as the History of Ideas* [1924], trans. John Hardy (London, 1984). I believe that 'cultural history' is a closer translation of the term *Geistesgeschichte* than 'history of ideas'.
130 Max Dvořák, *Die Illuminatoren des Johann von Neumarkt* (Vienna, 1901), pp. 35–127; Julius Schlosser, *Eine Fulder Miniaturhandschrift* (Vienna, 1892). See Hans Aurenhammer, 'Max Dvořák and the History of Medieval Art', *Journal of Art Historiography*, II (2010), pp. 2–16.
131 Diana R. Cordileone, *Alois Riegl in Vienna* (Farnham, 2014).
132 Franz Wickhoff, *Abhandlungen* (Berlin, 1913), p. 234.
133 Franz Wickhoff, 'Die italienischen Handzeichningen der Albertina', *Jahrbuch der Kunsthistorischen Sammlungen des Allerhöchsten Kaiserhauses*, XIII (1892), pp. clxxv–cclxxxiii; Matthew Rampley, *The Vienna School of Art History* (University Park, PA, 2013), p. 37.
134 Artur Rosenauer, 'Moriz Thausing und die Wiener Schule der Kunstgeschichte', *Wiener Jahrbuch für Kunstgeschichte*, XXXVI (1983), doi.org/10.7767/wjk.1983.
135 Hans Tietze, *Methode der Kunstgeschichte* (Leipzig, 2013), p. 335.
136 Gertrud Bing to Kenneth Clark, in Sears, 'Kenneth Clark and Gertrud Bing', p. 531.
137 Quoted in Ivan Gaskell, *Vermeer's Wager: Speculations on Art History, Theory and Art Museums* (London, 2000), p. 101.
138 Ibid., p. 141.
139 Udo Kultermann, *The History of Art History* [1966], Eng. trans. (anon.) (New York, 1993), p. 29.
140 Morelli, *Italian Painters*, p. 149.
141 Quoted in Frederick Bohrer, 'Photographic Perspectives', in *Art History*, ed. Mansfield, pp. 246–59 (p. 247).
142 Bernard Berenson, letter to Mary, 10 January 1896; letter to Isabella Gardner, 8 July 1908.
143 Thomas Crow, *Painters and Public Life in Eighteenth-Century Paris* (New Haven, CT, 1985).
144 Anita Brookner, *The Genius of the Future: Essays in French Art Criticism* (Ithaca, NY, 1971).
145 Pontus Grate, *Deux critiques d'art de l'époque romantique* (Stockholm, 1959).

146 Haskell, *Rediscoveries in Art*.
147 Eastlake, 'How to Observe'.
148 Frances Jowell, *Thoré-Bürger and the Art of the Past* (New York, 1977).
149 Albert Heppner, *Thoré-Bürger en Holland* (Amsterdam, 1938), pp. 15, 19.
150 Peter Hecht, 'Rembrandt and Raphael Back to Back: The Contribution of Thoré', *Simiolus*, XXVI/3 (1998), pp. 162–78 (pp. 166, 168).
151 Frances Jowell, 'Thoré-Bürger's Art Collection', *Simiolus*, XXX/1–2 (2003), pp. 54–119 (pp. 82, 96, 91).
152 Bode, *Leben*, p. 26; Haskell, *Rediscoveries in Art*, p. 146.
153 Tim Hilton, *John Ruskin* (New Haven, CT, 2002), p. 39.
154 Ibid., pp. 100, 90. See Michael Levey, 'Botticelli and Nineteenth Century England', *Journal of the Warburg and Courtauld Institutes*, XXIII/3–4 (1960), pp. 291–306.
155 Hilton, *Ruskin*, p. 94.
156 Ibid., pp. 555, 447.
157 James Dearden, 'John Ruskin, the Collector', *The Library*, XXI (1966), pp. 124–54 (p. 125).
158 Seymour Simches, *Le Romantisme et le goût esthétique du XVIIIe siècle* (Paris, 1964); Haskell, *Rediscoveries in Art*, pp. 108–10, 133–4; Frances Jowell, 'Thoré-Bürger and Eighteenth-Century French Art', in *Delicious Decadence: The Rediscovery of French Eighteenth-Century Painting in the Nineteenth Century*, ed. Christoph Vogtherr et al. (Farnham, 2014), pp. 71–85.
159 Gabriel Weisberg, *The Independent Critic: Philippe Burty and the Visual Arts of Mid-Nineteenth-Century France* (New York, 1993).
160 Edmond Goncourt, *Idées et sensations* (Paris, 1866); Dominique Péty, *Les Goncourt et la collection* (Geneva, 2003).
161 Donald Mallett, *The Greatest Collector: Lord Hertford and the Founding of the Wallace Collection* (London, 1979).
162 Helen Rees Leahy, '"For Connoisseurs": The *Burlington Magazine*, 1903–11', in *Art History*, ed. Mansfield, pp. 231–45 (p. 233).
163 Anne Helmreich, 'The Art Market and the Spaces of Sociability in Victorian London', *Victorian Studies*, LIX/3 (2017), pp. 436–49.
164 Morelli to Sir James Hudson (1871), p. 12.
165 Vincent Noce, *Descente aux enchères: les coulisses du marché de l'art* (Paris, 2002).
166 Philip Hook, *Breakfast at Sotheby's: An A–Z of the Art World* (London, 2014), p. 304.
167 Pierre Assouline, *Grâces lui soient rendues: Paul Durand-Ruel, le marchand des impressionistes* (Paris, 2002).
168 Jean-Paul Morel, *C'était Ambroise Vollard* (Paris, 2007).
169 Pierre Assouline, *L'homme de l'art: D.-H. Kahnweiler, 1884–1979* (Paris, 1988).
170 Mauro Minardi, 'Morelli, Berenson, Proust', *Studi di Menofonte*, XIV (2015), pp. 211–26 (pp. 214, 216, 221).
171 Bernard Berenson described Placci in *Rumour and Reflection, 1941–1944* (London, 1952).

172 Henry James, *Portrait of a Lady* [1882] (Harmondsworth, 1984), pp. 312, 316, 326, 354.
173 Viola Winner, *Henry James and the Visual Arts* (Charlottesville, VA, 1970).
174 Sergio Perosa, 'Henry James and Unholy Art Acquisitions', *Cambridge Quarterly*, XXXVII/1 (2008), pp. 150–63 (p. 160).
175 Henry James, *The Outcry* (London, 1911), pp. 40, 156, 167.
176 Strachey and Samuels, *Mary Berenson.*
177 Mary Ann Calo, *Bernard Berenson and the Twentieth Century* (Philadelphia, PA, 1994), pp. 21–2.
178 Bernard Berenson, *Italian Painters of the Renaissance*, 4 vols in 1 (London, 1952), pp. 4, 16, 13.
179 Ibid., pp. 45, 60, 67.
180 Ibid., pp. 109, 131.
181 Quoted in Ernest Samuels, *Bernard Berenson: The Making of a Legend* (Cambridge, MA, 1987), p. 29.
182 Ibid., pp. 365, 440.
183 Saltzman, *Old Masters, New World.*
184 Mario Casari, 'Bernard Berenson and Islamic Culture', in *Bernard Berenson: Formation and Heritage*, ed. Joseph Connors and Louis Waldman (Florence, 2014), pp. 173–205.
185 Ernest Samuels, *Bernard Berenson: The Making of a Connoisseur* (Cambridge, MA, 1979), p. 86.
186 Bernard Berenson, *The Study and Criticism of Italian Art*, 3 vols (London, 1901–16), vol. 1, pp. v, 2, 124–31.
187 Bernard Berenson, *Lorenzo Lotto* [1895] (London, 1956), p. xiv; Berenson, *Study*, vol. 1, pp. 46–69 (p. 49).
188 Ibid., p. viii.
189 Samuels, *Making of a Legend*, p. 38; Berenson, *Italian Painters*, p. xiii.
190 Berenson, *Italian Painters*, p. 61.
191 Berenson, *Homeless Paintings of the Renaissance* (London, 1969), pp. 236, 227, 233.
192 Berenson, *Study*, vol. 1, pp. v, vii.
193 Samuels, *Making of a Legend*, p. 8; Berenson, *Homeless Paintings*, p. 237.
194 Samuels, *Making of a Legend*, p. 402.
195 Berenson, *Study*, vol. 1, pp. 90, 92.
196 Quoted in Rachel Cohen, *Bernard Berenson: A Life in the Picture Trade* (New Haven, CT, 2021), p. 220.
197 Berenson, *Italian Painters*, p. 34; Berenson, *Lorenzo Lotto*, p. 91.
198 Berenson, *Italian Painters*, pp. 66, 83, 98, 195.
199 Samuels, *Making of a Legend*, p. 60.
200 Ibid., pp. 132, 234.
201 Ibid., pp. 166, 275.
202 Jeremy Howard, 'Art, Commerce and Scholarship: The Friendship between Otto Gutekunst and Bernard Berenson', in *Bernard Berenson*, ed. Connors and Waldman, pp. 33–68.

203 Colin Simpson, *The Partnership: The Secret Association of Bernard Berenson and Joseph Duveen* (London, 1987).
204 Philip Hook, *Rogue's Gallery: A History of Art and Its Dealers* (London, 2017), p. 79.
205 Cohen, *Bernard Berenson*, p. 220.
206 Cecil Gould, 'Ellis Kirkham Waterhouse', *Proceedings of the British Academy*, LXXII (2016), pp. 525–35.
207 Quoted in Cohen, *Bernard Berenson*, p. 229.

6 Globalization and Science

1 David Alan Brown, 'Bernard Berenson and Paul Sachs: Teaching Connoisseurship', in *Bernard Berenson: Formation and Heritage*, ed. Joseph Connors and Louis Waldman (Boston, MA, 2014), pp. 269–92.
2 Michel Laclotte, *A Key to the Louvre: Memoirs of a Curator* [2003], trans. Mark Pollizzotti (New York, 2004), p. 21; Philippe Costamagna, *Histoires d'oeils* (Paris, 2019), pp. 14, 34.
3 Costamagna, *Histoires d'oeils*, pp. 49, 51, 87.
4 Ben Grosvenor, 'Connoisseurship: Who Painted What, When and How to Tell' (2017), www.royalacademyofarts.org.uk, accessed 26 March 2025; Chantal Brotherton-Radcliffe, 'The Forensic Eye', www.theartssocietygrayshott.org, accessed 26 March 2025.
5 Edmund de Waal, *The Hare with Amber Eyes* (London, 2010).
6 Gabriel Weisberg, *The Independent Critic: Philippe Burty and the Visual Arts of Mid-Nineteenth-Century France* (New York, 1993), pp. 97–124, 223–43.
7 Dominique Péty, *Les Goncourt et la collection* (Geneva, 2003).
8 Edmond de Goncourt, *Outamaro: le peintre des maisons vertes* (Paris, 1891), pp. 4, 38, 49.
9 Edmond de Goncourt, *Hokousaï* (Paris, 1896), pp. 1–3.
10 Joanna Smalcerz, 'Introduction', in *Wilhelm Bode and the Art Market*, ed. Smalcerz (Leiden, 2023), pp. 1–15 (p. 1); Mario Casari, 'Bernard Berenson and Islamic Culture', in *Bernard Berenson*, ed. Connors and Waldman, pp. 173–205.
11 Emiko Yamanashi, 'Western-Style Painting: Four Stages of Acceptance', in *Since Meiji*, ed. J. Thomas Rimer (Honolulu, HI, 2012), pp. 19–33.
12 Richard Smart, 'The Secret World of Western Art Collection in Japan', *Spear's*, https://spearswms.com, 29 January 2016.
13 Minna Törmä, *Enchanted by Lohans: Osvald Sirén's Journey into Chinese Art* (Hong Kong, 2013).
14 James Pickford, 'Rich Collectors from China Switch Spending Power to Western Art', *Financial Times*, www.ft.com, 29 November 2013.
15 Philip Hook, *Breakfast at Sotheby's: An A–Z of the Art World* (London, 2013), p. 298.
16 See 'Departments', www.sothebys.com, accessed 15 August 2023.
17 'The Land of Colours', *The Economist*, 27 September 2025, pp. 78–9.

18 Denis Mahon, *Studies in Seicento Art and Theory* (London, 1947), p. 329.
19 Joullain quoted in Patrick Michel, *Le commerce du tableau à Paris dans la seconde moitié du XVIIIe siècle* (Villeneuve d'Ascq, 2007), p. 109.
20 Joseph Collins, 'British Pension Fund Buys Art', *New York Times*, 12 February 1978.
21 Hook, *Breakfast at Sotheby's*, pp. 289, 330; Orlando Whitfield, *All That Glitters: A Story of Friendship, Fraud and Fine Art* (London, 2024), p. 197. See Georgina Adam, *Big Bucks: The Explosion of the Art Market in the Twenty-First Century* (Farnham, 2014).
22 Charlotte Bydler, *The Global Art World, Inc.* (Uppsala, 2004), pp. 49–81.
23 Robin Pogrebin, 'Qatari Riches Are Buying Art World Influence', *New York Times*, www.nytimes.com, 22 July 2023.
24 Ming Tiampo, *Gutai: Decentering Modernism* (Chicago, IL, 2011), pp. 8, 18, 101.
25 Bydler, *Global Art World*, p. 67. See Reiko Tomii, 'The Discourse of (L)imitation', in *Globalization and Contemporary Art*, ed. Jonathan Harris (Chichester, 2011), pp. 344–56.
26 Dipesh Chakrabarty, *Provincializing Europe* (Princeton, NJ, 2000).
27 Partha Mitter, 'Interventions: Decentering Modernism: Art History and Avant-Garde Art from the Periphery', *Art Bulletin*, XC (2008), pp. 531–48.
28 Eugenia Bogdanova-Kummer, *Bokujinkai: Japanese Calligraphy and the Postwar Avant-Garde* (Leiden, 2020).
29 Essie King, 'David Hockney's Artistic Homages, from Picasso to Chinese Scrolls', www.myartbroker.com, accessed 13 January 2025.
30 Mariana Ribeiro da Silva Tavares, 'Entrevista com Beatriz Vasconcelos Coelho', PÓS, XI (2021), p. 7.
31 Barbara Mundy and Aaron Hyman, 'Out of the Shadow of Vasari: Towards a New Model of the "Artist" in Colonial Latin America', *Colonial Latin American Review*, XXIV/3 (2016), pp. 283–317; Aaron Hyman, 'Inventing Painting: Cristóbal del Villalpando, Juan Correa and New Spain's Transatlantic Canon', *Art Bulletin*, XCIX/2 (2017), pp. 102–35; Aaron Hyman, *Rubens in Repeat: The Logic of the Copy in Colonial Latin America* (Los Angeles, CA, 2021), pp. 20, 260.
32 Jorge Coli, 'Os falsos Aleijadinhos do MASP', http://amavelleitor.blogspot.com, 30 May 2018. See Myriam Oliveira et al., *O Aleijadinho e sua oficina* (São Paulo, 2002).
33 Cristina Carlisle, 'As Latin American Art Prices Rise, So Do Forgeries', *New York Times*, 6 October 1998; Hans-Jürgen Gehrke, quoted in Gabriella Angeleti, 'Spanish Dealer Claims to Find Long-Lost Frieda Kahlo Painting', *Art Newspaper*, www.theartnewspapercom, 1 July 2020.
34 Lassla Esquivel bio at IESA, www.iesa.edu/paris/news-events/faculty/esquivel, accessed 13 January 2025.
35 Cassatt quoted in Cynthia Saltzman, *Old Masters, New World: America's Raid on Europe's Great Pictures* (New York, 2008), p. 110;

on Marc, Eric Storm, *The Discovery of El Greco* [2006], trans. Marjolijn de Jager (Eastbourne, 2016), pp. 137–8. See Veronika Schroeder, *El Greco im frühen Deutschen Expressionismus* (Frankfurt, 1998).

36 Kenneth Clark, preface to Roger Fry, *Last Lectures* (Cambridge, 1939), p. ix.

37 Luciano Cheles, 'Piero della Francesca in Nineteenth-Century Britain', *The Italianist*, XIV (1994), pp. 188–260. Compare Luciano Cheles, 'Piero della Francesca et la peinture française', in *Fascinante Italie de Manet à Picasso (1853–1917)*, ed. Blandine Chavanne (Paris, 2009), pp. 59–65.

38 Umberto Morra, *Conversations with Berenson* [1963], trans. Florence Hammond (Westport, CT, 1975), p. 99; Carlo Ginzburg, *Indagini su Pietro* [1981], new edn (Milan, 2022), pp. 288–9.

39 Gabriele Finaldi and Neil MacGregor, 'Denis Mahon', *Burlington Magazine*, CLIII/1302 (2011), pp. 605–7; Mary Wakefield, 'The Man Who Rescued Caravaggio', *The Spectator*, 29 January 2005.

40 Hook, *Breakfast at Sotheby's*, p. 14.

41 Georgina Adam, *Big Bucks: The Explosion of the Art Market in the Twenty-First Century* (Farnham, 2014).

42 Terry Smith, 'The State of Art History: Contemporary Art', *Art Bulletin*, XCII (2010), pp. 366–83 (p. 366).

43 Rachel Cohen, *Bernard Berenson: A Life in the Picture Trade* (New Haven, CT, 2021), p. 100; Bernard Berenson, *Sketch for a Self-Portrait* (London, 1948), p. 193.

44 Anna Ottani Cavina, ed., *Dietro l'Immagine* (Turin, 2009), p. 13.

45 Richard Spear, *Caravaggio's Cardsharps on Trial: Thwaytes v Sotheby's* (London, 2020), p. 239. The case concerned the authenticity of a painting attributed to Caravaggio.

46 Quoted in Catherine Scallen, *Rembrandt, Reputation and the Practice of Connoisseurship* (Amsterdam, 2004), p. 235, from Charles Sedelmeyer, *The Adulteress before Christ* (Paris, 1912).

47 Cornelius Hofstede de Groot, *Echt of inecht? Oog of chemie?* (The Hague, 1925).

48 Martin de Wild, *The Scientific Examination of Pictures* (London, 1929); Walter Feilchenfeldt, 'Van Gogh Fakes', *Simiolus*, XIX/4 (1989), pp. 289–316; Stefan Koldehoff, 'The Wacker Forgeries', *Van Gogh Museum Journal* (2002), pp. 138–49; Esther van Duijn and Mireille te Marvelde, 'Hopman and De Wild: The Historical Importance of Two Dutch Families of Restorers', *Burlington Magazine*, CLVIII/1363 (2016), pp. 812–23.

49 Jonathan Lopez, *The Man Who Made Vermeers* (Boston, MA, 2009), pp. 107–9.

50 Garry Thomson, John Mills and Joyce Plesters, 'The Scientific Department', *National Gallery Technical Bulletin*, I (1977) pp. 18–28; John Walker, *Bellini and Titian at Ferrara* (London, 1956); Jill Dunkerton and Marika Spring, 'Titian after 1540', *National Gallery Technical Bulletin*, XXXVI (2015), pp. 6–39 (p. 15); Jaynie Anderson, 'Connoisseurship: Invention, Abandonment, Reinvention', in

A Companion to the Theories and Methods of Art History, ed. Geraldine Johnson (Hoboken, NJ, forthcoming).

51 Francesca Bewer, *A Laboratory for Art: Harvard's Fogg Museum and the Emergence of Conservation in America, 1900–1950* (New Haven, CT, 2010), p. 99.

52 Thomson, Mills and Plesters, 'Scientific Department', p. 20.

53 Noa Turel, 'Genius Disrobed: The Early Netherlandish Underdrawing Craze and the End of a Connoisseurship Era', *Journal of Art Historiography*, XVI (2017), pp. 1–16.

54 Erwin Panofsky, 'History of Art as a Humanistic Discipline' [1940], in Panofsky, *Meaning in the Visual Arts* (Garden City, NY, 1955), pp. 1–25 (p. 16); Spear, *Caravaggio's Cardsharps*, p. 311.

55 Ernst van de Wetering, 'The Invisible Rembrandt: The Results of Technical and Scientific Research', in *Rembrandt: The Master and His Workshop*, ed. Christopher Brown, Jan Kelch and Pieter van Thiel (New Haven, CT, 1991), pp. 90–105 (p. 90).

56 Ingrid Rowland and Noel Charney, *The Collector of Lives: Giorgio Vasari and the Invention of Art* (New York, 2017), pp. 10–13, 350–51, 357–9.

57 Samanath Subramanyam, 'How to Spot a Perfect Fake', *The Guardian*, 18 June 2018.

58 Dalya Alberge, 'AI Contradicts Art Experts', *The Guardian*, 27 September 2025, p. 9.

59 Max Friedländer, *On Art and Connoisseurship* (London, 1942), pp. 258–66.

60 Kenneth Clark, 'Forgeries', *History Today*, XXIX/II (November 1979), pp. 724–33 (p. 728).

61 Juliet Chippindale, 'The Madonna of the Veil', www.nationalgallery.org.uk, 30 June 2010.

62 Eric Hebborn, *Confessions of a Master Forger* (London, 1997), pp. 149, 218ff, 244, 255, 259, 303, 318.

63 Hélène Verougstraete and Jacqueline Couvert, eds, *La peinture ancienne et ses procédés: copies, répliques, pastiches* (Bruges, 2004).

64 Hélène Verougstraete, Roger van Schoute and Till-Holger Borchert, *Restaurateurs ou faussaires des primitifs flamands* (Ghent, 2004), pp. 110–59.

65 Hubert von Sonnenburg, 'A Case of Recurring Deception', *Metropolitan Museum of Art Bulletin*, LI/3 (1993–4), pp. 8–19 (p. 12).

66 Thomas Hoving, *False Impressions: The Hunt for Big-Time Art Fakes* (London, 1996), pp. 235–44.

67 Guy Isnard, *Faux et imitations dans l'art* (Paris, 1960), pp. 255–6.

68 Dalya Alberge, 'Art Market: Painting Withdrawn from Sale after Artist Declares It a Fake', *The Independent*, 19 May 1993.

69 Quoted in Guy Isnard, *Les pirates de la peinture* (Paris, 1955), p. 16.

70 Clifford Irving, *Fake! The Story of Elmyr de Hory, the Greatest Forger of Our Time* (New York, 1969).

71 Ibid., pp. 25, 68ff, 100. See Jonathon Keats, *Forged: Why Fakes Are the Great Art of Our Age* (Oxford, 2013), pp. 109–33.

72 Winnie Won Yin Wong, *Van Gogh on Demand: China and the Readymade* (Chicago, IL, 2014).
73 Abraham Bredius, 'A New Vermeer', *Burlington Magazine*, LXXI/416 (1937), p. 210.
74 Albert Blankert, 'The Case of Han van Meegeren's Fake Vermeer: The Supper at Emmaus Reconsidered', in *In His Milieu: Essays on Netherlandish Art in Memory of John Michael Montias*, ed. Amy Golahni, Mia Mochizuki and Lisa Vergara (Amsterdam, 2006), pp. 47–58.
75 Lopez, *The Man Who Made Vermeers*, p. 18. Of the many published versions of the story, this is one of the best informed.
76 Tamara Griggs, 'Ancient Art and the Antiquarian: The Forgery of Giuseppe Guerra', *Huntington Library Quarterly*, LXXIV/3 (2011), pp. 471–503 (p. 493); on this 'picaresque' topos, Sándor Radnóti, *The Fake: Forgery and Its Place in Art* (Lanham, MD, 1999), p. 13.
77 Jesse Lerner, 'Brígido Lara: Post-Pre-Columbian Ceramicist', *Cabinet Magazine* (Spring 2001), www.cabinetmagazine.org, accessed 16 August 2023; Daniel Schávelzon, *Arte y falsificación en America Latina* (Mexico City, 2009), pp. 36, 246.
78 Lopez, *The Man Who Made Vermeers*, p. 104.
79 Chantal Brotherton-Radcliffe, 'The Forensic Eye', www.theartssocietygrayshott.org, accessed 26 March 2025.
80 Guy Isnard, *Vrai ou faux?* (Paris, 1974).
81 John Gere, 'Philip Pouncey', *Proceedings of the British Academy*, LXXVI (1991), pp. 529–74 (p. 536).
82 Ibid., p. 535.
83 David Robertson, *Sir Charles Eastlake and the Victorian Art World* (Princeton, NJ, 1978), pp. 142–6.
84 Frédéric Elsig, *Connoisseurship et histoire de l'art* (Geneva, 2019), p. 9.
85 Sheryl Reiss and David Wilkins, *Beyond Isabella: Secular Women Patrons of Art in Renaissance Italy* (Kirksville, MO, 2000).
86 Clara Thomas, 'Anna Jameson: Art Historian and Critic', *Woman's Art Journal*, I (1980), pp. 20–22. See Meaghan Clarke, 'The Art Press at the Fin de Siècle: Women, Collecting and Connoisseurship', *Visual Resources*, XXXI/1–2 (2015), pp. 15–30; Meaghan Clarke and Francesco Ventrella, 'Women's Expertise and the Culture of Connoisseurship', *Visual Resources*, XXX/1–2 (2017), pp. 1–10.
87 Gladys Thomson, *Mrs Arthur Strong* (London, 1949); Mary Beard, *The Invention of Jane Harrison* (Cambridge, MA, 2000), pp. 14–29; Beard, 'Mrs Arthur Strong, Morelli and the Troopers of Cortés', in *Ancient Art and Its Historiography*, ed. Alice Donohue and Mark Fullerton (Cambridge, 2003), pp. 148–76 (pp. 159–64); J.C.M. Toynbee, 'Strong, Eugénie', *ODNB*, vol. III, pp. 97–8.
88 Caroline McCaffrey-Howarth, 'Lady Dorothy Nevill as Art Collector', *Interdisciplinary Studies in the Long Nineteenth Century*, XIX/31 (2021), pp. 1–26; Dorothy Nevill, *Reminiscences* (London, 1906), p. 237.
89 John Pope-Hennessy, *Learning to Look* (London, 1991), p. 37.

90 Mary Lago, *Christiana Herringham and the Edwardian Art Scene* (Columbia, MO, 1996).
91 Hannelore Nützmann, 'Ein Berufsleben: Frida Schottmüller', *Mitteilungen des Kunsthistorischen Instituts in Florenz*, XL (1996), pp. 236–44; Barbara Paul, 'Frida Schottmüller', in *Stadtbild und Frauenleben*, ed. Henrike Hülsbergen (Berlin, 1997), pp. 279–93; Gabriele Fattorini, 'Frida Schotmüller, 1872–1936', in *I conoscitori tedeschi tra otto e novecento*, ed. Francesco Caglioti, Andrea de Marchi and Alessandro Nova (Milan, 2018), pp. 127–38.
92 Deidre Robinson, 'Parsons, Betty', DA, XXIV, pp. 213–14.
93 Cesare Garboli and Cristina Montagnani, eds, *Bernard Berenson/ Roberto Longhi, lettere e scartafacci* (Milan, 1993), pp. 9–55. Anna Maria Ambrosini, ed., *Il mestiere del conoscitore* (Bologna, 2017), p. 487.
94 Roberto Longhi, *Opere* (Florence, 1967), vol. II, p. 321.
95 Giovanni Previtali, 'Roberto Longhi', *Belfagor*, XXXVI (1981), pp. 159–86.
96 Pasolini quoted in Ambra Cascone, *La città dei destini incrociati* (Padua, 2023), p. 122; Michele Tomasi, interview with Castelnuovo, *Bulletin Monumental*, CLXXIII (2015), pp. 3–4.
97 Pierre Rosenberg, 'Poussin et Roberto Longhi', in *Mestiere*, ed. Ambrosini, pp. 363–71 (p. 368); Laclotte, *Key*, p. 59.
98 Roberto Longhi, 'Un originale del Caravaggio a Rouen', *Studi caravaggeschi*, 2 vols (Florence, 1999–2000), pp. 2, 243–54; Laclotte, *Key*, p. 69.
99 Roberto Longhi, *Quesiti caravaggeschi* (Florence, 1968), p. 81.
100 Neville Rowley, 'Domenico Veneziano 1925: una predella ricomposta', in *Mestiere*, ed. Ambrosini, pp. 103–22.
101 Longhi, *Opere*, vol. IV, pp. 3–6. See Laura Cavazzini, 'Un polittico di Giotto ricomposto', in *Mestiere*, ed. Ambrosini, pp. 59–78.
102 Pope-Hennessy, *Learning to Look*, pp. 309–10.
103 Per Jonas Nordhagen, 'Robert Longhi (1890--1970) and His Method', *Konsthistorisk Tidskrift*, LXVIII (1999), pp. 99–116.
104 Previtali, 'Longhi', p. 183; Ginzburg, *Indagini su Pietro*, pp. 28, 307, 309.
105 Maria Cristina Terzaghi, 'Roberto Longhi e Caravaggio', in *Mestiere*, ed. Ambrosini, pp. 319–44 (p. 319).
106 David Tabbat, 'The Eloquent Eye: Roberto Longhi and the Historical Criticism of Art', in *Longhi: Three Studies* (New York, 1995), pp. ix–xxxiii; Andrea Mirabile, *Scrivere la pittura: la 'funzione Longhi' nella letteratura italiana* (Ravenna, 2009).
107 Gianfranco Contini, 'Contributi Longhiani', in *Altri esercizi* (Turin, 1972), pp. 101–26 (p. 123); Roberto Longhi, *Da Cimabue a Morandi*, ed. Gianfranco Contini (Verona, 1973), p. 402.
108 R. Longhi, 'Un ignoto corrispondente del Lanzi', *Proporzioni*, III (1950), pp. 216–30. See Marco Mascolo, 'Un "ignoto corrispondente"', *Prospettiva*, 161–2 (2016), pp. 157–86.
109 Cristina Montagnani, *Glossario Longhiano: saggio sulla lingua e lo stile di Roberto Longhi* (Pisa, 1989).

110 Bernard Aikema, *Pietro della Vecchia and the Heritage of the Renaissance in Venice* (Florence, 1990), p. 7.
111 Andrea Bacchi et al., eds, *Il mestiere del conoscitore: Federico Zeri* (2021), p. 45; Cavina, *Dietro l'Immagine*, p. 12.
112 Emanuele Lugli, 'Connoisseurship as a System: Reflections on Federico Zeri's *Due Dipinti, la filologia ed un nome*', *Word and Image*, XXIV (2008), pp. 162–75.
113 Federico Zeri, *J'avoue m'être trompé* (Paris, 1995), pp. 124–6. The text reproduces a series of interviews by Patrick Mauriès.
114 James Byam Shaw, 'Popham, Arthur Ewart', ODNB, vol. XLIV, pp. 889–90.
115 Christopher White, 'John Arthur Charles Gere', *Proceedings of the British Academy*, LXXXX (1996), pp. 367–88.
116 A colleague at the Louvre reported this to Pouncey: Gere, 'Pouncey', p. 532.
117 Jennifer Cooke, 'Frederick Antal or a Connoisseur Turned Social Historian of Art', *Migrating Histories of Art*, XIX (2018), pp. 99–110.
118 Anthony Griffith in Nicholas Turner, *The Study of Renaissance Drawings: The Contribution of Philip Pouncey* (London, 1994), p. 8.
119 Philip Pouncey, 'An Unknown Drawing by Leonardo da Vinci', *Apollo*, CVIII (1978), p. 405.
120 Philip Pouncey, *Lotto Disegnatore* (Vicenza, 1965), p. 12; Mario Di Giampaolo, ed., *Philip Pouncey: raccolta di scritti, 1937–1985* (Rimini, 1994), p. 177.
121 Giampaolo, *Pouncey*, pp. 139–46; Gere, 'Pouncey', pp. 536–7; Carlo Ginzburg, 'Piccole differenze: ekphrasis e connoisseurship', *Paragone*, LXXI (2020), pp. 98–116 (pp. 100–101).
122 Giampaolo, *Pouncey*, pp. 200, 159, 163.

7 Crisis

1 Quoted in Philip Hook, *Rogue's Gallery: A History of Art and Its Dealers* (London, 2017), p. 79.
2 John Brewer, *The American Leonardo* (New York, 2007), pp. 89–107.
3 Quoted in M. H. Miller, 'The Big Fake: Behind the Scenes of Knoedler Gallery's Downfall', *ARTnews*, www.artnews.com, 25 April 2016.
4 Scott Reyburn, 'Connoisseurship: Is It Time for a Comeback?', *Art Newspaper*, www.theartnewspaper.com, 5 August 2021.
5 Quoted in John Gere, 'Philip Pouncey', *Proceedings of the British Academy*, LXXVI (1991), pp. 529–74 (p. 534).
6 Quoted in Belinda Rathbone, *The Boston Raphael* (Jaffrey, NH, 2014), p. 262.
7 Quoted in Alan Wallach, 'Whither Connoisseurship?', *Panorama: Journal of the American Association of Historians of Art* (Fall 2015), doi.org/10.24926/24716839.1523.
8 Quoted in Robert Cumming, ed., *My Dear BB* (New Haven, CT, 2015), pp. 37, 52.

9 Longhi quoted in *Il mestiere del conoscitore*, ed. Anna Maria Ambrosini (Bologna, 2017), p. 491; Hans Tietze, *Lebendige Kunstwissenschaft: Zur Krisis der Kunst und der Kunstwissenschaft* (Vienna, 1925); Lothar Brieger, 'Die Krise in der Kunstwissenschaft', B.Z. *am Mittag*, 10 March 1931.

10 Federico Zeri, *Diari di Lavoro* (Bergamo, 1976); Giuliano Briganti, 'Ma quella del conoscitore è una specie in via di estinzione?', in *Affinità* (Milan, 2007), pp. 113–26; Gary Schwartz, 'Rembrandt Studies after the Age of Connoisseurship', *Annals of Scholarship*, x (1993), pp. 313–35.

11 James Beck, *From Duccio to Raphael: Connoisseurship in Crisis* (Florence, 2006), p. 29.

12 Maria Cristina Terzaghi, interview with Gregori, in *Il mestiere del conoscitore*, ed. Ambrosini, p. 21.

13 David Ekserdjian, 'Crowe and Cavalcaselle Then and Now', in *Exiles, Emigrés and Intermediaries: Anglo-Italian Cultural Transactions*, ed. Barbara Schaff (Amsterdam, 2010), pp. 357–74 (p. 371).

14 Philippe Costamagna, *Histoires d'oeils* (Paris, 2019), p. 246; Frédéric Elsig, *Connoisseurship et l'histoire de l'art* (Geneva, 2019), p. 139.

15 Payal Arora and Filip Vermeylen, 'The End of the Art Connoisseur?', *Information, Communication and Society*, XVI/2 (2013), pp. 194–214 (p. 205).

16 Bendor Grosvenor, 'On Connoisseurship', *Art History News*, 23 August 2012. See Reyburn, 'Connoisseurship'.

17 Mark Brown, '"Lost Caravaggio" Rejected by the Louvre May Be Worth 100m', *The Guardian*, www.theguardian.com, 28 February 2019.

18 Jonathan Harr, *The Lost Painting: The Quest for a Caravaggio Masterpiece* (New York, 2005); Sam Jones, 'Prado to Show Lost Work by Caravaggio', *The Guardian*, www.theguardian.com, 7 May 2024.

19 Peter Landesman, 'A Crisis of Fakes', *New York Times Magazine*, 18 March 2001.

20 Richard Dorment, *Warhol after Warhol* (London, 2023); Richard Polsky, 'The Story of Art Authentication Boards', MYARTBROKER, www.myartbroker.com, 30 August 2024.

21 Dalya Alberge, 'Legal Row Could Force Mystery Artist Banksy to Reveal His Name', *The Guardian*, www.theguardian.com, 9 March 2024.

22 Hook, *Rogue's Gallery*, p. 155.

23 Anna Tummers, 'Original or Copy', in *The Eye of the Connoisseur* (Los Angeles, CA, 2011), pp. 61–78 (pp. 75–6).

24 Béguin quoted in Vincent Noce, *Descente aux enchères: les coulisses du marché de l'art* (Paris, 2000), p. 333; see Kathleen Preciado, *Retaining the Original: Multiple Originals, Copies and Reproductions*, ed. Kathleen Preciado (Washington, DC, 1989); Maria Loh, 'New and Improved: Repetition as Originality in Italian Baroque Practice and Theory', *Art Bulletin* LXXXVI/3 (2004), pp. 477–504.

25 Jacob Burckhardt, *Recollections of Rubens* (London, 1950), pp. 204–13.
26 Charlotte Guichard, 'Du "nouveau connoisseurship" à l'histoire de l'art', *Annales: Histoire, Sciences Sociales*, LX (2010), pp. 1387–401.
27 Gary Schwartz, 'Rembrandt Research after the Age of Connoisseurship', *Annals of Scholarship*, X (1993), pp. 313–35 (pp. 316–17).
28 Tummers, *The Eye of the Connoisseur*, pp. 41–2.
29 Schwartz, 'Rembrandt Research', p. 331; Ernst van de Wetering, 'The Search for the Master's Hand: An Anachronism?', in *Künstlericher Austausch*, ed. Thomas Gaehtgens (Berlin, 1993), vol. I, pp. 627–30; Thomas Gaehtgens, 'Preface: The RRP: Past, Present, Future', in *A Corpus of Rembrandt Painting*, ed. Ernst van de Wetering et al., vol. IV (Dordrecht, 2005), pp. ix–xxxii.
30 Ivan Gaskell, 'A Rembrandt Puzzle and the Limits of Connoisseurship', paper given at the symposium 'Hans Heinrich Thyssen as an Art Collector', Museo Nacional Thysse Bornemisza, Madrid, 2021.
31 Svetlana Alpers, *Rembrandt's Enterprise: The Studio and the Market* (Chicago, IL, 1988); Hilton Kramer, 'Rembrandt as Warhol: Svetlana Alpers's "Enterprise"', *New Criterion,* 6 April 1988. See Josua Bruyn, 'Rembrandt's Workshop: Function and Production', in *Rembrandt: The Master and His Workshop*, ed. Christopher Brown et al. (New Haven, CT, 1991), pp. 68–89.
32 Suzi Gablik, 'Connective Aesthetics', *American Art*, VI/2 (1992), pp. 2–7.
33 Hans Belting, *The End of the History of Art* [1983], trans. Christopher Wood (Chicago, IL, 1987).
34 Marquard Smith, ed., *Visual Culture Studies* (Los Angeles, CA, 2008).
35 Kobena Mercer, ed., *Cosmopolitan Modernisms* (Cambridge, MA, 2005).
36 Partha Mitter, 'Interventions: Decentering Modernism: Art History and Avant-Garde Art from the Periphery', *Art Bulletin*, XC (2008), pp. 531–48 (pp. 534–7). See Partha Mitter, *The Triumph of Modernism: India's Artists and the Avant-Garde, 1922–1947* (London, 2007), pp. 7–10.
37 Mitter, *Triumph of Modernism*, p. 18.
38 Hugh Honour and John Fleming, *A World History of Art* (London, 1982).
39 Carlo Ginzburg, 'Storia dell'arte da vicino e da lontano', *Mitteilungen des Kunsthistorischen Institutes in Florenz*, LXI/3 (2019), pp. 275–85.
40 Stephen Deuchar, 'Whose Art History? Curators, Academics, and the Museum Visitor in Britain in the 1980s and 1990s', in *The Two Art Histories: The Museum and the University*, ed. Charles Haxthausen (New Haven, CT, 2002), pp. 3–13.
41 Adam Kuper, *The Museum of Other People, from Colonial Acquisitions to Cosmopolitan Exhibitions* (London, 2024).
42 *The Economist*, 16 March 2024, p. 80.

43 Amy Zegart, 'Re-Imagining Espionage in the Era of Artificial Intelligence', https://hai.stanford.edu, 17 August 2021.

44 Carina Popovici, 'Two AI Models Produced Different Results when Authenticating a Raphael Painting', *Artnet*, 24 October 2023. See Jo Lawson-Tancred, *AI and the Art Market* (London, 2024), pp. 23–4, 40.

45 Greta Harris, 'AI Meets Old Masters in the Fight to Authenticate Paintings', *Financial Times*, www.ft.com, 2 March 2024.

46 'Johnson', 'Rise of the Cyborgs', *The Economist*, 3 December 2022.

47 Dalya Alberge, 'Flushed Out: Duchamp's Greatest Concept Is Not His Own Work, Say Historians', *The Observer*, 15 October 2023.

48 Hannah Ghorashi, '"You develop a sixth sense": Richard Polsky on His New Warhol Authentication Service', *ArtNews*, 28 October 2015; Dorment, *Warhol*, pp. 84, 232–5.

49 Belting, *End*; Belting, *Likeness and Presence: A History of the Image before the Era of Art* [1990], trans. Edmund Jephcott (Chicago, IL, 1994); Arthur Danto, *After the End of Art* (Princeton, NJ, 1997), p. 47.

50 Quoted in Schwartz, 'Rembrandt Research', pp. 313, 332.

51 Guichard, 'Nouveau connoisseurship', pp. 1395–7; Preciado, *Retaining the Original*; Jaynie Anderson, 'Connoisseurship: Invention, Abandonment, Reinvention', in *A Companion to the Theories and Methods of Art History*, ed. Geraldine Johnson (Hoboken, NJ, forthcoming).

52 Christine Peltre and Philippe Lorenz, eds, *La notion d'école* (Strasbourg, 2007).

53 Gablik, 'Connective Aesthetics'; Claire Bishop, 'The Social Turn: Collaboration and Its Discontents', *Artforum International*, XLIV (2006), pp. 178–83.

54 Luigi Lanzi, *Storia pittorica dell'Italia* [1792–8], ed. Martin Capucci, 3 vols (Florence 1968), vol. I, p. 13.

55 Morelli quoted in John Fleming, 'Art Dealing and the Risorgimento I', *Burlington Magazine*, CXV/838 (1973), pp. 4–17 (p. 12).

56 Hans Tietze, 'Master and Workshop in the Venetian Renaissance', *Parnassus*, XI/8 (1939), pp. 34–45.

57 Charles Seymour Jr, 'Fatto di sua mano', in *Festschrift Ulrich Middeldorf*, ed. A. Kosegarten and P. Tigler (Berlin, 1968), pp. 93–105; Wendy Sheard and John Paoletti, eds, *Collaboration in Italian Renaissance Art* (New Haven, CT, 1978); Annabel Thomas, 'The Workshop as the Space of Collaborative Artistic Production', in *Renaissance Florence*, ed. Roger Crum and John Paoletti (Cambridge, 2006), pp. 415–30.

58 Elsig, *Connoisseurship*, p. 57.

Conclusion: Can We Trust Connoisseurship?

1 Frédéric Elsig et al., 'Le connoisseurship et ses revisions méthodologiques', *Perspective*, III (2009), pp. 344–56.

2 Jean Baptiste Du Bos, *Réflexions critiques sur la poësie et la peinture* (Paris, 1719); Jonathan Richardson, *Two Discourses* (London, 1719), p. 141.

3 David Ebitz, 'Connoisseurship as Practice', *Artibus et Historiae*, IX (1988), pp. 207–12.

4 Oskar Bätschmann, 'Der Holbein-Streit: Eine Krise der Kunstgeschichte', *Jahrbuch der Berliner Museen*, XXXVIII (1996), pp. 87–100.

5 John Brewer, 'Evaluating Evaluation', in *The American Leonardo* (New York, 2007), pp. 89–107.

6 Jonas Nordhagen, 'Roberto Longhi and His Method', *Konsthistorisk Tidskrift*, LXVIII/2 (1999), pp. 99–116 (p. 111).

7 Bernard Berenson and Roberto Longhi, *Lettere e scartafacci, 1912–1957* (Milan, 1993), pp. 134–5; M. Natale, ed., *Lettere 1946–1965, Federico Zeri, Roberto Longhi* (Milan, 2021).

8 *Fortnightly Review*, 1 October 1891, p. 509.

9 Bernard Berenson, *Sketch for a Self-Portrait* (London, 1949), p. 39.

10 John Pope-Hennessy, *Learning to Look* (London, 1991), p. 140; Denis Mahon quoted in Bernard Lahire, *This Is Not Just a Painting* [2015], trans. Helen Morrison (Cambridge, 2019), p. 386.

11 Richard Spear, *Caravaggio's Cardsharps on Trial: Thwaytes v Sotheby's* (London, 2020), pp. 143, 187, 205, 255.

12 Bredius to Sedelmeyer, quoted in Catherine Scallen, *Rembrandt, Reputation and the Practice of Connoisseurship* (Amsterdam, 2004), p. 233.

13 Kate Steinitz, *Pierre-Jean Mariette and le Comte de Caylus* (Los Angeles, CA, 1974), p. 35; Mariette to Bottari, 5 January 1765, in *Lettere*, ed. Erminia Gentile Ortona (Rome, 2022), p. 566.

14 Giovanni Morelli, *Italian Painters* [1890], trans. Jocelyn Ffoulkes, 2 vols (London, 1892–3), vol. I, p. 235.

15 Berenson to Paul Sachs, quoted in Rachel Cohen, *Bernard Berenson: A Life in the Picture Trade* (New Haven, CT, 2013), p. 223.

16 Lahire, *This Is Not Just a Painting*, p. 3.

17 Spear, *Caravaggio's Cardsharps*, pp. 223, 237.

18 Ibid., pp. 72, 75.

19 Ibid., pp. 191, 226, 317–19. The novelty of this task for a judge is noted by Linda Danil, 'Thwaytes v Sotheby's', *Law, Culture and the Humanities*, XVII/2 (2017), pp. 1–15 (p. 1). On Judge Black, see John Brewer, 'Evaluating Valuation: Connoisseurship, Technology, and Art Attribution in an American Court of Law', in Brewer, *The American Leonardo: A 20th-Century Tale of Obsession, Art and Money* (London, 2009), pp. 89–107.

20 John Russell, 'David Carritt, English Art Critic, Historian and Dealer, Dies at 55', *New York Times*, 5 August 1982.

21 Malcolm Gladwell, *Blink: The Power of Thinking without Thinking* (New York, 2005); Daniel Kahneman, *Thinking Fast and Slow* (New York, 2011).
22 John Gere, 'Philip Pouncey', *Proceedings of the British Academy*, LXXVI (1991), pp. 529–44 (p. 535).
23 Press Release, 'The Last Caravaggio', www.nationalgallery.org.uk, accessed 26 March 2025.
24 Max Friedländer, *On Art and Connoisseurship* (London, 1942), p. 173.

FURTHER READING

This list is limited to books in English.

Texts by the connoisseurs themselves include Jonathan Richardson, 'An Argument in Behalf of the Science of a Connoisseur', in *Two Discourses* [1719] (Menston, 1972); Gustav Waagen, *Treasures of Art in Great Britain* (London, 1854), with caustic comments on aristocratic owners who are confident in the authenticity of their Old Masters; Giovanni Morelli, *Italian Painters* [1892–3] (London, 2012), which can be read as a drama set in the art world as well as a milestone in connoisseurship; Bernard Berenson, *Rudiments of Connoisseurship* [1902] (New York, 1962); Barbara Strachey and Jayne Samuels, eds, *Mary Berenson: A Self-Portrait from Her Letters and Diaries* (London, 1983); Max Friedländer, *On Art and Connoisseurship* (London, 1942; reprinted Boston, MA, 2024), whose reflections are both witty and perceptive; Kenneth Clark, *Another Part of the Wood* (London, 1974); John Pope-Hennessy, *Learning to Look* (London, 1991).

For a general overview of connoisseurship, Carol Gibson-Wood, *Studies in the Theory of Connoisseurship from Vasari to Morelli* (New York, 1988).

On the seventeenth century, Jonathan Brown, *Kings and Connoisseurs* (New Haven, CT, 1995), a European panorama that privileges collecting rather than connoisseurship.

On Italy, see Genevieve Warwick, *The Arts of Collecting: Padre Sebastiano Resta and the Market for Drawings in Early Modern Europe* (Cambridge, 2000), and Frances Gage, *Painting as Medicine in Early Modern Rome: Giulio Mancini and the Efficacy of Art* (Philadelphia, PA, 2016). On the Netherlands, North and South, see Anna Tummers, *The Eye of the Connoisseur* (Los Angeles, CA, 2011), and Jeffrey Muller, *Rubens: The Artist as Collector* (Princeton, NJ, 1989). On France, see Thomas Puttfarken, *Roger de Piles' Theory of Art* (New Haven, CT, 1985); Kate Steinitz, *Pierre-Jean Mariette, the Comte de Caylus and Their Concept of Leonardo* (Los Angeles, CA, 1974); Krzysztof Pomian, *Collectors and Curiosities* (Cambridge, 1990); and Kristel Smentek, *Mariette and the Science of the Connoisseur in Eighteenth-Century Europe* (Farnham, 2014).

On England, see David Howarth, *Lord Arundel and His Circle* (New Haven, CT, 1985). On the eighteenth century in England, see Iain Pears, *The*

Discovery of Painting: The Growth of Interest in the Arts in England, 1680–1768 (New Haven, CT, 1988); Carol Gibson-Wood, *Jonathan Richardson* (New Haven, CT, 2000); and Cinzia Maria Sicca, ed., *John Talman: An Early Eighteenth-Century Connoisseur* (New Haven, CT, 2008).

On Winckelmann, see Alex Potts, *Flesh and the Ideal: Winckelmann and the Origins of Art History* (New Haven, CT, 1994), and Katherine Harloe, *Winckelmann and the Invention of Antiquity* (Oxford, 2013).

On Latin America, see Aaron Hyman, *Rubens in Repeat: The Logic of the Copy in Colonial Latin America* (Los Angeles, CA, 2021).

On the long nineteenth century (1780–1914), see Francis Haskell, *Rediscoveries in Art* (Oxford, 1976), a pioneering history of changes in taste; David Robertson, *Sir Charles Eastlake and the Victorian Art World* (Princeton, NJ, 1978); Susanna Avery-Quash and Julie Sheldon, *Art for the Nation: The Eastlakes and the Victorian Art World* (London, 2011); Jaynie Anderson, *Giovanni Morelli's Scientific Method of Attribution* (Strasbourg, 1992); Helen Davies, *Sir John Charles Robinson and His Role as a Connoisseur and Creator of Public and Private Collections* (Oxford, 1992); Ernest Samuels, *Bernard Berenson: The Making of a Connoisseur* (Cambridge, MA, 1979); and *Bernard Berenson: The Making of a Legend* (Cambridge, MA, 1987).

On the twentieth century and beyond, see Catherine Scallen, *Rembrandt, Reputation and the Practice of Connoisseurship* (Amsterdam, 2004); Jonathan Harr, *The Lost Painting: The Quest for a Caravaggio Masterpiece* (New York, 2006), which reads like a thriller; James Beck, *From Duccio to Raphael: Connoisseurship in Crisis* (Florence, 2006); and John Brewer, *The American Leonardo: A Twentieth-Century Tale of Obsession, Art and Money* (New York, 2007), which focuses on the 1929 trial *Hahn v Duveen*. See also Georgina Adam, *Big Bucks: The Explosion of the Art Market in the Twenty-First Century* (Farnham, 2014); Bernard Lahire, *This Is Not Just a Painting: An Inquiry into Art, Domination, Magic and the Sacred* (Cambridge, 2019), which views the art world with an anthropological eye; Richard Spear, *Caravaggio's Cardsharps on Trial: Thwaytes v Sotheby's* (London, 2020), an account of a trial in which the author was an expert witness; and Susanna Avery-Quash and Barbara Pezzin, eds, *Old Masters Worldwide* (London, 2020).

On fakes (among many other studies), see Mark Jones, ed., *Fake? The Art of Deception* (London, 1990); Thomas Hoving, *False Impressions: The Hunt for Big-Time Art Fakes* (London, 1996); Eric Hebborn, *The Art Forger's Handbook* (London, 1997); Sándor Radnóti, *The Fake* (New York, 1999); Jonathan Lopez, *The Man Who Made Vermeers* (New York, 2008) on the rise and fall of Han van Meegeren; and Winnie Won Yin Wong, *Van Gogh on Demand: China and the Readymade* (Chicago, IL, 2014).

ACKNOWLEDGEMENTS

As usual, I have received good advice and useful references from a number of people: Melissa Calaresu, George Katsibokis, Robin Milner-Gulland, Laura Moretti, Tamsin Palmer, Ulinka Rublack, Nigel Spivey, Paul Taylor and Mark Thurner. Six people kindly read and commented on a draft of this essay: Jaynie Anderson, who also shared an unpublished article; Luciano Cheles, who also sent me his valuable articles on the reception of Piero della Francesca; Paolo Coen, who also invited me to speak on this topic to his students at the University of Teramo; Ivan Gaskell, who made many helpful observations as well as inviting me to lecture at Bard Graduate Center; Carlo Ginzburg, who suggested that I add case studies and sent me the second edition of his *Indagini* (effectively a new book); and my wife Maria Lúcia, who once again read a manuscript of mine and offered valuable suggestions for its improvement.

PHOTO ACKNOWLEDGEMENTS

The author and publishers wish to express their thanks to the sources listed below for illustrative material and/or permission to reproduce it. Some locations of artworks are also given below, in the interest of brevity:

Alamy: 7 (© ABC/courtesy Everett Collection); Archivio storico dell' Accademia delle Scienze, Turin: 4; Bridgeman Images: 1 (Mondadori Portfolio), 5 (© Marcello Mencarini, all rights reserved 2026), 19 (© Towneley Hall Art Gallery and Museum); Chatsworth House: 14; courtesy Childs Gallery, Boston: 30; Cleveland Museum of Art, OH: 18; Frick Digital Collections, New York: 31; Galleria d'Arte Moderna, Palazzo Pitti, Florence: 21; Gallerie degli Uffizi, Florence: 12; Girton College, University of Cambridge: 25; from Albert Hahn, *Het land van Rembrandt* (Amsterdam, 1906), photo Getty Research Institute, Los Angeles: 27; Library of Congress, Prints and Photographs Division, Washington, DC: 24; The Metropolitan Museum of Art, New York: 2; Musée Albert Kahn, Boulogne-Billancourt: 6; Musée du Louvre, Paris: 11, 13; Museum Yamato Bunkakan, Nara: 28; Muzeum Narodowe, Warsaw: 17; National Galleries of Scotland, Edinburgh: 23; National Portrait Gallery, London: 16; Östasiatiska museet, Stockholm: 29; Philadelphia Museum of Art, PA: 20; Princeton University Art Museum, NJ: 8; private collection: 26; RKD – Netherlands Institute for Art History, The Hague: 9; photo Sky/www.findagrave.com: 3; Städel Museum, Frankfurt am Main: 22; Villa Medicea di Castello, Accademia della Crusca, Florence: 15 (photo Sailko/Wikimedia Commons, CC BY 3.0); Wikimedia Commons: 32 (public domain).

INDEX

Illustrations numbers are indicated by *italics*